T0330136

The Revival of Modern Austrian Economics

Other books by the author

The Making of Marx's Critical Theory: A Bibliographical Analysis, 1983.
Marx's Critique of Political Economy: Intellectual Sources and Evolution, two volumes, 1984 and 1985.
Essays in Political Economics: Public Control in a Democratic Society, by Adolph Lowe, edited with an Introduction by Allen Oakley, 1987.
Schumpeter's Theory of Capitalist Motion: A Critical Exposition and Reassessment, 1990.
Classical Economic Man: Human Agency and Methodology in the Political Economy of Adam Smith and J.S. Mill, 1994.
The Foundations of Austrian Economics from Menger to Mises: A Critico-historical Retrospective of Subjectivism, 1997.

The Revival of Modern Austrian Economics

A Critical Assessment of its Subjectivist Origins

Allen Oakley

The University of Newcastle, Australia

Edward Elgar

Cheltenham, UK • Northampton, MA, USA

Published by
Edward Elgar Publishing Limited
Glensanda House
Montpellier Parade
Cheltenham
Glos GL50 1UA
UK

Edward Elgar Publishing, Inc.
6 Market Street
Northampton
Massachusetts 01060
USA

A catalogue record for this book
is available from the British Library

Library of Congress Cataloguing in Publication Data
Oakley, Allen.
The revival of modern Austrian economics : a critical assessment of its subjectivist origins / Allen Oakley.
Includes bibliographical references and index.
1. Austrian school of economists. 2. Economics. 3. Subjectivity.
I. Title.
HB98.0254 1999
330.15'7—dc21 98–42886
CIP

ISBN 1 85898 540 4

Typeset by Manton Typesetters, 5–7 Eastfield Road, Louth, Lincs, LN11 7AJ, UK
Printed and bound in Great Britain by MPG Books Ltd, Bodmin, Cornwall

For Renate

Contents

Preface

In the development of economic thought, Austrians have come to be identified with a research programme that gives serious recognition to a subjectivist and individualist understanding of human action as the metatheoretical foundation of economics. Alex Shand's summary of matters Austrian and neoAustrian announces that 'Austrians are subjectivists' and that subjectivism is seen in their 'prevailing attitude to all social phenomena' (1980, pp. 11, 12). That the idea has been of profound significance for economics in general was emphasized by Friedrich von Hayek in his much-quoted claim that 'it is probably no exaggeration to say that every important advance in economic theory during the last hundred years was a further step in the consistent application of subjectivism' (1955, p. 31).

Our attitudes towards these references to the subjectivism pursued by Austrians should depend crucially upon what we believe constitutes the full scope of the principle and its proper application. Comments such as Shand's, to the effect that, while 'no two Austrians have ever completely agreed on methodology, there does seem to have been broad agreement on the basic concept – subjectivism' (1980, p. 13) rather beg the question. An unfortunate characteristic of Austrian economics since its foundation by Carl Menger has been the paucity of serious endeavours explicitly to define and defend the complete ontology of human subjectivism with which it purports to be concerned. It is evident from my previously reported research (Oakley, 1997a, 1997b) and in the further evidence to be elicited in its continuation below, that this disinclination to be specific and coherent about the realistic meaning and full import of their key metatheory has afflicted the work of all founding contributors to Austrian economics.

Nonetheless, it is now generally accepted that the sort of subjectivism that is found in Austrian economics is one that goes beyond the narrow focus on agents' preferences and valuations that is the limit of its neoclassical version. All Austrian subjectivism is 'radical' in this sense and extends to encompass the specifically temporal problematic of agent deliberations and decision making by means of expectations formed under conditions of uncertainty and limited knowledge. Ludwig Lachmann's suggestive testament in this respect was that 'the first, and most prominent, feature of Austrian economics is a radical subjectivism, today no longer confined to human preferences but extended to expectations'. For this reason, he went on, Austrians emphasize an 'awareness of the protean character of time' and 'a distrust of all those formalizations of economic experience that do not have an identifiable source in the mind of an economic actor' (1978b, pp. 1f). From these perspectives, it is especially challenging to reflect upon what such a particular meaning of subjectivism would lead us to expect of its 'consistent application' to an understanding of economic phenomena as Hayek suggested. Such reflection drives a potential wedge between what may be defined as a complete and realistic subjectivism and the particulars of the delimited versions that can be extracted from the Austrians' writings. The issue thus posed, and to be addressed at length in my inquiries, is the extent to which these latter should be taken to define the limits of the principle as it affects economics. My conclusion will be that no Austrian's treatment of subjectivism can be taken to be definitive once the fullest potential extent of its status and meaning is explicated.

In the critical assessment of Austrian subjectivism that is pursued below, the particular objective is to re-examine the endeavours of Hayek and Lachmann to develop defensible subjectivist research programmes by building on the legacies of Friedrich von Wieser and Ludwig von Mises in particular. My intention in pursuing this inquiry is to show that these Austrians' subjectivism and individualism brought a human vitality to our understanding of economic phenomena. To this end, I elicit the very real contributions that each has made in his own way to a rendering of economics that is conscious of the irreducibly human ontology of its substantive objects. I am concerned to emphasize, too, that the Austrians comprise one of the few schools of economics that, in treating it explicitly as a human science, have then been prepared to give fundamental recognition to the consequent distinctive metatheoretical implications and demands made on theory formation. They have, with varying degrees of conviction, argued that economic methodology and epistemology are distinct from what is encompassed within the positivism and instrumentalism of the physical sciences. The Austrians' primary concern has been to preserve the ontological insight that all economic phenomena are the consequence of individual, but situationally conditioned and directed, subjective human actions. In doing so, their methodology has put realist ontological consistency before the demands of physical scientism and formal analytical elegance.

The present study takes up the story of Austrian subjectivism where Mises appears as the main bridge into the twentieth century for the passage of these ideas, from the second generation contributions of Wieser to those of Hayek. Mises and Hayek each confronted mainstream microeconomics with the subjectivist alternative. Their vision of economics as dealing with processes that are constituted by the collective effects of individual human action set in real time presented analytical problems that the orthodox of the profession were not prepared to confront. Ludwig Lachmann, a German who was Austrian by adoption, emerged to play the 'devil's advocate' for a more comprehensive, and thus more intractable, range of subjectivist principles. Recognizing these additional demands compounds the effect that subjectivism has on the way in which economic phenomena should be understood, and on the construction of the theory that purports to provide accounts of their generation. But, in the end, it will be my finding that even this most 'radical' of Austrians did not take us far enough into the depths of subjectivism as the most apt metatheoretical foundation for a reconstructed economics. Lachmann skated over the surface of the subjectivist problematic, just as I find Mises and Hayek to have done. Their different legacies for the revival of interest in Austrian themes in the 1970s, and for the factionalized neoAustrian schools of thought spawned as a result, have left much need for further inquiry and methodological development in order fully to reconstruct economics on subjectivist foundations.

In doing research of the kind that is required for the writing of such a book as this, the 'tyranny of distance' between Australia and Europe is an ever-present impediment in many respects. In my case, the tyranny is mitigated by frequent trips to Austria, where my colleague Karl Milford of the University of Vienna always provides just the right balance of scholarly assistance and personal inspiration. I thank him for his contributions to this book, without implicating him in its conclusions.

Allen Oakley,
Medowie, Australia

1. Introduction

1.1 SUBJECTIVISM IN ECONOMICS AS A HUMAN SCIENCE

What sets all versions Austrian and neoAustrian (or Modern Austrian) economics irrevocably apart from the mainstream of neoclassical orthodoxy is its concern to represent economics as a human science. In giving primacy and emphasis to the human ontology of its objects, Austrian economics takes on a realist and humanist philosophical orientation that is quite foreign to the instrumentalism, rationalistic objectivism and equilibrium pretensions of mainstream analyses. This distinction has a number of quite profound implications for the metatheory upon which Austrian economics is founded. Most fundamentally, some form of subjectivism, along with its complement of individualism, provide the common, differentiating essences of 'Austrianness'.[1] The immediate import of this common ground is that Austrians give priority to understanding the individual human origins of observed (empirical) economic phenomena. They adopt the premise that the real world in all its dimensions is inherently meaningful and/or intelligible in its essential structure, a structure that exists independently of any subjective ordering of its elements by observers. In formulating their inquiries, Austrians are most concerned to ask ontological questions about the inherent qualities of the real world, with epistemological questions about our knowledge of it taking a secondary role. Their realism is Aristotelian in its origins and defends discursive representations of reality that claim existential validity. Such realism is to be understood both in an ontological sense, meaning that the external world exists more or less as we find it, and in an epistemological sense, meaning that we can and do know about the structures, relationships and operations of this external world.

In these particular respects, then, the Austrian founders of subjectivist economics with whom we will be concerned here have all been explicitly conscious of and given priority to the metatheoretical issues of being, existence and knowledge that underpin human scientific inquiry. It was their consciousness of subjectivism that led them to attribute priority to ontology over methodology and epistemology in constructing their research programme for economics. They believed that economic inquiry should begin from a fully explicit ontology of the phenomena concerned, and that the methodology of discursive analytical representation should subsequently be designed to ensure the retention of the maximum degree of ontological integrity and realism. Only then can judgements be made about the epistemological status and limits that apply to the analyses produced. As Karen Vaughn observes so appositely, for Austrians now and in the past, 'there is *something* "out there" that economists have been trying to describe ...'. This 'something' has sufficient orderliness, she continues, for us as analysts to make continuing valid generalizations at a certain level of abstraction and for us as individual agents 'to live most of our catallactic lives with some sense of continuity and predictability' (1994, p. 161, original emphasis).

To begin, I consider the nature of subjectivism as the actual and potential foundation of Austrian economics. Subjectivism in the human sciences, including economics, is a mode of thought about the origins of the empirically observed object phenomena with which those sciences are concerned. Primacy is ascribed to the ontology of individualism in that it is the collective outcomes of individual human actions that account for the appearance of all such phenomena. There can be no question of a unique meaning being given to the concept of subjectivism or to its complement, individualism. For this reason, I should indicate explicitly the general metatheoretical principles that will be guiding my present retrospective inquiries.

Two tenets of subjectivism are pertinent to its use by economic analysts (cf. Hutchison, 1994, p. 189). First, the fundamental and dedicated focus of subjectivism is on the mental and cognitive processes of active human subjects that mediate in giving meaning to external physical objects and to social structures, institutions and relationships. The perceptions, interpretations and knowledge concerning the external physical and social world that direct and shape action are thus limited by and relative to the self-conscious human subject. External objects as they exist in the given reality that surrounds human subjects have a resulting dual existence for a properly defined subjectivism: in their physical or virtual existence, they have particular independent and existential qualities and quantitative dimensions, *and at the same time* they have a dependent and evaluated existence as meanings attributed to them by human subjects who perceive and grasp them cognitively. In the extreme of its idealist form, subjectivism does not acknowledge this dualism and both physical and non-physical entities are rendered as having no existence beyond the conceptual constructions that subjects ascribe to them. That is, real entities can have no independently definable and ascertainable influence in the shaping of human activities. This is because activities are devised and driven only by the purely subjective and relative beliefs, conceptions and motivations of atomistic, isolated individuals. By contrast, in its realist form, the subjectivist perspective adopted by analysts will treat the natural–physical as well as the human–creative and social–relational entities that active subjects confront and utilize as having an independent existence that is prior to any individual's attention to them. And, most significantly, the realist will argue that the existential world of real things directs and shapes what human subjects know about it in ways that can be explicated. However, there can be no unique 'correspondence' between the subject's world of concepts and the qualities of the reality represented, for, in their cognitive capacities, subjects are limited, fallible and subjective in their grasp and interpretation of the world around them.

The other and consequent tenet of subjectivism is that such a realist perspective leads us to consider human subjects primarily as *agents* with given mental and cognitive constitutions that are the products of their innate qualities, their biographically accumulated experiences and their contemporary situational environment. Subjectivism, then, relates directly to human beings as *homo sapiens,* the only extant member of the species 'homo' and one that has the *capacity for wisdom* implied by the appellation 'sapiens'. But human beings have also proved themselves to have an additional capacity of immediate concern to economists: that is the capacity *to act with self-interest and purpose* towards their environment in the light of their wisdom, as implied by their equally applicable identification as *homo agens* (cf. Mises, 1966, p. 14). This additional inherent motivational and teleological quality of human beings is significant in defining subjectivism in economics because it directs our attention to those particular actions that have deliberated and purposeful character and that originate in self-conscious, reasoned decisions and choices. All actions are not of this kind, but only those with such characteristics constitute the origin of phenomena of concern to economics.

It is in this sense that human subjects as economic agents are envisaged by subjectivists as pursuing the satisfaction of their hierarchy of needs and wants by means of interacting with their physical and social environment. Where such needs and wants originate, in human biology and/or in human society, may be a matter of debate. But the important realization is that resources available for achieving such satisfaction must be considered as scarce relative to demand for them in the case of human actions relevant to economics. Agents must deliberate and make choices on the basis of their own, individual interpretations and understandings of the problems and environments that they confront. Whatever may be the limitations of this understanding that come from lack of information and/or shortcomings of the agents' cognitive capacities, their actions as individuals are to be understood as the result of the meaning *they* attribute to the environment and to the *telos* of the pursuit of *their* objectives. In these respects, *interpretation* is inescapably of the essence in all human science, in that it conditions the ontological form of the objects of those sciences through its influence on the actions of agents.

Both of the principles essential to subjectivism, the focus on cognitive processes and on the individual acting agents to whom these processes are attributable, have an ontological orientation in the sense that they relate to the nature and origin of a part of existent reality. The part of reality concerned here is the world of phenomena that are generated by subjectively grounded and situationally conditioned and directed human action. With its direct focus on the deliberated, creative and purposive actions of individual but specifically situated agents, subjectivist human science proceeds to give priority to the fact that its phenomena, the objects of investigation, are the products of such actions. It is this ontology of phenomena that is to be elicited by realist economic inquiry with the objective of making particular human actions and their phenomenal consequences intelligible in the form of representational theoretical argument. These preliminary observations lead me to address several key questions raised by advocating a subjectivist metatheory for economics. First, what can be said by way of generalization about the individual nature of active subjective agents and their agency? Secondly, because agents do not operate as isolated atomistic individuals, it is necessary to pose the question: what role does the external situational environment play in directing and shaping human action, and thus in determining the ontology of economic phenomena? Thirdly, if the collective actions of situated and conditioned human agents are taken to be the origin of economic phenomena, what methodological principles can legitimately be applied in order to provide for discursively valid representations of such phenomena? Fourthly, what epistemological status can be ascribed to the analyses that result from the applications of this methodology to accounting for and making predictions about economic phenomena?

1.2 A SUBJECTIVIST ONTOLOGY OF ECONOMIC PHENOMENA

The effect of such definitional essentials as just outlined is to give subjectivism the status of an ontological principle of human science and to separate it from the pseudo-subjectivism of the orthodox microeconomic analyses, centring on the 'pure logic of choice', that rose to prominence after the 1870s. Such orthodoxy has the human agent modelled as *homo oeconomicus,* a puppet-like being with a remarkable degree of omnipotence, who mechanically responds to preferences and circumstances with a logically rational choice that is entailed by the premises and conditions established by assumptions. Spiro Latsis refers to such a model as amounting to the application of situational determinism as a means of objectifying human agency for methodologically driven reasons. The result is a body of 'decision makers without decision procedures', for, as he observes: 'It is part and parcel of the neoclassical programme to specify situations which uniquely determine behaviour' so that its practitioners 'concentrate on the logic of the agent's situation and are spared the complexities of the psychology of the agent in that situation' (1972, pp. 210, 211). Under these assumed conditions, positing different patterns of preferences with maximum utility as the singular human objective does not render such choice truly subjectivist. More than this, indeed, the substantive determinism of the deductive logic as it flows from premises to conclusion negates any effective choice on the part of the agent. The pseudo-human agent *homo oeconomicus* is less than a *homo sapiens cum agens* in not really needing to use wisdom in making choices in pursuit of self-conscious goals. All the knowledge he requires is presumed given to him and the ends and means manifested in his conduct are preordained. He is an omniscient being for whom the future is also logically certified and carries no risk or uncertainty. What all this adds up to is that the objective formalism imposed on economic action by the invention of *homo oeconomicus* can only be seen as a way of avoiding the issue of agent subjectivism altogether.[2]

By contrast, the real-world human agents of concern to subjectivist economists embark on life's journey with a psychosomatic constitution that includes those congenital physiological and genetic characteristics that predetermine the physical and intellectual capacities of individuals. Subjectivism pursues an existentialist image of human nature and being as far as it is relevant to the economic facets of the life-world. In doing so, it begins from the fundamental proposition that, as isolated individuals, in an absolute and ultimate sense, human beings are free and self-responsible entities who may choose, decide and act in any manner they consider appropriate at the time. But, most especially, subjectivism adopts the principle that *human being is dominated by human action.* In their lives as active subjective agents, individuals draw upon their innate characteristics and capacities in order to design their actions. These characteristics are compounded by the acquired profile of qualities and knowledge that are the result of their respective biographies as unique beings who have internalized the effects of a range of cumulative, externally imposed experiences. All such qualitative dimensions vary widely, and agents are able to act only within the limits of their capabilities and interests. At this level, agents' conduct is grounded in and characterized by ever-present dimensions of autonomy and contingency.

It should be recognized, though, that in practice the freedom of agents is never absolute. It is conditioned and conditional, for in nearly all aspects of their life-world, human agents exist, make decisions and do their periodic choosing and acting within and through some particular situation consisting of a multiplicity of facets and conditions. For our purposes, an agent's external situation comprises a complex totality of natural and humanly created environmental conditions made up of physical, spatial, social and institutional dimensions. Such situational exigencies are, then, for many short-term human imperatives, *given* as effectively inherited by agents from period to period. But note that a dual influence is involved here. For, while it is all too easy to treat situational conditions as merely externally imposed limitations on the human condition and human actions, such a view is seriously misleading because it fails to pay due regard to the dimension of situations that provides the *possibilities and facilities* for action open to agents. So, although situations do have a significant coercive effect for agents to contend with, there is also a degree of volition in the actual way they interpret and choose to use them. They provide many of the means by which agents can operate in their own best interests if they understand how and are prepared to cooperate optimally with the demands that their structural situations make. The effect of situational influences in all circumstances is to introduce a counterweight of delimited proportions to the pure capriciousness and spontaneity of human action. This delimitation allows for the psychology of interpretation and for a tentative and conjectural remainder in all situational explanations of conduct. There is, then, a balance in the origins of human conduct between existential, psychologically based contingency and situational containment.

More specifically, on a day-to-day basis, agents confront and are called upon to work within the bounds of rules and roles that are often manifested in institutional structures as particular elements of containment and facilitation. Institutions are significant because they comprise established and acknowledged social and economic relationships and practices that exist and are maintained in a specific form over time. As such, they must occupy a key position in the formulation of the interaction of agents and structures as played out through rules and roles. In particular, the existence of agreed rules and roles facilitates mutual comprehension and assessment of interdependent actions by agents. Institutions should not be envisaged as rigid or immutable, but rather as the result of accepted practices that have evolved, and continue to do so, because they prove to be functionally efficacious and mutually advantageous for the agents concerned. But any general acceptance by agents of the functional status of rules and roles within an institutional complex should also not be allowed to obscure the serious import of the contingencies that remain in the operations that comprise human agency.

The first source of a contingent remainder is a consequence of the very nature of the way agents interpret, engage and thereby instantiate the virtual (non-physical) dimensions of their situations. Concerning rules in particular, it is to be noted that, in the main, they are not analogous to those of games such as chess, where the rules exist independently of any particular game or players, and where, in any game, the only moves used and allowed are those strictly consistent with the rules. More appropriately, rules and the actions they direct exist in conjunction with one another. As a consequence there can be no unique relation between any particular action and a rule or rules (cf. Giddens, 1979, p. 65). Moreover, some rules may be altered over time in response to agents' perceptions of changed circumstances and from their recursive reflection on the mix of expected and unexpected consequences of their actions. The result is that rules do not travel well through time or space, thus mitigating against any attempt to apply them as objective and generally applicable intertemporal criteria for understanding and predicting agent conduct. For similar reasons, care is also needed in applying role categories in order to ensure that they are not represented as so functionally deterministic in their effect as to pre-empt the self-consciousness of deliberation, decision and action that should be the centrepiece of any theory involving human agents. What should be stressed is that, while social structures as frameworks for action ultimately comprised of roles, it is the actual forms of action that manifest those roles that is significant for understanding human phenomena. It is thus on practices, which emerge from role prescriptions by virtue of agents' actions, that subjectivists should focus while remaining mindful that agents are attached to such roles without their conduct being fully determined by them (cf. Giddens, 1979, p. 117).

Another dimension of subjectivist contingency is made apparent by the fact that different aspects of economic role prescriptions call for different profiles of agents' capabilities, some innate, some learned, if they are to be serviced optimally. The general condition required for agents to optimize the use they make of the situations through which they must act is that they have the will and ability to make interpretations and calculations in their deliberations that are sufficiently near to correct. Clearly, the intellectual capacities, along with the preparedness to apply them to the necessary knowledge and information gathering and processing, that agents bring to their problem situations will vary widely. Moreover, what limited knowledge and information are actually available, as well as their processing, have a pecuniary cost. The result is that there will be resource limitations to consider when arguing the deliberation processes of agents. Most importantly, it is wholly inappropriate to represent agents as homogeneous in either of these respects. We need to confront the contingent consequences of their differential cognitive limitations and individual differences of knowledge and information access quite squarely. In particular, agents are generally incapable of meeting the demands of strict rationality and optimization, contrary to what is so often assumed in orthodox economics. Even if we allow them a complete comprehension of their situations, as far as these can be known, the complexity of the relevant knowledge, information flows and calculations that they would be called upon to work on in their deliberations remains beyond the normal capacities and concerns of most agents. When we do focus upon the procedures of reasoning applied to actually knowable circumstances, we find that what agents can achieve is heavily circumscribed. That is, the rational capacities of human agents are delimited in the particular sense that they attend to only a small, relevant part of the complex reality around them. They must make a highly simplified model of their world and use it when deliberating and choosing prior to acting. It is not that rationality has no import at all, it is rather that, in applying their reasoning abilities, agents can only ever seek to approximate what might actually and unbeknown exist as an optimum for them.

Yet a third contingency-inducing problem confronted by all agents is that their agency is chronically and irremediably set in an unceasing flow of real time. They have, therefore, an unavoidable obligation somehow to cope with all the perfidiousness that characterizes the future. Agents' deliberations and decisions involve coming to grips with the future to an extent that gives them confidence that they can forecast what will happen as a consequence of their actions with a personally satisfactory expected degree of accuracy. The relevant deliberation processes should be explicitly recognized as encompassing the cognitive capacity of agents to be creative and originating. These processes are essentially grounded upon the creative imaginations of the agents, for there exist no other means of dealing with objects that have had, as yet, no experiential manifestations for them to draw upon. Acts of choice and decision thus have an uncaused originating dimension. They create a wholly new beginning to events that have no necessary logical ties to what preceded them. It is a fundamental fact which human agents must face in their deliberations and decisions that, in the strictest sense, there can be no information about the future. It designates the period of time on the other side of the 'epistemological wall' that divides the time that has passed, about which facts can be known in some usually accepted senses, from the time yet to come, the constitution of which cannot be 'known' in any meaningful sense. 'Information' about the future has an effectively infinite price. Indeed, it is not that the future is merely uncertain, it is a dimension that has no existential form that can be 'known' in the usual sense at all.

Endeavours to model future outcomes and their causes, and to deal with them rationally, are an integral part of the human agents' predicament. Agents contemplating action are forced to confront the 'void of time' that constitutes the future and effectively to transcend it, at least at the mental level. They must do something, for all choices and decisions to act in the present are only meaningfully based on some pertinent pattern of beliefs about the future. The fact that all agents must accept is that the possible range of alternative imagined scenarios is necessarily incomplete and uncompletable. However, as far as we are concerned with it here, that range is not open-ended. The idea of relevance suggests that, for better or for worse, it will only encompass future scenarios which have some reasonable foundation in experience and knowledge. What this view suggests is that the only way agents can devise the actions necessary to realize a particular projected state of their existence is to resort to what they know already in the belief that sufficient of it will remain relevant in the future. The significant dilemma for agents now is how much of their resources to devote to purchasing and subjecting to calculation information about the past in an effort to throw light on the future. The outcome of this choice must remain contingent, for there are no ex ante criteria by means of which to assess the optimal set of information inputs to their deliberations. Indeed, even ex post, for future reference, there can be no way of knowing whether or not the information used was optimal or what outcomes other unchosen alternative scenarios would have brought. And, because the current choice has irrevocably changed the agents and their situations, ex post reflections can only provide insights that are of limited future relevance. Nonetheless, the foundations for scenarios deemed possible can only comprise agents' expectations formed from some more or less subjective interpretation of the relevant past and calculations about the meaningful future that they believe will follow from it. The minimum requirement is the belief that according to agents' present knowledge the projected action would have been feasible, in that the necessary means would have been available if the action had occurred in the past. Along with this must be the belief that no obstacles fatal to the intended outcome of the action have arisen since it was last attempted.

To say that orthodox economics has had difficulty coming to grips with these time-related puzzles is no news. All endeavours to escape the true significance of it for the construction of economic theory have ended by making the problem disappear in the interest of methodologically imposed criteria. Closed collective stochastic certainty, comprising probabilities that sum to unity, is just no realistic substitute for the open-ended contingent nature of true uncertainty that must be coped with by forming expectations. Indeed, it may well be argued that the very concept of objectively grounded calculation itself has unwelcome connotations in relation to subjective economic agency. By the very nature of the origin of expected future scenarios, as imagined sequences derived largely from subjective interpretation and creative reason applied to current knowledge, and because the range of them is necessarily open-ended and uncompletable, it is evident that they could not inherently possess a closed probability distribution for agents to discover. There is, too, the more subtle point that, because the effects of a chosen action are irrevocable, no pre-experimentation with the alternative scenarios is possible, so that the actual consequences of the unchosen options can never be known. Agents may like to defy the real nature of these conditions, even though they are rife in the sort of decisions to be made in economic matters, and *impose* a probability set of their own invention as a mode of formalizing their reason and salving their ignorance. But this, too, is an arbitrary and subjective procedure, the viability of which depends on finding a legitimate means of deciding the parameters of the probability distribution. As far as economists are concerned, resort to such a representation of agency as realistic would require some empirical evidence that actual decision makers use such procedures.

If there is to be any legitimate potential for subjectivist economic theory with some degree of reliable predictive capacity, it must represent and explicate the deliberations that lead to decisions and actions as a balancing of containment and contingency. Devising subjectivist understandings and explanations does not justify any conclusion that there can be no place for predictions in economics. What is required is that we 'soften' the demands of prediction by allowing that explanation need not be reducible to, and exclusively validated by, predictions. This does not rule out the quite different claim that properly developed representative explanations should enable us to make some sort of predictions about economic events. There can be no doubt that these explanations and derived predictions, that are to follow from subjectively grounded hermeneutical understandings of human actions, require strict methodological and epistemological circumscription. In particular, it can be granted that the sort of predictions to be made are not likely to be as quantitatively or temporally specific about *individual* events as those possible in astronomy or in physics experiments. Rather, the provision of generalized and regularized argument and predictions in economics should be limited to a degree of specificity sufficient to identify an event as qualitatively typical of its class and to remain consistent with the limited degree of quantitative and temporal regularity exhibited by that class of event. In short, the characteristics of predictions should not be expected to transcend the epistemological limitations of the explanations from which they are devised.

Realists should call up two potentials of human agency again at this point, for they give us the clues to the way we might proceed. First, it is a fact that agents inherit given and existentially independent structural situations within and through which the vast majority realize they must volitionally operate if they are to serve their own interests to maximum effect. And, for each particular economic problem, for each functional category of action, for each consequent role prescription perceived by agents, there will exist a common set of structured situational features upon which they will be able to depend and to whose demands they may well be prepared to conform as the only available means of realizing their own objectives. Secondly, it is a fact that, although agents undertake all their actions strictly as individuals in an existential sense, the uncoordinated and unintended collective consequences, while extremely complex, are not chaotic to any intractable extent. The challenge for a revised approach to theory construction in economics is to explicate just how the realities of individual and collective situations simultaneously facilitate, contain and constrain what individual agents decide to do when confronted by particular categories of economically pertinent problematical conditions.

Any such achievement will, though, require an agreement that allowing methodological preconditions concerning the analytical form, and the definitude of its derived results, to have any priority in theory construction is not a viable option. The dominant criterion of theory construction must be that there is a sufficiently identifiable representation of the subjective ontological character of the object phenomenon to ensure that the underlying human realities of its generation can be explicitly accounted for and understood. Just what the methodology turns out to be, along with its epistemological ramifications, must be accepted as the necessary condition for the realization of these more meaningful and practically useful objectives. Some methodological principles that may be consistent with and further these ontological priorities are to be explored in the next section.

1.3 FROM ONTOLOGY TO METHODOLOGICAL PRINCIPLES[3]

One implication of the alternative subjectivist principles introduced above is that human phenomena are properly interpreted as being of a quite different ontological status from those objects that are of interest in the physical sciences. Scientific interest in the physical world is centred on the belief that most of it comprises permanent elements and regularized relationships that are subject to laws. Change, where it is at issue at all, is of a gradual, long-term and evolutionary character. Repetition of predefined and regularized phenomena is anticipated because either a system is directly observed as closed in its constitution, or it is *ostensibly* replicated as closed in experimental situations. Inductive observations of repeated conjunctions of event sequences are accepted as evidence of causality. And these observations are taken to be the exclusive source of knowledge, because nothing more need be known about event origins than what the senses deliver. Universalist and generalized, logico-deductive argument makes immediate sense on ontological grounds in devising causal explanations of such events in much of the world of nature because of these qualities.

By contrast, for subjectivists, the notion of 'causality' in accounting for human action and its observed consequences is not identifiable with that associated with the regularities of the physical world. Whereas the apt questions to be asked about a physical event are empirical and concerned with how it happened, the appropriate inquiry for the human realm is *why* an event occurred, in the sense of '*for what humanly attributable reason?*' Except in theology, such ontologically oriented '*why?*' questions that ask for reasons have no place in the physical realm. The dimensions of cognition peculiar to human scientific inquiry that follow from these observations are usually summarized under the objective of *Verstehen,* implying a search for *understanding* in terms of the set of reasons why phenomena are as they are. Inquiries about human phenomena, including those of economics, involve a process that must contend with contingent characteristics stemming from exigencies of human nature that are not found in devising physical explanations. Most significantly, there is no analogous sense in which physical objects can be considered as exclusively the voluntarist, contingent and open-ended products of human belief, motive, interpretation, creativity, meaning, choice and action. This is why subjectivists do not accept the immediate application of physical science methodology or its epistemological standards to investigations concerning human activity. All science has a place for observation in establishing what phenomena are *there* to be explained. And the rules of logic and consistency of argument are fundamental to all scientific exposition. Nevertheless, in the case of the human sciences, the subjectivist ontology of its objects is so distinctive as to require an independent effort to devise suitable methodological principles and to accept the epistemological consequences.

In pursuing these metatheoretical implications of subjectivism, the philosophical vision of economic phenomena as the products of situated human agency that will be adopted below is one that is consistent with *realism.* A straightforward *general* definition of realism must include the notion that, for analysts, the ultimate objects of any scientific inquiry have an existential status that is quite independent of any activities of those analysts. So it is that Norton Jacobi (1990, pp. 23f) defines realism for both analysts and active agents as requiring primarily that an affirmative answer be given to the 'primitive' question: does anything exist other than the phenomenal contents of our experiences? A second stage to the definition then claims that an underlying reality exists independently of our experience of it and that any such experience is to be understood as generated by the perceived existential form of that reality. These claims then suggest the further question: what is the nature of the relationship between this underlying reality and the phenomenal constitution of our experience? There are various degrees of correspondence that can be posited in response, but the significant point is that they all presuppose a dualism between an independent existential reality and our experience of it.

In the definition of Tony Lawson, this realist perspective claims that 'the world is constituted not only by *experience*, and by the *actual* objects of experience such as events and states of affairs, but also by (irreducible) *structures*, powers and mechanisms and so on that may not be directly perceivable but which underlie the events of experience and govern them' (1994d, p. 132, original emphasis). If this basic dualism between the domains of experience and the real is accepted, it is then necessary to proceed carefully to define the different perspectives of active agents and observer analysts implicit in the above observations about realism. There is a sense in which phenomena as we experience them, both as agents and as analysts, are *representations* rather than replications of an external reality in our minds. The mind, that is, provides an interpreting mediation through which we grasp cognitively what we observe. There is implied, as a consequence, what has been called a 'layered ontology' of all that exists for the agent and for the analyst. In this model of ontology, 'actual' actions and events and other manifested phenomena are the products of a 'deep' layer comprising mechanisms, rules and powers that are accepted and adopted from the independent (intransitive) structures and relationships that make up agents' physical and social situations. These direct and shape the actions that generate the 'actual' phenomena on which observation is to focus. Observations of phenomena at the 'surface' empirical level are then constituted for agents as experiences, perceptions and impressions. (cf. Fleetwood, 1995, pp. 79ff; Lawson, 1994b, pp. 7f). But, in the case of the human sciences, it is to be recognized that the 'layers' as they involve *active agents* are distinct in some key respects from the concerns of the scientific analysts who observe them. This distinction is a result of the fact that agents with given abilities and experiences deliberate, choose and act on the basis of their interpretations of a particular set of external environmental conditions that have an 'actual' existence. From their experiences, perceptions and impressions of these conditions, they confront constraints on and draw facilities for their actions in the form of the 'deep' mechanisms, rules and powers that have implications and influences they are prepared to accept. By contrast, observer analysts seeking to understand the results of agents' actions must interpret what they perceive to be 'actual' phenomena as the products of this prior interpretation process and all that has gone into it.

Most importantly, however, it is to be recognized that, for analysts, this pursuit of realism allows no guarantee of any one-to-one synchronization and correspondence between the characteristics of these layers. The 'deep' layer has a prior and independent existential status that is always the origin of 'actual' action and event phenomena generated by active agents. But these phenomena may exhibit transfactual elements, elements that are *apparently* out of kilter with what have become established as the regular causal and formative forces of their 'deep' origins. The import of such irregularity of 'actual' actions and events is that there exist in particular observed cases some additional, atypical and contingent dimensions of human agency involved in the generation process that impede or distort the manifested phenomenal forms. Moreover, the empirical layer of action and event perceptions and interpretations introduce a further transitive dimension into the ontology. Here the mind of the transcendental subject agent is the mediating entity, with the necessary consequence being that any element of the 'actual' situational environment can be variously interpreted. That is, interpretations instigated by experience, perception and impression are the products of a diverse mental and cognitive processing that has its roots in the genetic and cumulative experiential qualities of the individual mind.

The challenge for human scientists is to identify and work with any regularities of appearance and consistency of linkages to 'deep' origins that can be identified in their 'actual' object phenomena. It is quite an insufficient basis for understanding and explanation for such identification to be left at the surface level of any observed action and event regularities. Penetration to the intransitive, 'deep' domain of the generative origins is essential if the observations are to have any regularized theoretical representation that the analyst can posit as a realist account of the way an action or event comes to occur. Acceptance of such a vision of reality leads on to the ontologically grounded transcendental realist metatheory of science in which the very purpose of investigations is to identify and articulate these 'deep' dimensions as they contribute to the generation of the empirical phenomena on which analysts focus. In the human sciences, the realism has a transcendental quality because the ontology is devised by reasoning about 'what the world must be like, given that certain phenomena (and especially generalized human practices) are observed' (Lawson, 1994b, p. 28, n5; cf. pp. 8ff).

For subjectivist economists, transcendental realism demands explicit recognition that it is essentially mental processes that constitute the underlying reality of the observed phenomena that are their objects of inquiry. The inference must be, then, that economists are to form thought constructs which can effectively represent in discursive form the deliberative processes and consequent decisions of agents which result in the object actions and events. Mental representation is thus a process that involves some particular specification of the intransitive structures of the reality, mediated by their sensory appearance and the active intervention of the mind. Here there emerges a very difficult, unavoidable and all but intractable problem for all human scientists: that of access to the structures and processes of other minds. It is to be recognized that, the idea of a layered ontology having been established, the 'deepest' level of all in the otherwise intransitive layer is the *transitive* dimension of agents' mental processes. This transitivity is aggravated by the additional fact that so much of agents' cognitive activity, as it is of concern to economists, relates to deliberating and making decisions about actions which have outcomes in the future. The significant concern for human science that emerges is that the creative mental processes of the active agents comprise an integral part of the 'deep' ontology underpinning object actions or events. These processes have an existential status that is highly subjectivist but no less real than the intransitive dimensions within which they are situated. And, to compound the difficulty, there are amongst these latter dimensions those that depend for their very existence on the instantiated results of agents' past and present creative actions. In their endeavours intellectually to grasp and discursively to represent an understanding of the origins of observed actions and events in realist terms, subjectivist analysts always confront an interpretive task. In this general sense, their investigative strategy must be *hermeneutical.* The crucial point is that it is only hermeneutics that enables the analyst of human phenomena to give priority to ontological integrity, for it *begins* from the notion of agents as voluntaristic but purposeful, conditioned and situated beings. So it may be validly argued that,

> if we hold that the proper object of economics is human *subjects*, is the *meaningful* behavior of human agents, it follows that we cannot get hold of our object in an appropriate manner unless we have a means of incorporating into our scientific accounts the understanding that agents themselves have of their own action, since this is, in the case of humans, constitutive of the meaning of the action itself. (Madison, 1988, pp. 6f, original emphasis)

Such hermeneutic procedures in human science are concerned to provide an interpretive understanding of the meaning structures upon which agents ground their actions. Subjective agents act on the basis of interpretations of their problems and environment by means of their multidimensional cognitive characteristics and abilities. Defining what agents can and do know, and establishing how and the extent to which they apply what they know, are issues requiring explicit attention. Analysts who aim to understand what these observed agents do must then be prepared to devise *an interpretation of the agents' interpretations* by means of their own subjectively conditioned cognition. That is, economists and other human scientists must contend with a 'double' hermeneutic in the sense that their science is not only essentially a 'mode of understanding, but also has for its object the understanding that economic agents *themselves* have of what as economic agents they do' (ibid., p. 6, original emphasis) .

In these procedures, there is the ever-present danger of scientific nihilism as a consequence of idealism and relativism, and a number of objectivist critics have rejected hermeneutics on this ground. It must be said, though, that such concerns carry most weight when the extreme of an idealist form of subjectivism is presumed to be at issue. The import of this presumption, should it be made, is expressed in Steve Fleetwood's summary that, while 'the existence of an external entity is ... recognized, *any structure humans perceive in it is the result of the cognitive capacity of the mind, not the objective properties of the entity*' (1995, p. 18, original emphasis). The entailed effect is to render '*hermeneutical foundationalism*' as the only possible form of the hermeneutic approach. This, according to Fleetwood, is a 'version of extreme subjectivism' in which the claim is made that 'the social world is entirely conceptual in nature, that is, the social world is not merely concept-*dependent*, but concept-*determined.* Put another way, the social world is *exhausted* by the conceptions that agents hold' (ibid., original emphasis). It is clear from my argument so far about the nature of subjectivism that a different metatheoretical perspective concerning its hermeneutical implications is adopted here.

It is Lawson's notion of *critical realism* (1997, pp. 157f), as the crucial strategic principle combining a realist social ontology and the metatheory of science he refers to as transcendental realism, that I will maintain is the most fundamental starting point for subjectivists in search of a methodology. The reason for this, expressed in Lawson's words, is that critical realism 'shares with the hermeneutic tradition the understanding that economics, unlike natural science, deals with a pre-interpreted reality, a world already conceptualized by lay agents in their activities, and like that tradition it acknowledges the epistemological consequences of this' (Lawson, 1994e, p. 71). However, he goes on to assert that any combination of the hermeneutic and subjectivist traditions insists on a vision of 'social material' as 'exhausted by its conceptual component' (ibid.). My alternative is to envisage critical realism and hermeneutics as consistent, compatible and complementary methodological strategies required to maintain a subjectivist ontology. Hermeneutics is to be envisaged as the means of inquiry that will enable economics to achieve the 'deep' analytical insights that are the hallmark of critical realism. That is, in order to probe beneath the manifested 'surface' phenomena as they are observed and reach their 'deep' origins, analysts in the human sciences cannot avoid interpretation of the subjective and situated human agency involved. They are required to devise by interpretation discursively reasoned accounts of these origins that are consistent with the observed phenomena appearing as they do.

In order to do this, the interpretations of analysts are to form an integral part of the application in economics of the *retroductive* methodology, referred to by Lawson as 'primarily concerned not with the flux of events … but with identifying and understanding the necessary relations, mechanisms and so on that govern or condition it' (ibid., p. 70). Analysts achieve the required insight by relying upon their individually characterized capacities for introspection, classification and extrapolation when specifying the nature of the 'deep' domain and the place of active agents within it. They are called upon to interpret the nature, and assess the extent, of agents' dependence upon their prestructured situations in forming and choosing their action responses. That is, there will exist, for every human action and event, 'deep' origins which comprise some balance between contingent voluntarism and situational conditioning and containment. Subjectivists must confront this existential fact and come to grips with it methodologically as best they can. To this end, retroduction employs *as-if reasoning* by means of which analysts devise argument which 'consists of moving (on the basis of analogy, among other things) from a conception of some phenomenon of interest to a conception of some totally different type of thing, mechanism, structure or condition, that is responsible for, or facilitative of, the given phenomenon'. The consequence is that 'the task of science is to describe all that must be going on (whether or not adequately comprehended by the [active] agents involved) for some manifest social phenomenon, for some set of practices or activities, to be possible' (Lawson, 1994b, pp. 22, 23).

It is appropriate to emphasize at this point that there is little sense in a science for which the objective is accounting ex post *only* for singular and unique concrete phenomena that occur once and cannot be repeated in exactly the same form. Despite the open-ended, subjectivist origins of their object phenomena, hermeneutists are confronted by the challenge of identifying some degree of generality and objectivity in those phenomena necessary to render critical realist discursive analysis the basis for science. This will require some defensible identification and classification of *typical forms* of agency that can be accounted for with a minimum of voluntaristic intrusions. Realism is preserved if the typification of actions and events within some taxonomy of categories maintains sufficient ontological integrity for actual actions and events as they are observed to be linked to their 'deep' origins in spite of the abstractions that must be involved.

In order to improve on the state of economic theory and its predictive acumen from a realist and subjectivist perspective by employing typified categories, the requirement is that we ask about the specific factors that contribute to the contingency and openness of economic systems that deny us the use of typification.[4] These factors should then be seen as counterbalanced by the fact that agents always operate in and through the constraints and facilities provided by some inherited and objectively existent situation of common relevance to agents in a certain category, a fact that brings some degree of closure to the nature of their actions. The consequence for analysts in economics is that agents' actions and events should refer to particular type categories rather than to individual examples of such events. Critical realist accounts claiming understanding of the typical and implying a potential for prediction will, nevertheless, always be fallible and contingent, and thus subject to rejection on critically reasoned grounds.

Three crucial concerns surface here to impede the epistemological reach of critical realism and ontological typification in economics. One is the widely accepted notion that agents' personal knowledge, as it is applied in dealing with practical matters, is not always discursively available even to agents themselves. This supraconscious level of knowledge is used by agents without its becoming part of the explicable reasoning that precedes action. Another concern is the capacity of human beings to be creative, so that there will be no unique correspondence between any problem, together with its existential conditions, and a particular agent's action response to it. A final consideration is the also widely accepted view that, whatever may be the reasoned intentions of agents in carrying out some action, its consequences will generally include elements that were not part of those intentions. Observing the particular *results* of actions, therefore, can never be a wholly reliable indicator of agents' actual motives and intentions. In a strict sense, then, for the reasons implied in these concerns, it is an impossible task for the analyst bent on retroductive investigation to break into the mental constitution that underpins the observed actions of subject agents. But it is, nonetheless, the task that actually confronts human scientists intending to provide an understanding of what human agents do. Understanding and explaining human phenomena requires that economists make some metatheoretically defensible endeavour to resolve the problems thus posed.

1.4 A LOOK AHEAD

My theme is subjectivism as the metatheoretical foundation for what has become known as Austrian economics. In the chapters that follow, I examine and critically assess the ideas of each of the main contributors to this foundation over the generations stretching from Carl Menger (1840–1921) to the 1970s revival and beyond. As I have previously considered this theme at length with emphasis on the work of Menger and Ludwig von Mises (1881–1973), the next two chapters here provide only limited summaries of their particular contributions as subjectivists (see Oakley, 1997b). Chapter 2 deals briefly with Menger as the ultimate founder of Austrian subjectivism. His second generation successors were Eugen von Böhm-Bawerk (1851–1914) and Friedrich von Wieser (1851–1926), but only the latter was able to keep the Mengerian subjectivist thesis going in Austrian economics. Also in Chapter 2, I find that Wieser had some quite profound insights in this direction, and that his legacy was to be transmitted to later generations of Austrians mainly through the efforts of his most renowned student, Friedrich von Hayek (1899–1992). Chapter 3 explains that it was Mises who attempted the task of carrying forward the subjectivism of Menger into this century. His writings during the period leading up to the 1970s became, as a consequence, the main bridge between the founder and the ultimate revival of subjectivist economics. However, it was to be Hayek who produced the most extensive and penetrating subjectivist contributions to the maintenance of a separate Austrian economics. Chapters 4 to 8 are devoted to the many facets of his core thesis that, if economics is to be Austrian, it must be grounded on subjectivism and give emphasis to the actions of the individual human agent.

As the extent of my coverage suggests, pursuing this thesis led Hayek into wide-ranging researches. He began as an erstwhile formal theorist, but, as is shown in Chapter 4, he was always destined to have the ideas of subjectivism overtake his theoretical endeavours. From a very early date, the idea that human agency must matter in understanding economic activity intruded into some of his most abstract and formalistic writings. Hayek's encounter with the economics of socialism provided him with the opportunity to elicit the virtues of capitalist free market organization and to conceive of its competitive basis as a process. Chapter 5 shows how this generated his vision of an economic order in which the challenge for analysts was to understand the collective consequences of individual actions as they are shaped by the structures of the market and constitute the processes that generate its outcomes. It was the immanent distribution of knowledge amongst agents that emerged in this context as the key means by which the process of competition between them creates an unplanned order out of their unilateral choices and decisions.

From the beginning of his career, Hayek pursued an interest in understanding the way the human agent functions as an individual and in the society of others. His psychological research and the understanding of cognitive processes and reason that he worked up, together with his subsequent inquiries concerning the shaping of individual action by external situational circumstances, are the themes of Chapters 6 and 7. To conclude my Hayek studies, I reflect upon the contributions he made to providing a methodology that is consistent with the demands of subjectivism as the essential requirement for understanding and accounting for economic phenomena. He rejected scientism, the direct adoption of physical science methodology by the human sciences, but his progress towards putting something in its place was minimal. Indeed, as is argued in Chapter 8, he lost some of the impetus to do so when he retreated towards the notion that, somehow, all scientific inquiry is the same and that only the degree of complexity of its objects varies. Human science, including economics, confronts the most complex of objects, but its methodology should aim to maintain the epistemological standards of physical inquiry as far as possible. It could do so, Hayek ultimately believed, by means of the appropriate preparation of its objects prior to analysis.

The German, Ludwig Lachmann (1906–90) was intellectually an Austrian by adoption. He was a contemporary of Hayek's who made his mark on subjectivist economics by developing the claim that the others had missed much that is important in the subjectivist thesis. His 'radical' version of the theme enabled him to play the 'devil's advocate' in the 1970s revival of Austrian economics. But, as is explained in Chapters 9 and 10, his subjectivist journey began many years before. He had always been concerned to promote the problematic of including the role of human agency in any understanding of economic phenomena. For him, this meant the explicit inclusion of the exigencies of human volition, real time and uncertainty, and the need for agents to plan their actions with the aid of expectations about the future. The result was a representation of all economic phenomena as processes flowing from the uncoordinated independent actions of individual agents with no inherent means of bringing order to the outcomes. In such a kaleidic vision of the economy, equilibrium could have no place and the notion of order had to take on a different hue. And, as Lachmann realized, the results for methodological design were profound. In Chapter 10, we will find him facing up to the challenge of *Verstehen*, understanding, as the objective of economics and, consequently, delving all too briefly into the potentials of typification and hermeneutics as apt methodological strategies. As the final chapter concludes, though, in these endeavours he joined his antecedents and his contemporary Hayek in leaving much scope in the post-1970s revival of subjectivist economics for difference of opinion and for further development. The result of their varied and inconclusive legacy has been factionalization amongst the small number of neoAustrian contributors who have been prepared to carry on the pursuit of economics as a strictly human science. The intellectual progress and substantive penetration of this pursuit have been impeded as a consequence.

NOTES

1. Barry Smith elicits several characteristics of Austrian philosophy more generally that can be considered to have set it apart during the second half of the nineteenth century, and he concludes that each of the eight elements listed played no role in the German traditions of the same period. The most significant of these characteristics for my present purposes have been included in the outline that follows (Smith, 1990a, pp. 266ff; 1990c, pp. 214f).
2. Another means of doing so is behaviourism that attributes understanding to observation of action alone. This may well give some purpose to the experimental study of human action, or its simulation by animal substitutes, but it inclines investigators to isolate their conclusions from the essentially subjective mental and cognitive processes that precede and produce action.
3. In the brief metatheoretical outline to follow, I have drawn upon a number of extant sources in the literature, sometimes without specific citations. As will become apparent, it has been the reading of Tony Lawson's many contributions that has afforded me the most insight (1988, 1989, 1994b, 1994c, 1994e, 1997). But appropriate general acknowledgements are also due to Steve Fleetwood (1995), Norton Jacobi (1990) and Uskali Mäki (1988a, 1990).
4. Any immediate realist claim to such generality and objectivity can only be potentially secure in the strictest sense if the system that comprises the phenomenon and its generative origins is *closed* rather than open. *System closure* requires the extrinsic condition that a

particular set of external causes can only and always be linked reliably to particular effects *and* the intrinsic condition that any particular effect has a constant and singular set of causes (Lawson, 1989, pp. 241ff). However, the problem for realists in the human sciences is that all systems that are their objects of investigation are *open* rather than closed in these respects. Lawson, for example, notes that 'for the realist, a constant conjunction of events can be expected to occur only under certain special conditions – those in which the operating of some enduring causal mechanism is effectively isolated from the effects of other mechanisms. It is only in such a case that there may be one-to-one correspondence between the acting of some causal entity and actual events'. He concludes that 'for many realists a situation or system in which a constant conjunction of events holds – which I ... refer to as a *close system* – is considered ... to be the exceptional case rather than the general rule' (ibid., p. 240, original emphasis). In economics, the extrinsic condition is violated by the independent dynamics and ever variable influence of the situational environment confronted and interpreted by agents and the intrinsic condition by the immanent flux of the various contingent elements of subjectivist conduct that characterize agents.

2. A historical sketch of seminal Austrian subjectivism

2.1 CARL MENGER

It is well recognized in the historical literature that the founder of Austrian economics as it is characterized in the present day was Carl Menger (Oakley, 1997b; cf. Vaughn, 1990, 1994). Such recognition has caused a move away from the reading of him as but one of the trinity of marginal theorists who reoriented economics towards what is now its dominant neoclassical form (Jaffé, 1976). His achievement comprised much more than any contribution to marginalist thought that he may have made, and his theoretical reforms really take us into a vision of the economy that cannot be confined within neoclassical tenets. The deep-seated subjectivism he espoused and his emphasis on processes, in particular, were just too profound in their implications for the methodology and substance of economics to be readily set out in any formalized expression. He had an ostensible desire to develop a universal and exactly argued body of theory, but expressing his key arguments in any Walrasian-like model never proved to be desirable or possible. Moreover, the prominence Menger gave to subjective value theory was but one element in a much broader appreciation of the implications of subjectivism in economics. In his main writings, the focus was on the subjective nature and origin of all economic phenomena as the products of individual human decisions, choices and action.

It is to Menger that we owe the enduring insight that economics is a subjectivist science. It concerns itself primarily with phenomena that are generated by the deliberations, plans and actions of individuals in that most fundamental of human preoccupations, the endeavour to satisfy material and other essential needs and wants. He depicted agents as engaging in activities dedicated to maximizing this objective within the bounds of their given environment, situational conditions and individual capacities. The relevant operations of production, exchange and distribution in which agents participate are all geared to this objective one way or another, and it is these operations, carried out as processes set in time, that constitute the vitalist vision of the economy perceived by Menger. Agents exhibit all the characteristics that render their conduct contingent with respect to any given problem and situation. They act according to various combinations of their innate characteristics and free-will, together with their desires, beliefs, preferences, values, knowledge, information and expectations. Their deliberations and plans relate to the future and are thus always replete with uncertainty, in spite of which agents must act economically. In doing so, agents expose their fallibility; they endeavour to mitigate their uncertainty as far as possible through obtaining knowledge and information, but they are often forced to act on incomplete states of both; they reveal their limitations as calculators; and they make errors of judgement.

The result of these insights for Menger was a theoretical exposition which, for all its imprecisions and incompleteness, tried to capture the essential idea that subjectivist economics is about human agency and the processes it generates. It is not about mere states of the economy because it deals with systems in time in constant flux, so that it is an inherently dynamic rather than a static inquiry. He was no equilibrium economist in any systematic sense as a consequence. Although his writings included references to the potential for individual and partial equilibria to exist, the essential thrust of his vision was towards non-equilibrating processes. However, his intense and wide-ranging subjectivist wisdom, and his consciousness of time in human affairs, were to take him beyond what he could formally include in his attempts at formulating discursive representations of the phenomena on which he focused. Nevertheless, it is apparent that he was well aware of virtually all of the dimensions of human agency that should be included in a subjectivist metatheory, and that he sensed the analytical intractability that resulted. Menger's Austrian successors were to confront a difficult task in carrying forward the real meaning and extent of his subjectivist vision for economics.

2.2 FRIEDRICH VON WIESER

No less an authority than Friedrich von Hayek himself has informed us of the Mengerian bona fides of the second generation Austrians: Eugen von Böhm-Bawerk and Friedrich von Wieser were students of Menger's work in the sense that 'they decided to make the fulfilment of his teaching their lifework. It was mainly through … [their] work … that Menger's ideas were developed and spread' (Hayek, 1992, p. 46). But of these two, it was only Wieser who turned out to be philosophically and metatheoretically inclined.[1] He preserved a fundamental interest in the subjectivist roots of economic conduct and adopted for further development Menger's main insights into the nature and role of human agency in economics. Wieser's position on subjectivism and its methodology, as a representative of the Austrian School, was summed up for the most part in the three contributions to be examined here: first, his

1911 review (1994) of Joseph Schumpeter's *Das Wesen und der Hauptinhalt der theoretischen Nationalökonomie*; second, some relevant pieces from his magnum opus, *Social Economics* (1967), a 1927 translation of the work that appeared in two identical 'editions' in 1914 and 1924, *Theorie der gesellschaftlichen Wirtschaft*; and third, the *Law of Power* (1983) that was originally published only a few months before his death in 1926 as *Das Gesetz der Macht*.

One of Wieser's most explicitly subjectivist metatheoretical pieces was his richly insightful 1911 review of Schumpeter's errant methodological and substantive challenge to mainstream Austrians of the time in *Das Wesen und der Hauptinhalt der theoretischen Nationalökonomie*. Schumpeter rejected the notion that methodology in economics is of primary importance and requires explicit attention in isolation from substantive matters. It was his alternative claim that an appropriate methodology would simply emerge out of the substance of the phenomena addressed in the theory formation process. As Wieser observed, 'Schumpeter ... believes at the end that he can attain a unifying methodological way of thinking – "Methodology must not be the first but the last chapter of a system" – and he confidently expects that from his way of working "something like an epistemology of economics or a contribution thereto" will develop' (Wieser, 1994, p. 286). Wieser's sole intention was to give a critical account of the success or otherwise of this approach. He did so in order to expose the misrepresentation evident in Schumpeter's claims to have adhered to established Austrian principles.

In particular, while there were similarities in the results of his analyses, he had deviated from the demands of the 'psychological method' in arriving at them (p. 286). Wieser's belief was that 'anyone who accepts our results must also accept our method; they cannot be divorced from one another' (p. 287). The crucial reason for this was that a subjectivist interpretation of economic phenomena made specific demands on, and set epistemological limitations for, the legitimate methodology to be employed in understanding them. Wieser put it categorically that, as an economist, 'I believe that I must keep within the boundaries of my science and must avoid making epistemological claims or even couching my testimony on the substance of economic understanding in terms which are foreign to common experience' (p. 292). In failing fully to recognize the subjectivist premises upon which economics depends as prior to the pertinent methodology, what Schumpeter had actually done was to impose an approach to analysis that he simply presumed to be legitimate without further reflection upon the ontological nature of the object phenomena to be dealt with.

Wieser's critical reaction was to assert that 'I do not believe that Schumpeter's methodology has really grown out of the material in the way that he says, for ... [in] reality he brings in, without knowing it, his methodological concept ready-made from outside: he is under the spell of the epistemology which has recently been developed by the exact natural sciences' (p. 287). Most striking is Wieser's reference here to the forcing of analyses in economics to meet the predilections of physical science methodology without concern for the loss of ontological integrity with respect to the true subjectivist origins and nature of its object phenomena. Schumpeter was, he believed, so 'blinded by the success of the exact natural sciences, he takes their way of thinking as a model even where it in no way suits our material'. In particular, his 'methodological concept infringes the psychological foundations of our results' (p. 287). His conclusion was that 'Schumpeter would have described the substance of theoretical economics more fully and more simply if he had not wanted to portray its nature according to his method' (p. 302).

By contrast, Wieser was adamant that, whatever the methodological consequences, subjectivism must remain the foundation for understanding human action in economics. For economic analysts, the 'subject-matter is ... the consciousness of a person engaging in economic activity with his treasure-house of universal experience, that is, the experience possessed by every practitioner and which every theoretician finds ready in him as a practitioner without his first needing to gather it by means of special scientific methods' (Wieser, 1994, p. 289). 'Schumpeter's procedure was to observe economic facts from outside alone, just as natural scientists do with phenomena, whereas the psychological method observes them above all from inside one's consciousness. It does so because from there it can observe incomparably more and in more depth than from outside'. Wieser continued: 'The best method will always be the one which yields the most knowledge; here ... it is the psychological method, because it uses the most favourable observation post. In the store of common economic experience, it finds all the most important facts of economics assembled, and why should it not draw on them at the source?' (pp. 290f). His conclusion was to claim a priority for subjectivism in any economics: 'There has never been a theoretical school of economics which would have worked without these psychological overtones; the psychological school differs from all the older ones only in that it has created a method from their naive process' (p. 297).

To add to this subjectivist emphasis, Wieser revealed an even more profound insight into the problematic of the human mind as it must be confronted by analysts: 'The mind works unconsciously and cannot give an account of why the facts appear and disappear in it; there is something more under the threshold of consciousness on which it depends, which we do not control and which is as foreign to our sense as external nature' (ibid., p. 291). The implications of this fact of life for analysts was that their methodology took on what amounts to a hermeneutical orientation. In economics, this orientation is bound to leave a metatheoretical remainder for analysts to confront, as he realized: 'It should not be forgotten that external observations have a metaphysical background too, and just as the natural scientist overcomes it, we can do so too with regard to internal observation' (p. 292). Schumpeter's contrary view, which followed from his imposed scientific method meant that, 'by avoiding introspection, ... [he] hopes not only to steer clear of the risk of engaging in metaphysics and avoid everything of an a priori nature, but also to obtain the further great advantage of bypassing a whole range of difficult controversies with which theory has become burdened' (p. 293). What Wieser had realized was that the difficulties at root in these controversies were inherent in the nature of the subject and could not be resolved by methodological strategies alone.

For Wieser, the key metatheoretical problem of economics was how to ensure consistency between the substance of theoretical analyses and the ontological realities of the phenomena that are the objects of those analyses. These realities, as he was clearly aware, involved the exigencies of human action as the origin of the phenomena. He had some very explicit things to say about this problematic when he considered the nature of simplifying assumptions required to ensure analytical tractability. To begin with, 'the assumptions which the psychological school uses are all empirical. However numerous they are, they must all be supported by the facts.' (ibid., p. 294) Among other things, given the realism being sought, this posed the question, 'why does the [psychological] school use assumptions, a seemingly artificial aid, at all?' (p. 294). The reason given by Wieser was one that related explicitly to the subjectivist ontology of object phenomena in economics. He believed that, as analysts, we 'depend on them because of the circumstances under which we make our observations. We can only make *observations into thoughts* with the aid of the visual memories of the facts which we store in our consciousness; direct observation of the working psyche is denied to us'. As he realized, too, 'experimentation ... is denied to us by the nature of our object; we cannot even attempt it to the limited extent to which it is available to scientific psychology'. The resulting implication was that in economics especially, 'a theory which wishes to exploit the rich substance of common economic experience has to develop a whole range of assumptions in order to make its observations into thoughts, one after the other, under secure control' (p. 294, emphasis added).

Whatever its ontological complexity and raw intractability, an observed economic phenomenon must be represented by building on assumptions that are not hypothetical, arbitrary or artificially formalized. The procedure envisaged by Wieser here was one in which the analyst must recognize that assumptions have a 'usefulness or appropriateness [that] depends on their truth. In this it is wholly acceptable that they do not always offer the whole truth' (p. 294). That is, empirically sound simplifications comprise the essence of acceptable assumptions, for just as 'the natural scientist does in experimentation', we as economists must also 'isolate when making observations into thoughts; the complex experiences cannot be interpreted as a whole, we have to split them into their elements in order to understand what they mean; only then are we in a position to deduce the overall effect by assembling the discrete units' (p. 294). This procedure, Wieser continued, 'requires one to deviate from the straight truth to the extent that the elements never enter one's consciousness individually; but this is surely a permissible deviation … [for] after all, the ultimate intention is to reach full agreement with the facts, and therefore theory does not lose its empirical nature by making use of isolation' (pp. 249f).

A further implication of this simplification process posited by Wieser is that it may need to include an idealizing of assumptions. As he stressed, though, this extension is not an invention of Austrian economists, for 'it has been used since people begun [*sic*] to think scientifically' (ibid., p. 295). These idealized elements of reality 'contain less than the whole truth', but 'in them we elevate the empirical case in thoughts to the level of the highest possible perfection'. And as a subjectivist, the most obvious example he could give was that of assuming 'the existence of a model person engaging in economic activity such as has never actually existed and never can' (p. 295). But if properly constructed, such typifying assumptions 'in no way render our theory unempirical, for they too are always only made in order to understand reality, and therefore they are only temporary assumptions which in the end have to be corrected' (p. 295). So it is, then, that an idealizing assumption is used, 'like isolation, as a temporary aid in order to deduce rules under simplified conditions which are only then applied to the complex conditions of reality' (p. 295).

Wieser went on to build much of the metatheory revealed in the critique of Schumpeter into his *Social Economics*, written over the years from 1911 to 1914. He emphasized from the outset that the focus of the work was to be on the 'psychological' approach to economics 'because the theory takes its point of departure from within, from the mind of the economic man' (Wieser, 1967, p. 3). But he wanted to distance his subjectivist economic analyses from any notion that they constitute 'scientific psychology' per se or have any links to its physiological foundations. To this end, his claim was that 'the observations concerning the inner life of man, which our "psychological" theory of economics develops, have been made by it independently', and he based this on the belief that 'our discipline does not seek and could not find direct aid from this source' (p. 3). Economics should not 'follow the sequence of ideas in the individual consciousness beyond the point at which prompts to action are explained. It should … avoid any more penetrating psychological analysis' (p. 4).

Most importantly, he maintained the thesis that economics is founded upon the commonsense experiences of all human agents: 'The sphere of economic theory has the same limits as ... common experience' and the 'task of the theorist ends at the boundary of common experience' (ibid., p. 4). Thus he argued in strongly subjectivist terms that 'it is the problem of economic theory to exhaust scientifically the content of everyday economic experience and to interpret it' (p. 3). To do so required the additional belief that the analyst 'finds in the consciousness of every economically active human being a wealth of experiences which are [the] common property of all' and that 'these are experiences which every scientist shares with the layman, without resort to special scientific instruments' (p. 4). More specifically, they comprise 'experiences concerning the facts of the outer world, as for example, the presence of goods of various sorts; experiences concerning the source and current of the economic activity of mankind' (p. 4). Wieser felt that these characteristics of its object phenomena gave economic inquiry a distinct scientific advantage by comparison with the non-human sciences. He posed his position rhetorically: 'Can we conceive of economic theory refusing to draw from a fountain-head so inexhaustible in its riches, so dependable in its purity!' and concluded that 'it will be the natural method of its investigations, to follow the guidance offered by our recollection of the course and significance of the economy which is practically familiar to all of us' (p. 4). In all of this argument we find Wieser quite ready to confront the necessarily subjectivist nature of the metatheoretical foundations of economics. Its phenomena were clearly the products of active human agents and could only be understood and represented as such analytically. The next step was to inquire about a methodology that could ensure that the ontology of such phenomena is preserved in economic theory.

For Wieser, 'the method of economic theory is empirical. It is supported by observation and has but one aim, which is to describe actuality' (ibid., p. 5). Of course, as he noted, any human 'actuality' would be too complex to grasp theoretically in its immediately observed state. Therefore 'economic theory does not attempt to describe the actual in its entirety, as purely empirical sciences are wont to do' (p. 5). And as the required methodology was to be such as to preserve ontological integrity in the abstract terms of the theory, this implied the need to resort to typification as a mode of ensuring the presence of the ontologically defining characteristics of a phenomenon. As a result, the economist 'endeavours to place before us the typical phenomenon, the typical development, and to eliminate whatever may be subordinate, accidental or individual' (p. 5). According to Wieser, then, because 'complex experiences cannot possibly be interpreted as wholes' they must be 'isolated and separated into their elements in order that their effects may be known. The elements, moreover, must ideally be protected from all disturbing influences, in order that the pure effect may be recognized'. And, beyond this, when the disturbing factors are re-introduced in the pursuit of realism, 'they in their turn must be stripped of everything accidental in order to study their typical progress' (p. 5). Perhaps in an effort to comfort his readers, he maintained, too, that this methodological position was not, in itself, all that different from that thought valid in the natural sciences. Just as 'isolation and idealization' are the instruments of economic inquiry, these 'have always been the instruments of man pursuing other truly empirical sciences, for example, the exact physical sciences. Like the naturalist performing an experiment, the theoretical economist is bound to isolate, when making observations' (p. 5).

From this point, Wieser argued that further progress in the design of economic theory requires that 'side by side with the isolating assumptions which embrace less than the entire truth', the analyst must 'form numerous idealizing assumptions which embrace more than the truth' (ibid., p. 5). Such idealizations are 'conscious transformations of the known' that are 'designed to accentuate [its] essential features' so as to simplify experience and render it analytically tractable (p. 6). As an example of idealization, Wieser gave that of the assumed 'existence of a model man, a man such as actually has never existed, nor can ever exist' (p. 5). However, his vision of 'economic man' was one which, in principle, would include dimensions beyond the narrow confines of that employed by Classical economists. They 'stopped at abstractions too remote from actuality, and hence unequal to the task of making it fully intelligible', for they 'have not appreciated correctly the very elements of economic life'. The reason for this was that 'their fundamental assumptions are not rooted in adequate observation' (p. 7). In this respect, any economic theory founded upon representing human agency must move rapidly beyond any constrained definition of isolated 'economic man'. It 'should discern the community of interests, but no less should it recognize power, the conflict of motives and the economic evil. It should furnish a sound theoretical basis for freedom and also for restrictions of freedom' (p. 9). And, as already indicated, Wieser believed that integral to the required 'observation' in economics were the revelations of introspection. So, because 'the object of investigation is man in a condition of activity', it is possible that, as analysts, 'our mind ratifies every accurate description of the processes of his consciousness by the affirmative declaration that such is the case, and by the compelling feeling that it must be so necessarily. ... In these cases we, each of us, hear the law pronounced by an unmistakable inner voice' (p. 8).

In forming these abstractions from reality, the analyst 'raises the empirical fact reflectively to the highest degree of perfection conceivable. But the most perfect state is at the same time the most simple and the most readily understood'. It is then a required extension of this procedure that, in order to understand reality, the analyst must 'step by step by a system of decreasing abstraction … render his assumptions more concrete and multiform' (ibid., p. 6). Moreover, it will be a further requirement that the theorist join forces with historians, statisticians and political analysts in order finally to bring theory to its full meaning and significance in the context of reality. They can provide empirical details that economic theory necessarily avoids, because, although it must be empirical in its origins, as explained above, it cannot be immediately empirical in and of itself. But 'from its very beginning it looks towards a union with the methods of purely empirical science for whose efforts it prepares the ground' (p. 7).[2]

The substantive structure and contents of the *Social Economics* cannot be pursued in any detail here. Suffice it to say that Wieser applied his methodology of decreasingly abstract analyses in designing the approach to what was, overall, a heavily subjectivist inquiry. We are informed that the four parts of the study are such that 'the first starts with the most idealized assumptions. The later ones proceed by decreasing abstraction to conditions of reality' (ibid., p. 9). Most significantly in the present context, it is apparent that the modelling of human agency was an essential part of this progressive methodology. And even a desultory perusal of the work reveals a continual primacy of human action, first of all in isolation and then in situ within a structure of social relations and institutions. Specifically, the 'theory of the "simple economy" in the first book begins with the idealizing assumption that the subject is a single person' in the form of 'an ideal economic subject' (pp. 9, 10). This idealized agent is 'in full possession of his powers [and] he obeys economic principles and is liable neither to error, passion nor weakness'. And, because 'mankind is treated as a unit' at this stage, there can be 'no more consideration of conflicting interests or of economic justice than there would be in the economy of a Crusoe' (p. 10). Wieser's subjectivist awareness was further highlighted by his qualified use of rationalism and utilitarianism. The simple economy arguments were developed by focusing on the 'effects of economic purposes on economic processes' involving a single agent without consideration of 'the conditions that accompany the formation of the socio-economic powers' (p. 19). This focus on purpose was made more specific by assuming that agents strive for 'the greatest usefulness of economic action' in order to emphasize 'the maximum influence of purpose on national economy' (p. 20). But Wieser hastened to add that his abstract vision of human agency 'does not imply that we are either rationalist or utilitarian'. For, as he explained, 'we expect to show later by a process of decreasing abstraction what diminution of this maximum is required by typical conditions' (p. 20). This suggests a consciousness of the fact that agents are delimited in their capacities to realize the maximization of their economic well-being and that criteria other than utilitarian concerns will be included in their motivations for economic action.

In the second stage of the work, devoted to what Wieser called the 'theory of exchange', the single agent is situated in a social context and must relate to others. It is the 'exchange contract' that acts as 'the coordinating instrument that binds the individual economies into the national economy' (ibid., p. 150). He emphasized such 'exchange' as a mode of inter-agent contact and mutual influence. These contacts were perceived as the result of the fact that 'man is too weak to assure his preservation and to develop his life if he stands as an isolated individual', and it is 'the egoistic interest that grows from an appreciation of weakness … [that] leads to social organization' (p. 155). So, although 'in part, men are … led by [self-] conscious deliberation', there is a fundamental 'social impulse … operative; man is by nature a social being' (p. 155). So it is that 'in social communion they receive those psychological restraints which sustain them. Each man feels his steps controlled by his family, his associates and his surroundings'. The reference here was to 'the rules of economic life [that] are creations of society, just as are the laws of property. The individual forces called into play to carry these laws into effect have also been socially trained' (p. 37). This extension to the social context requires the recognition of two crucial characteristics of situated agents. First, the analyst must 'consider the inequality of possessions as well as the inequality of personal aptitudes due to natural talents and education'. For this reason, the analyst must 'modify the idealizing assumption of the modern householder in so far at least as to place in his stead the types of the principal classes of society in all their most important gradations' (p. 11). Secondly, 'a complete economic theory is now bound to describe, as well as the principal types, the displacements brought about by the occurrence of power, especially of the capitalistic power' (p. 11).

These were vital steps forward by Wieser in recognizing and modelling the true nature of human action, most especially because it enabled him to present the outcome of market competition more realistically than had been possible using the assumed perfections of the 'invisible hand'. Under perfect competition, with homogeneous and omnipotent human agents, it may be assumed that 'self-interest is being forced into subserviency to the general welfare. One may take it for granted that the power of competition will direct selfseeking efforts towards that goal and [one] may acquiesce in a theory of the economic society, which merely analyses it into a sum of individuals' (p. 11). But, in situating individualized agents in a social context that makes due allowance for the realities of the market, attention must be drawn 'to the full extent of the conflict waged between power and weakness. Thereafter it will be possible to acknowledge social unity only if more effective unifying forces than self-interest are observed, forces that are strong enough to bend even the most powerful' (p. 11). In these real-world circumstances, 'in order to be convincing … a modern economic theory requires for its completion *a more profound theory of society*' (p. 11, emphasis added). This challenge of properly situating the individual subjective agent in a realistically defined social environment was one which all Austrian subjectivists had to face.

For Wieser, it was only appropriate to depict human agents as decisively conditioned by a situational environment that shapes and directs virtually every aspect of their character and actions. At the most essential level of human existence and identity, 'even the consciousness of self – the inner assurance of each man that he is a being apart from all others – is influenced by social forces, and thus takes a direction that is not entirely personal. There are innumerable breaches in consciousness through which social influences enter, impelling it to courses prescribed by society' (ibid., p. 160). He also made it plain that, as well as being subject to the morals and laws of his time, the agent is more broadly 'a creature of his period and his environment – of his nation, his class and his profession. That which appears as individual in him is a particular form of the typical manner of life ... [that] he receives through ... education' (p. 158). And, while it is self-evident that the agent's 'knowledge and skill are the result of his education' both formal and informal, Wieser extended this notion to include a 'social education [that] penetrates to the very heart of his individual being. Needs, impulses and egoism itself are dominated by social powers' (p. 158). He went even further to assert that 'man's senses are socially determined' in the sense that the actual impression they make on the agent is a matter of interpretation that is mind-dependent, with the mediation of the mind itself influenced by its social conditioning (p. 159). This meant that how agents respond to sensory input is likewise affected by social forces: 'the impulses to activity are not purely personal. For the average man they are entirely dependent upon the practice of his time and environment for their direction and their strength'. The will to act is 'schooled impulse; even more than the impulse itself, will is socially developed' (p. 159). As a consequence, the individual is in a situation in which 'his Ego is not satisfied unless it finds itself in all important respects at one with society. If one is truly socially educated, his Ego departs from him and finds its end in society; it ceases to be purely personal and becomes social egoism; it wishes to conform in all respects to law and custom and in general to the social forces of the economy' (p. 161). So, in case of economic action in particular, 'the direction and standard of economic endeavour cannot be determined entirely personally', for the most basic motivations and objectives are 'interpreted by everyone in the light of his social environment' (p. 159). And 'in most matters a man accepts the social code of the industrial or social group of which he is a member' (p. 161).

What all this meant for Wieser was that a narrow form of individualism could be of limited relevance in economics. For, to understand the processes of the economy, 'one must first perceive the readiness of the individual to range himself in the social order. One must see him as a social being who develops through social education' (ibid., p. 163). He concluded that 'the current individualist concept of the economic principle is a theoretical idealization' from which the analyst 'must make a transition, by decreasing abstraction, to the social concept that is actually current, if ... [he] would understand the concrete phenomena of life' (p. 160). He summed up the importance of giving economic analysis its proper social setting by arguing that 'an economic theory that should suffice for our times is inconceivable without a social theory that is consistent with the fact of power' (p. 154). His view of the situational conditioning of agents began from the premise that 'the theory of the simple economy only explains the condition of the isolated and idealized individual economy that follows its laws of motion without restraint'. But in the social economy, 'these individual units meet from all directions. Indeed, they clash with great force'. Economic analysts should seek to 'ascertain whether their conjunction does not alter their law of motion' and to establish the conditions under which 'the individual movements are so well coordinated that the spirit of the economy is fulfilled for all participants'. And, where this is the case, they 'must ask by what power the individuals, each of whom independently follows his own law, are held to a common purpose and enabled to work to a single end' (pp. 151f).

But, be this social conditioning as it may, Wieser was determined to maintain a properly defined and qualified *individualist* position as integral to his subjectivism. For 'one cannot get away from ... [the] fundamental concept, that the individual is the subject of social intercourse. The individuals who comprise society are the sole possessors of all consciousness and of all will'. And, while 'one must hold himself aloof from the excesses of the individualistic exposition, ... the explanation must still run in terms of the individual' (ibid., p. 154). On this basis, it must be made evident that 'it is in the individual that one must look for those tendencies that make the social structure – that dove-tail ... in such a manner as to give the firm cohesion of social unity and at the same time provide the foundation for the erection of social power' (p. 154). It was this notion of power that Wieser used in its broadest sense to imply all dimensions of direction and control, volitional and coercive, that agents experience and accept from their situations (pp. 154f).

As Wieser noted briefly, the social environment in which agents find themselves and through which they operate is composed in part of institutions. Examples that were cited as important were money, the market, the division of labour and the national economy in which all the others are included (ibid., p. 162). He was aware that such institutions 'are so harmonious in structure as to suggest that they are the creation of an organized social will'. But, in fact, he pointed out that most of them 'can only have originated in the cooperation of periodically independent persons' so that 'the service of individual forces working together and working in successive generations, through centuries and millennia, toward the same end, may slowly build great economic structures'. That is, making reference to Menger, Wieser concluded that they had emerged as the unintended and undesigned product of combined individual actions through 'gradual historical evolution, which takes account of the powerful factor of time' (pp. 162, 163). In a similar way, change would come only slowly to institutions via such evolutionary processes. For individuals, 'the older institution creates a historical force because of its binding power'. But, although 'the individual is helpless against the historical force of old institutions ... [and] must take them as he finds them', some may initiate particular changes which accumulate into unintended transformations over time (p. 166).

Wieser further extended the dimensions of situations in which socialized agents find themselves in the economy by moving to introduce government institutions in the third stage of his analyses. In the 'theory of state economy', as he called it, the state is given an integral role in determining the structures and operations that constitute economic processes instigated by agents' actions. Wieser's view was that, 'if the co-operation of the state is needed in order that the well regulated current of the economic process be secured, economic theory, on its part, will have to describe in its most general features the influence which it exerts' (ibid., pp. 11f). At this point, though, he sidestepped the obvious normative questions about the extent and role of government in the economy broached by this proposed extension. For his purpose, he claimed that 'theory ... takes for granted an ideal state' even though 'it is well aware that the law deduced by it for a state of this sort, does not find concrete application in a single instance' (p. 12). Economics per se has no need to go beyond this step of further decreasing the abstraction involved in its analyses, with any idealization of the state in the economy being based upon abstractions from the observed realities of the time. And, by implication, much the same reasoning would apply to the fourth stage of opening up the 'state economy' to include institutions that make up the 'world economy' (p. 12).

What became increasingly apparent to Wieser as a result of his highly subjectivist economic inquiries and exposition in *Social Economics* was that some human agents have characters and/or are so placed within the structural conditions of the capitalist system as to be able to exercise various patterns of coercive power over others. This dimension of the system so concerned him that he devoted the last years of his life to another magnum opus directed at understanding it. The *Law of Power* (1983) was originally published, only a few months before his death in 1926, as *Das Gesetz der Macht.* Most importantly for the present context, implicit in its wide-ranging theoretical, historical and contemporary inquiry into the nature and consequences of power is a subjectivist image of socialized and situated individual human agency that carries over from that depicted in *Social Economics*. Wieser reiterated his vision of agents as what he now called '*synchronized members of society*' (1983, p. 64, original emphasis). For an agent, 'the ego feeling, by which a person recognizes himself in his innermost as being distinct from others ... is being influenced by unnoted but compelling social powers, thus being given a direction which is no longer purely personal'. This vision thus allows for agent consciousness that 'has untold points through which social influences can penetrate it and which guide it, to its very depths, into the socially well-worn tracks' (p. 64). So, in deciding upon actions, agents will have an 'ego feeling ... [that] is not satisfied unless it finds itself at one with society in all principal respects' (p. 64).

All this social obligation, nonetheless, remains consistent with the notion of an essential freedom for agents. Conformity entails a sacrifice for the individual: 'in a social group ... [an agent] must partly sacrifice his own personality ... at the very least a *sacrifice of independence of his will*' (p. 69, original emphasis). But Wieser referred to this social containment as a *sacrificium voluntatis* to stress its ultimately volitional nature. The basis for such voluntary restraint in actions was that it allows the agent to become 'part and parcel of a strong collective force which wins greater successes'. In this sense, 'success categorically demands collective action, and therefore even the most independent mind subjects itself to the collective will. Individuals do not want to stay apart from each other, but spontaneously arrange themselves in rank and file, all of them rendering consciously the strongly felt sacrifice of their own will'. By this means, 'every person becomes the active agent of the collective will which he translates into purposeful actions by means of his will' (p. 69).

At the same time, the work is constructed around what Wieser called the 'Law of Small Numbers', which argues that the differentiated agents who wield effective power are few in number and readily identified within the hierarchies that constitute the institutional structures of economy and polity. What this means for a subjectivist economics is that individual agents confront an additional, probably more constructed, dimension of situational influence on their conduct. This takes the form of the need to make choices about recognizing and obeying the dictates of other agents by virtue of their systemically or functionally imposed authority. As Wieser emphasized, this is an immanent form of power in which agents are effectively divided into leaders and followers within institutional organizations of various scopes. From this perspective, 'all constitutions are merely *variants of an ever recurring basic form*. Their *substance* always concerns the *division of power between leader and masses*' (ibid., p. 35, original emphasis). What emerges is a mix of continuing cooperation and potential tension between those so classified that must be understood as to their joint operation and effects on economic and political outcomes. For 'in social life leaders and masses have their certain functions which ... must be jointly active. If an association is to be able to act it must have both organs' (p. 35). And such powers of leaders over followers penetrates to all levels of the human life-world. Individual agents simply cannot exist independently of the power of others: 'There *is no such thing as an "individual for himself"*; it would not be viable' (p. 63, original emphasis). The difference between agents operating in their private life and in their social life is only a matter of degree. The power structures that surround them reach all their decisions and actions, although less so in the private than in the social spheres. As Wieser put it, 'personal energy manifests itself mostly only in the degree of independence by which the general norms are adapted to the personal circumstances', and 'there are probably few households which completely flout the social model; most of them accommodate themselves closely to it' (p. 63).

When we look back over the subjectivism of Wieser as it has been elicited here, we find a number of fundamental and durable contributions to our understanding of economics as a science of individual and collective human action. It simply did not occur to him to model the human agents responsible for the generation of economic phenomena as isolated, omnipotent and purely rational beings. They are, as realism in subjectivist economics demands, always of limited capacity and fallible, but at the same time socially and institutionally situated and conditioned in ways which enable them to transcend some of their shortcomings as active individuals. Agents were depicted as consciously and voluntarily using their inherited situations as means to guiding their actions towards acceptable if not maximized outcomes. For Wieser, it was this subjectivist ontology of economic phenomena that had to take priority in matters of methodological choice. The method of decreasing abstraction was indicative of this requirement in that it recognized from the outset that fully empirically specified phenomena would be intractable as analytical objects. But the method of beginning with abstract concepts to represent the essential features of reality was in principle acceptable because the intention was always to proceed immediately to render the concepts increasingly empirical. The analytical powers of analysts would then take care of the amount of detail that could ultimately be included in the formal argument and thus set the epistemological boundaries for economics as a science. Of course, some key points of pertinence to a fully fledged subjectivism remained missing from Wieser's account. These included, most especially, the exigencies of time and ignorance as these affect agents' decisions and actions. But as we will find in the work of Hayek to be analysed below, there was much that he found to be of enduring relevance in the legacy of the Austrian who had been his main formal teacher.

2.3 TRANSITION TO THE TWENTIETH CENTURY

After the turn of the twentieth century, the methodological and epistemological concerns resulting from an emphasis on the human exigencies of economics, as they had been confronted by Menger and carried forward by Wieser, faded in importance. Of what became the third generation of Austrians, it was only Mises who initially kept alive the broader implications of subjectivism for economics. Austrian contributions more generally began to appear increasingly like the generic marginalist doctrine that was to dominate twentieth-century orthodox economics, already widely accepted as being necessarily a theoretical, axiomatic–deductive discipline. Mises was soon joined by Hayek in undertaking metatheoretical inquiries in the 1930s and beyond and, for these two, such endeavours oriented towards developing an extended subjectivism remained of immediate, if not exclusive, concern. However, although their ideas can be seen to have been derived in part from strategically critical readings of Menger's seminal thoughts about subjectivism in economics, their understandings of what remained most significant in the work of their mentor varied. Consequently, considerable differences exist between their individual contributions to the extension of his subjectivist ideas, with some of these comprising complementary elements in the extension, while others pointed beyond themselves to separate paths of development (cf. Kirzner, 1994c, pp. ixff).

It was to be Ludwig Lachmann's vision of subjectivism that ultimately stood out, in that his immediate concern was with some of the deeper-seated and more analytically awkward dimensions of subjectivism. It is readily apparent that he had been influenced by the intellectual heritage of Menger and by the writings of Mises and Hayek that appeared more or less concurrently with his own. But Lachmann was very discerning in choosing just those aspects of the Mengerian legacy and the work of its inheritors that were complementary to his own, more penetrating, ideas for a subjectivist research programme. He was, then, to a significant extent responsible for reinforcing and integrating some of the incompletely worked out subjectivist ideas of Menger, and for extending the reach of the subjectivism of Menger's more conservative Austrian successors.

NOTES

1. Böhm-Bawerk's most explicit venture into the metatheoretical realm came in his 1891 paper, 'The historical vs the deductive method in political economy' (1994). All that warrants comment here concerning this contribution is that, in his methodological discussion, it was evident that he had not misplaced his subjectivist orientation and concerns entirely. In developing his argument, the examples he cited emphasized an agent-centred

vision of economic issues. He gave a further fillip to this notion by suggesting that perceptions of economics as needing 'a sound psychological foundation' were appropriate, and he added the observation that 'it would not surprise me if in the future this school should come to be called the "psychological school of political economy"' (p. 123). In no extant literature, though, did he undertake any serious pursuit of these metatheoretical concerns.

2. It is of interest to note in passing that it was this methodology, rooted in the need to preserve ontological integrity in economic analyses, that Wieser felt militated against the use of mathematical expression. While he granted a necessary status to mathematics in arguing theory, its use could only be restricted to the most abstract stages. Only an 'investigation confining itself to this narrowest group of theoretical problems, a group open to extreme idealization, may resort to mathematical expression as the most exact instrument for formulating results' (1967, p. 13). For once an investigation moves 'by decreasing abstraction to the remaining problems of theory [it] will find itself compelled to discard, in its further advance, the mathematical formula'. Indeed, Wieser's belief was that, because the purpose of economics defined subjectively was to provide an understanding of 'the meaning of economic action', then 'none of the great truths of economic theory, none of their important moral and political applications, has been justified by mathematical means' (p. 13).

3. The legacy of Ludwig von Mises

3.1 INTRODUCTION

Much of Mises's thought on the praxeological foundations for subjectivist economics is a mixture of ontological claims about the nature of human action and the epistemological positions that may be adopted in the search for formal knowledge about such action and its phenomenal results. From an ontological perspective, Mises's emphasis was upon situated and conditioned human agents as the active generators of the phenomena that constitute the objects of study. Epistemological argument shifted his focus to observer-analysts in the sense that it is concerned with what they can legitimately claim to know about the world of human action and phenomena. He recognized that the two philosophical dimensions are intimately related in that the epistemological status of claims to knowledge of an object world are dependent upon and shaped by the ontological nature of the objects. It is for this reason that claims to realist knowledge in the human sciences were apparently more difficult to defend than in the sciences of nature. The variable and contingent origins of human phenomena in individual actions give such phenomena an appearance of impermanence and disorder that defies scientific generalization. The temptation, all too obvious in so much of orthodox economics, is to impose the required permanence and order by assumption. Mises, as with all subjectivists, refused to take this naive escape route.

Establishing the nature of the interface between these two philosophical dimensions in Mises's subjectivist economics is no straightforward matter. Nonetheless, as I intend to establish in summary form in this chapter, the pursuit is warranted (cf. Oakley, 1997b, ch. 7). In particular, I will use his writings on these themes to elicit, and thereby to expose the limitations of, the insights into the essential problematic of subjectivism that were the legacy of this founder of Austrian economics.

3.2 PHILOSOPHICAL ORIENTATIONS

It is evident that, in choosing to ground his economics in what he believed to be a priori axioms of human action, Mises was inclined to argue them in formally logical terms as prior to, and apparently isolated from, particular observations of their empirical manifestation. Such is also the dominant perception of the very idea of a priori knowledge: that is, as logically arranged mental categories that exist prior to and independently of observer experience. However, the implication of such a definition for the status of a priori knowledge is not necessarily so restricted. Rather, it may be argued that the coherence and content of such knowledge is attributable to one of two alternative sources (Smith, 1990a, pp. 275f).

The first involves the domination of cognition and concept formation that flows from experience by the imposed structural and categorial qualities of the observing mind, whatever the source of these qualities may be argued to be. In this 'impositionist' case, the claimed knowledge of observed reality is the mediated product of the mind's pre-existing capacities to deliver a particular logical coordination and order to an inflow of raw sensory experience. The alternative 'reflectionist' version of the a priori holds that knowledge expresses the primary existential order discovered in the essentials of reality and immediately grasped by the mind. The claim is that cognition and concept formation are processes that *report rather than construct* the ordered and intelligible state of reality. Clearly, this latter form of a priori knowledge must be thought of as making ontological statements about the existential nature of reality as it is in itself, something that the 'impositionist' stance could never claim to do. A priori knowledge claims that depend exclusively upon the imposition of pre-existing mental constructs are appropriately thought of as Kantian, while the 'reflectionist', ontologically connected a priori claims are a heritage of Aristotle's essentialism and realism. It is to be emphasized that, in both cases, knowing reality involves drawing upon the imbedded character of observation and experience. This was not so for the third philosophical position confronted by Mises. Baden neoKantianism held that knowledge claims were to be defended axiologically rather than as dependent upon or consistent with experience. Knowledge accordingly comprised concepts expressing the values of the observer rather than the ontology of the object.

Mises found himself confronted by all of these alternative backgrounds to the pursuit of knowledge. As an Austrian educated scholar, he stood simultaneously within two distinct Germanic intellectual heritages. These have recently been identified and cogently argued out by Barry Smith (1986a, 1986b, 1990a, 1990c; cf. Kauder, 1957). Summarily put by Smith, 'Austria and Germany are different' (1990c, p. 212). The particular difference at issue concerns their fundamental philosophical traditions and a number of important philosophical principles that they espoused. In terms of the ontological connections encompassed by the conceptual constructs of the mind, the German strand was inclined to follow the legacy of Kant's epistemology of the a priori, with its synthetic but unreal representation of knowledge based on experience. Some followed the Baden neoKantian revision of Kant's epistemology as a rationalistic theory of concepts isolated from experience, but validated by axiological premises (see Parsons, 1990). In the sharpest contrast to these Kantian pursuits is the evidence that Austrians were influenced by the Aristotelian heritage of realism, with its emphasis on knowledge as an expression of the ontological form of observed objects. It is quite evident, as will be shown, that each of these traditions impinged upon Mises to some extent at the outset of his search for the proper foundations for the human sciences in the 1920s (1960). The joint legacy of these influences then remained prominent throughout his work.

Mises looked back to Carl Menger as the father of the Austrian tradition from which he took his intellectual cues (Mises, 1978, pp. 33, 121f, 127). In some prominent quarters, Austrian intellectual life was under the influence of the realism and essentialism of Aristotelian and scholastic thought (Kauder, 1957; Johnston, 1972, pp. 68, 290ff; Smith, 1990a, 1990c). Menger's acceptance of ontologically rooted 'exact theories' in the realm of human conduct was arguably a consequence of this influence. The point upon which Menger depended was that 'Aristotle had insisted that there are qualities, for example, of action or knowledge or of more complex social phenomena, which are knowable a priori' (Smith, 1986a, p. vii). And, more graphically put, 'the ontological grammar of economic reality that is sketched by Menger can be seen … as providing a pre-empirical qualitative framework in whose terms specific empirical hypotheses can be formulated' (Smith, 1990a, p. 279).

One scholar who recognized that this alternative realist epistemology had been carried forward into Mises's work was Emil Kauder. He wrote of Mises as referring to praxeology comprising 'reflection about the essence of action' that maintained 'the ontological character of economic laws' (Kauder, 1957, p. 417). According to Kauder, Mises could be aligned with both Wieser and Böhm-Bawerk as carrying forward the Aristotelian roots of subjectivism in the very particular sense that 'all three authors are social *ontologists*. They believe that a general plan of reality exists. All social phenomena are conceived in relation to this master plan' (ibid., p. 417, original emphasis). Kauder's insight here hints at the theme that will be pursued in more depth in the section below on praxeology and empirico-historical economics: that the ontological status and content of praxeology, even in its purest form as expressing the essence of rational human action, was emphasized by Mises as a consequence of this Aristotelian heritage.

By contrast, other students of Mises have rejected the idea that this orientation is to be found so prominently displayed in his work. Lachmann, for example, in assessing Mises's relationship to Menger, cited the latter's adherence to Aristotelian realism and essentialism in which 'exact laws' captured ontologically 'essential as well as necessary relationships between phenomena'. But, apropos of Mises, Lachmann concluded that 'in this respect Mises was unable to follow his master. He was no essentialist'. And, although 'to him reason was inherent in human action, to be sure, ... few of what are usually regarded as typical manifestations of the Aristotelian tradition in European thought he found to his taste' (1982a, p. 35).

Barry Smith's reading stands in contrast to Lachmann's. In Smith's work on the philosophical origins of Austrian economics, Mises's thesis of praxeology is assigned epistemologically to the Kantian camp (Smith, 1986b, pp. 8, 18; 1990a, p. 279). But this assignment is qualified by the suggestions that Mises was inclined to adhere to an analytical rather than synthetic perception of praxeological constructs and that he did not explicitly espouse an 'impositionist' conception of the a priori (Smith, 1990a, pp. 280f). In so conflating the a priori with an analytical logic, what appeared to be certain, nevertheless, was that his position could not be compatible with 'reflectionism' because analytical concepts and arguments have no ontological content. Now, in spite of such metatheoretical directions being clearly evident in Mises's writings, Smith also suggests that most of his praxeological understanding of economic phenomena actually fits into the Aristotelian mould as synthetic and realist. This turnaround comes in what Smith calls 'Mises's *practice*' as distinct from his 'methodological self-interpretations' (ibid., p. 282, original emphasis). Smith denies Mises's awareness of the realist perspective as fundamentally relevant, observing that 'we know ... that there is an Aristotelian alternative to the Kantian form of apriorism. This alternative seems not to have been explicitly recognized as such by Mises' (p. 279).[1] It is the word 'explicitly' that is significant here. For Smith, there is a very definite Aristotelian connection to be found implicit in the extended scope of Mises's economic analyses, which 'represent one of the most sustained realizations of the Austrian Aristotelian idea in the literature of economic theory' (p. 282). The broad sweep of Mises's economic inquiries made it necessary for him to give the core axiom of human rationality a substantive form and context. Smith's finding is that there exists in Mises's work an ontologically grounded, pre-empirical structural framework comprising 'a family of a priori categories and categorial structures' (p. 283). These are so diverse and extensive that they could not have been derived from any singular axiom of rational human action by purely analytical arguments. He concludes, therefore, that they must rather have had their origin in the order inherent in economic events and are, therefore, aptly treated as ontologically rich, *synthetic* discursive representations of a slice of reality. This essentialist approach to the causal interpretation and understanding of economic phenomena brought Mises into line with his Aristotelian heritage.

However, it remains unclear from Smith's analyses what meaningful status can ultimately be attributed to the axiom of rational action and some closely related categories. Rational action appears to become just another member of the 'family of a priori categories'. In Smith's otherwise helpful diagrammatic representation of the 'family' relationships involved in Mises's praxeological foundations for economic inquiry, the really critical issues are avoided (ibid. pp. 283ff). There are boxes containing the labels 'agent', 'choice', 'knowledge' and 'expectations', but there is no accompanying consideration of the ontological meaning, if any, given to them in Mises's writings. They are, without doubt, ontologically rich categories with an essential status in understanding economic action as rational or otherwise. But, as will be argued below, making them parts of a universal a priori structure for realist economic inquiry defies the contingent nature of the human agency to which they refer.

It is readily made apparent, however, that juxtaposed to this Aristotelianism, Mises sought his epistemological foundations by reaching into and selectively adopting certain key principles of Kantian and neoKantian thought. Lachmann commented that Mises sought 'a reputable philosophical position that would supply him with enough intellectual armor to withstand the onslaughts of positivism and to espouse the cause of rationalism in human affairs'. And, although Lachmann shied away from giving us details, he read Mises as 'driven to seek refuge in NeoKantianism', but added the rider: 'How far this endeavor was successful is a matter of debate. Some have held that no epistemology that fails to grant major status to experience is entitled to claim affinity with Kant' (1982a, p. 36). These observations fail fully to explicate Mises's position, for, as will be shown, his rationalism cannot be consistently identified with the ontologically unreal conceptual forms envisaged by the Baden neoKantians. Upholding my argument then negates Lachmann's concern that, in Mises's rationalism, there is a neglect of the Kantian thesis that knowledge originates in experience. It will become evident in this respect that Mises's epistemology of the a priori was closely akin to Kant's in the very particular sense that both demanded experiential input in order to make meaningful claims to know anything about reality.

Parsons is the most recent interpreter to devote some sustained inquiry to Mises's Kantian and neoKantian connections.[2] After quoting the above comments by Lachmann, he, too, is diverted towards the notion that 'although Mises's neglect of experience may indicate a break with Kant, it also reveals a continuity with neo-Kantianism' (Parsons, 1990, p. 297). Parsons grants some affinity between Mises and Kant, but adds that, 'despite these similarities, Mises's intellectual heritage leaves him susceptible to a critique from the position of Kant' (p. 310). The main objection in Parsons's Kantian critique of Mises that is of concern in the present context is the treatment of time and its link to his allegedly extreme rationalist view of knowledge. On the treatment of time, Parsons's criticisms are ontologically oriented and he finds Mises to have lacked completeness in dealing with the implications for agents' conduct of this vital facet of economic decision making. It will be suggested below, however, that the criticism levelled by Parsons is more aptly attributed to Mises's revealed lack of philosophical sophistication in pursuing appropriate epistemological principles than to any failure to appreciate the extent of the ontological problem. It is quite apparent in Mises's arguments that he understood the problematic of time in relation to the subjectivism of human action. Indeed, he did so in very much the same terms as George Shackle, but lacked the inclination to pursue the issues further.

It should be mentioned in passing, though, that Parsons picks up one point in Kant's own concerns about reason in relation to the treatment of the import of time. He quotes Kant's second thoughts on the issue to the effect that reason per se is autonomous and out of time (Parsons, 1990, p. 314). It is my understanding that this was precisely the position taken by Mises. He warned of confusing timeless logical constructions that comprise reasoning per se, such as that employed in mathematics, with the logical essentials of human action (Mises, 1966, pp. 99f). Reason is projected into time by the fact that the ontology of action has a necessary time dimension. And recognizing that the intended status of praxeology as prior to, but for practical purposes never independent of, the manifested phenomena of economics proper is also relevant here. For, once this is allowed for, the epistemological puzzles of how time enters our knowledge of human action seems less significant. Moreover, if Kant was in doubt about the matter, Mises could hardly have been expected to sort it out.

Parsons is on less certain ground in attempting to tie the time problem to Mises's epistemology, claiming that 'for Mises, knowledge was understood rationalistically, as involving analytical judgements' (Parsons, 1990, p. 312, cf. p. 315). As will be elicited below, while there is evidence of Mises's neoKantianism and accompanying conceptual rationalism, there is also much in his writings to counter such an attribution. Passages that align him with the vital role of experience in the constitution of knowledge, as found in Kant's synthetic a priori and in the epistemological import of Aristotle's realism, are readily identified. Parsons concludes on rather too heavily philosophical grounds that 'Mises's science [of economics], like logic and mathematics, was ... concerned with universally valid knowledge' and that, 'in common with Baden [neoKantians], he defined knowledge rationalistically: it involved the analysis of concepts, independently of possible experience' (p. 318). My interpretation will indicate that, in making this claim, Parsons has taken a very narrow perspective and thus left much aside that is of relevance in understanding Mises's contribution to the foundations of Austrian subjectivist economics.[3]

What are we to make of these contrasting readings of Mises's ontological premises and epistemological connections? As will become apparent below, there is clear evidence that, at certain points in his work, Mises thought of the concepts and arguments of praxeology in epistemological terms as analytical and thus ontologically isolated from and prior to any empirical forms of action. Somehow, from this perspective, purely rational action was a conceptual form that had an unreal existence. In this respect, contrary to Smith's claim that Mises did not adopt the 'impositionist' position on a priori knowledge, my reading suggests that this was an integral part of his many Kantian and neoKantian moments in applying the concept of rational action. As conceptual forms, Mises frequently inferred that the axioms of human action are, in and of themselves, ontologically empty.

But, as already suggested, there is juxtaposed and contrasting evidence of equal cogency that, at other points, he thought of the praxeological axioms as existentially present in observed action. This facilitated his 'reflectionist' and realist references to the ontology of human action and phenomena. He made many explicit claims that the axiom of rational action could be identified within the phenomena of reality. Such claims render it unnecessary to pursue Mises's 'practice' to elicit that it was a 'reflectionist' realism that gave his praxeology its epistemological grounding and that gave the essential shape to his subjectivist economics. The potential difficulty with such intellectual ecumenicism, consciously or unconsciously espoused, was that the Austrian and German philosophical traditions were fundamentally incompatible in their ontologies and related epistemologies. Ultimately, Mises was left with a chronic ambivalence that continued throughout his career to impair the precision of his metatheoretical writings and of the interpretations that may reasonably be given to them. This dilemma can only be addressed by identifying some rationale in his work for giving dominant weight to one or the other of these alternative orientations.

3.3 PRAXEOLOGY FROM THE KANTIAN PERSPECTIVE

Mises revealed a fundamentally Kantian orientation in grounding his metatheory when he wrote that 'the human mind is not a tabula rasa on which external events write their own history. It is equipped with a set of tools for grasping reality' (Mises, 1966, p. 35). So, although 'life and reality are neither logical nor illogical, they are simply given', it is logic that is 'the only tool available to man for the comprehension of both'. And, 'as far as man is able to attain any knowledge, however limited, he can use only one avenue of approach, that opened by reason' (ibid., pp. 67f; cf Mises, 1990, p. 48). More generally expressed, 'what we know is what the nature or structure of our senses and of our mind makes comprehensible to us. We see reality, not as it "is" and may appear to a perfect being, but only as the quality of our mind and of our senses enables us to see it'. In this respect, Mises stressed that 'we must never forget that our representation of the reality of the universe is conditioned by the structure of our mind as well as of our senses' (Mises, 1962, pp. 18, 19).

Particularly in the case of praxeology, 'its concepts and theorems are mental tools opening the approach to a complete grasp of reality'. More specifically, Mises's position was that 'all experience concerning human action is conditioned by the praxeological categories and becomes possible only through their application. If we had not in our mind the schemes provided by praxeological reasoning, we should never be in a position to discern and to grasp any action' (Mises, 1966, pp. 38, 40; cf. 1962, p. 16). Most important here were the matters of the origin and status of these tools and the meaning attributed to the 'reality' that is to be grasped. The tools, he wrote, comprise 'the logical structure' of the mind and are acquired by the human being 'in the course of his evolution from an amoeba to his present state' (Mises, 1966, p. 35). Mises's claim was, then, that human science is grounded in a praxeology that is not dependent on discovering the ontological realities of human conduct, ordered and coherent or otherwise, for praxeology 'is not derived from experience; it is prior to experience. It is, as it were, the logic of action and deed' (Mises, 1960, pp. 12f). He reiterated his belief that its categories emanate from the logical structure of the human mind. In this sense they are, in a clearly 'impositionist' sense, 'the necessary mental tool to arrange sense data in a systematic way, to transform them into facts of experience .' (Mises, 1962, p. 16).

Consistently with such Kantian fundamentals in their neoKantian guise, Mises also held that, in cognition and mental representations, the concepts involved 'are never and nowhere to be found in reality; they belong rather to the province of thought' (Mises, 1960, p. 78). And, even more unequivocally expressing the 'impositionist' requirement, 'it is true ... that between reality and the knowledge that science can convey to us there is an unbridgeable gulf. Science cannot grasp life directly. What it captures in its system of concepts is always of a different character from the living whole' (p. 46). On another occasion, he expressed the same strongly neoKantian sentiments: 'The imaginary constructions that are the main – or, as some people would rather say, the only – mental tool of praxeology describe conditions that can never be present in the reality of action. Yet they are indispensable for conceiving what is going on in this reality' (Mises, 1962, p. 41). This preserved a neoKantian void between conceptual forms and the experiential sensations of reality that led the mind to form them.

Read in isolation, the implication of the arguments elicited so far is that the order and coherence of the agents' cognitive grasp of the world around them is a product of some 'imposed' a priori capacity and quality imbedded in the mind itself. However, the inferred isolation of the aprioristic logic that comprises praxeology from any ontology of action and its phenomenal results needs to be interpreted with some care if Mises's ultimate intention is to be correctly understood. It turned out that he was no committed Kantian in any sense and, as we are about to see, often shifted ground towards a realist perspective that gave priority to ontological concerns about the origin and nature of human phenomena.

3.4 MISES AND REALIST EPISTEMOLOGY

If the Aristotelian ontological perspective is to be identified in Mises's work, it is fundamental that he be shown to have believed in a number of particular ontological theses (Smith, 1990a, pp. 266ff). First, he held that an inherent order and coherence can be discovered in the real world of the phenomena of human action. This takes the form of structured relationships between essential constituent elements that have universal status. Secondly, while the existential nature of this reality is considered to be independent of human cognition, that cognition is capable of grasping its essentially pre-ordered constitution. Thirdly, experience and cognition of the object world comprise a mix of universal elements and other individual characteristics.[4] My position here is that there are in Mises's writings some very definite statements that conform to this realist orientation and its required ontological premises.

First of all, it was Mises's expressed view in this connection that human agents can only grasp the reality around them if the ontological presumption is made that it has an innately and essentially coherent form to which they can gain cognitive access. He wrote of the idea that 'no thinking and no acting would be possible to man if the universe were chaotic, i.e., if there were no regularity whatever in the succession and concatenation of events' (Mises, 1962, p. 19, cf. pp. 21f). Moreover, 'in a world without causality and regularity of phenomena there would be no field for human reasoning and human action. Such a world would be a chaos in which man would be at a loss to find any orientation and guidance. Man is not even capable of imagining the conditions of such a chaotic universe' (Mises, 1966, p. 22). The potential for such a paralysing state of humankind is overcome by the fact that 'the first and basic achievement of thinking is the awareness of constant relations among the external phenomena that affect our senses' (Mises, 1962, p. 20). This means that, in the human sciences, conceptual forms must, as a first principle, immediately grasp and express in discursively rational arguments the irreducible existential 'essentials' of human action that are present within the superficial disorder of human affairs. Most importantly in the present context, Mises expressed his 'reflectionist, belief that praxeology is 'not arbitrarily made, but *imposed upon us by the world in which we live and act and which we want to study*. ... [It is] not empty, not meaningless, and not merely verbal. ... [It comprises] – for man – the most general laws of the universe, and without them no knowledge would be accessible to man' (ibid., p. 14, emphasis added).

For Mises, we know that a subjectivist interpretation and understanding of the world of human phenomena meant recognizing first and foremost that the human being perceives action as 'the essence of his nature and existence' (Mises, 1966, pp. 18f). As 'the characteristic feature of man is action', Mises reasoned that 'the study of man, as far as it is not biology, begins and ends with the study of action' (Mises, 1962, p. 34). Praxeology is, he argued, a theory in which human reason manifested as action in pursuit of particular ends is ontologically causal. And, because active human agents, taking a perspective from their current life-world situation, self-consciously seek to better their condition, the causality is teleological (Mises, 1966, pp. 23, 25; cf. 1962, pp. 7f). They can only achieve this generalized objective by choosing means they individually believe will achieve the ends envisaged. On this basis, Mises concluded that action and its observed results cannot be anything but the existential manifestations of reason applied to problematic circumstances.

What we find here is the suggestion that Mises intended to preserve the immediately ontological content and context of his concepts: thus praxeological propositions refer 'with the full rigidity of their apodictic certainty and incontestability to the reality of action as it appears in life and history. Praxeology conveys exact and precise knowledge of real things' (Mises, 1966, p. 39; cf. 1990, p. 15). And, with an even more apparent realist and 'reflectionist' orientation, Mises continued with the argument that 'the starting point of praxeology is not a choice of axioms and a decision about methods of procedure, but reflection about the essence of action. There is no action in which the praxeological categories do not appear fully and perfectly' (Mises, 1966, pp. 39f). Since the categories of praxeology 'have enabled man to develop theories the practical application of which has aided him in his endeavours to hold his own in the struggle for survival and to attain various ends that he wanted to attain, these categories provide some information about the reality of the universe' (Mises, 1962, p. 16). So, as a means of understanding individual agency, praxeology 'does not deal in vague terms with human action in general, but with concrete action which a definite man has performed at a definite date and at a definite place. But, of course, it does not concern itself with the accidental and environmental features of this action and with what distinguishes it from all other actions, but only with what is necessary and universal in its performance' (Mises, 1966, p. 44). It was, then, Mises's belief that the a priori categories of praxeology in some sense manifest a universal reality of human action that exists imbedded in the complex, individual empirico-historical phenomena of economics. The evidence for this belief was compounded by his methodology of separately identifying, but then arguing the necessary integration of, the a priori of praxeology and the investigation of actual economic phenomena. This is the theme developed in the next section.

3.5 PRAXEOLOGY AND EMPIRICO-HISTORICAL ECONOMICS

Mises identified what he called 'two main branches of the sciences of human action' as praxeology and history (Mises, 1966, p. 30; cf. 1962, pp. 41ff). In the case of economics, this dualism was made explicit: 'There is economics and there is economic history. The two must never be confused' (1966, p. 66). For 'economics is not history. Economics is a branch of praxeology' and 'economic history ... needs to be interpreted with the aid of the theories developed by economics' (1962, p. 73). There was in his writings, however, an apparent inclination quite inappropriately to identify the term *economics* exclusively with *praxeology*. He posed 'the main question that economics is bound to answer' as 'what the relation of its statements is to the reality of human action whose mental grasp is the objective of economic studies' (1966, p. 6). It is crucial that we notice his wording here. In distinguishing '*economics*' from '*economic studies*', he can only have meant the former as exclusively a branch of praxeology and the latter as focusing upon instances of real-world human action. If praxeology was to provide the legitimate grounding for the study ('mental grasp') of empirico-historical economic phenomena, then the epistemological relationship between the two levels of argument must be precisely established. At issue is that, if *economics as praxeology* is to be the foundation for analyses that can enable us to understand and account for economic conduct and phenomena in the real world, it must be explicitly shown that its concepts can be ontologically grounded. In this respect, then, care is needed when dealing with what is often loosely referred to as 'Mises's economics', for, when interpreting him, we should maintain a clear distinction between the logic of praxeology and any argument concerning the manifestation of the axiom of rational agent action in economic phenomena.

The general objective of both praxeology and the study of empirico-historical phenomena 'is the comprehension of the meaning and relevance of human action'. More specifically, Mises argued that 'the cognition of history refers to what is unique and individual in each event of class or events' (ibid., p. 51). Praxeology, by contrast, with its cognition confined to conception in the form of universals and general categories, is 'a theoretical and systematic, not a historical, science. Its scope is human action as such, irrespective of all environmental, accidental, and individual circumstances of ... concrete acts' (p. 32, cf. p. 51). In line with its rationalist principles, it is from 'the unshakeable foundation of the category of human action [that] praxeology and economics proceed step by step by means of discursive reasoning. Precisely defining assumptions and conditions, they construct a system of concepts and draw all the inferences implied by logically unassailable ratiocination' (p. 67). The issue that this assertion raises for the present context is the epistemological status to be ascribed to this 'system of concepts' constructed for the purposes of economic analysis. Mises saw the problem as one of explicating 'how a purely logical deduction from aprioristic principles can tell us anything about reality' (Mises, 1990, p. 11).

The import of this question is to be found in his emphasis that, while praxeology is an a priori and purely general science of human action, its rationale and utility are only realized through its embodiment in discursive explanations of observed object phenomena. He was not the builder of a system of theoretical concepts for its own sake, but rather saw theory as the foundation for causal investigations of those facets of the empirical world that interest particular analysts. That is, at the level of empirico-historical interpretation and understanding, 'the science of human action deals only with those problems whose solution directly or indirectly affects practical interests ... [and] by giving preference to the problems encountered under the actual conditions in which action takes place, our science is obliged to direct its attention to the facts of experience' (ibid., pp. 30f).

Thus Mises was ultimately very careful to explain the intentions and meaning of his praxeological metatheory and the distinctive view of theoretical conception to which it led him. It is important to emphasize first of all that his a priori axioms about human conduct, and the economic theories he constructed from them, could never have been intended to be ends in themselves for economists. The scope of the insights into human action claimed by the conceptually expressed axioms was very restricted and limited to universal dimensions of rational action that Mises thought all of us as human beings know to be always and everywhere correct and applicable in practice. Moreover, by virtue of their explicitly delimited definition, these essentials can be nowhere manifested in their 'raw' form. For they are conceptual structures that, even if they could be shown to have an ontologically connected 'reflectionist' form, represent merely the consistent existential core of an infinite range of empirically determined and manifested actions.

Consistently with this severe delimitation of praxeology, Mises stressed that 'the end of science is to know reality. It is not mental gymnastics or a logical pastime. Therefore praxeology restricts its inquiries to the study of acting under those conditions and presuppositions which are given in reality' (Mises, 1966, p. 65). Empirically, 'the experience with which the sciences of human action have to deal is always an experience of complex phenomena. Historical experience as an experience of complex phenomena does not provide us with facts' for the reason that every such experience 'is open to various interpretations, and is in fact interpreted in different ways' (ibid., p. 31; cf. 1990, pp. 10, 18, 40). The ultimate challenge for praxeological theory is to serve as the foundation for the understanding and explanation of empirico-historical economic phenomena whose origin and constitution extend well beyond the axiomatics of rational agents' actions. Therefore, argued Mises, references to experience as the context in which theory always appears 'does not impair the aprioristic character of praxeology. Experience merely directs our curiosity toward certain problems and diverts it from other problems. It tells us what we should explore, but it does not tell us how we could proceed in our search for knowledge' (Mises, 1966, p. 65, cf. p. 66). In this respect, then, 'theory and the comprehension of living and changing reality are not in opposition to one another. Without theory, the general aprioristic science of human action, there is no comprehension of the reality of human action' (pp. 38f). Mises reinforced this idea by stating the principle that economic inquiry 'adopts for the organized presentation of its results a form in which aprioristic theory and the interpretation of historical phenomena are intertwined' (p. 66).[5]

What emerges from this analysis of Mises's expressed views is that he envisaged praxeology as an *existential and realist* foundation for meaningful empirical economic inquiry. Praxeology did not, and was never intended to, embrace what we have come to call economics in our usual parlance, and Mises was remiss in his failure to make sure that this was obvious to his readers. Praxeological accounts of human rationality had no independent status, as all human action of concern to science and active agent observers has to have an empirically specific purpose and meaning that befits its problematic and its situational conditions. At no time did he claim that any human agency and its resulting phenomenon as it is studied in economics could be attributed to praxeological action in a pure form. Mises knew well that active human agents were not legitimately or meaningfully depicted as existentially rational in this situationally isolated and sterilized sense. The tenets of praxeology were for him, and could only be, conceptual forms that, in themselves, expressed the essential roots of all human action. They stood as separable, but never in isolation from some empirical manifestations. Analytically, rational action was intended by Mises to be a means of giving some core of coherent regularity to the complexity of observed action and its results. The issue remains, though, as to whether or not the axiom of rational action can be defended as an ontologically realistic core for economics, as he required. The realities of human agency, even as Mises himself understood them, suggest not.

3.6 THE ONTOLOGY OF CONTINGENT HUMAN AGENCY

As was indicated at the outset, the subjectivist metatheory for economics requires that its object phenomena be explicitly dealt with as the products of human action: that is, of human action that is the result of individually conditioned and reasoned deliberation about the pursuit of an objective by what are presumed, under the circumstances and on the basis of available information, to be the most apt means. This simple notion begs a number of pertinent questions that are important in assessing an endeavour such as Mises's to found economics on epistemological principles that are consistent with such subjectivism. These questions relate first of all to specifics about the nature of human agents and their capacities to undertake reasoned deliberations. They also relate to the characteristics of the inputs to those deliberations that flow from the problematic situations confronted by agents: in particular, what can agents know about their circumstances and the alternative means available? These are questions about the ontology of situated human agency and their answers affect the potential for realist epistemology to be defensible in subjectivist economics. The focus here will be on the extent to which Mises was conscious of and provided answers for such questions.

Praxeology comprised what Mises claimed were the a priori essentials of all self-conscious, deliberative human action that stems from teleologically directed choice. So stated, it was *an immediately ontological thesis* which ostensibly tells us about the nature of action in all sorts of situations. Mises summarized the ontological essentials of choice and action as he saw them by claiming that 'Man is a rational being; that is, his actions are guided by reason'. It followed that 'the proposition: Man acts, is tantamount to the proposition: Man is eager to substitute a state of affairs that suits him better for a state of affairs that suits him less'. But, continued Mises, 'in order to do this, he must employ suitable means. It is his reason that enables him to find out what is a suitable means for attaining his chosen end and what is not' (Mises, 1958, p. 269; cf. 1962, p. 11). He believed emphatically that this fundamental thesis of human rationality in choice and action is unchallengeable: 'No talk about irrationality, the unfathomable depths of the human soul, the spontaneity of the phenomena of life, automatisms, reflexes, and tropisms, can invalidate the statement that man makes use of his reason for the realization of wishes and desires' (Mises, 1966, p. 67). At issue is the meaning that can really be given to the claim, 'man makes use of his reason'. For Mises it constituted an axiom about agents' conduct upon which much depended. But it tells us very little and neglects a number of vital matters concerning human agency.

The foundation of praxeology was the axiom of reason manifested as action as an actual quality of living human agents. This belief inescapably involved Mises in making claims that were specifically psychological.[6] That is, the axiom necessarily refers to particular qualities and capacities of the mind and its processes: 'Thinking and acting are the specific human features of man. They are peculiar to all human beings' (ibid., p. 25). To this he added that 'the characteristic feature of man is precisely that he consciously acts. Man is Homo agens, the acting animal' (Mises, 1962, p. 4). Furthermore, it is reason that is 'man's particular and characteristic feature' (Mises, 1966, p. 177). So, Mises argued, 'a priori thinking and reasoning on the one hand and human action on the other, are manifestations of the human mind. The logical structure of the human mind creates the reality of action. Reason and action are congeneric [*sic*] and homogeneous, two aspects of the same phenomenon' (Mises, 1962, p. 42; cf. 1966, p. 25).

As far as Mises was concerned, such considerations gave human agency a regularized core upon which observers could rely. When observing other agents, he believed that the one thing we can be sure of is that the other employs a logic of thought that is identical to our own. All human agents have introspectively grounded knowledge of all things fundamentally human. As Mises put it, we have our own 'insight into the principles of human reason and conduct ... [and] we have this insight in our mind' (Mises, 1990, p. 9). Thus 'what we know about our own actions and about those of other people is conditioned by our familiarity with the category of action that we owe to a process of self-examination and introspection as well as of understanding other people's conduct. To question this insight is no less impossible than to question the fact that we are alive' (Mises, 1962, p. 71). Therefore he reasoned that 'we have, being human ourselves, a knowledge of what goes on within acting men' (Mises, 1990, p. 8). Each individual is 'himself an acting being' who in dealing with others 'knows what it means to strive after ends chosen' (ibid., p. 48; cf. 1960, p. 130). Mises believed that, because 'both human thought and human action stem from the same root in that they are both products of the human mind' (Mises, 1990, p. 11), we can conceive of the actions of others as having meaning to them 'as a purposeful endeavour to reach some goal' (ibid., p. 9). And, 'being himself a valuing and acting ego, every man knows the meaning of valuing and acting. ... It is impossible to imagine a sane human being who lacks this insight. It is no less impossible to conceive how a being lacking this insight could acquire it by means of any experience or instruction' (Mises, 1958, p. 283).

These *existential* referents of reason and action common to all human agents that have ever lived apparently brought real ontological content to the apparently isolated concepts of praxeology. Mises thought of the essential rationality of human action as very real in and of itself. As he summarized his position, we 'conceive activity as such, its logical (praxeological) qualities and categories. All that we do in this conceiving is by deductive analysis to bring to light everything which is contained in the first principle of action and to apply it to different kinds of thinkable conditions' (Mises, 1990, p. 9). That is, the analyst of human phenomena finds the causal teleology of their generation in the rational action of the active agents as it is shaped by the exigencies of the conditions under which it is carried out. The conceptual grasp and understanding of the phenomena are immediately at one with their ontological origin and the epistemology presumed could not be anything but realism. The indications are that we should interpret Mises as giving the 'reflectionist' position more weight than the 'impositionist' alternative in establishing the a priori in praxeology.

However, there existed for Mises some difficulties that act as a counterweight to this presumption. These are to be found in the essential qualities of individual human agents that he presented as the grounds for the praxeological understanding. Such qualities apparently followed from the realities rather than the pure logic of their capacities to reason and then act in accordance with the circumstances. His belief was that there exist three 'general conditions of human action' and that 'man is the being that lives under these conditions. He is not only *homo sapiens*, but no less *homo agens* ... [as] the essential feature of humanity' (Mises, 1966, p. 14). That is, man as the only extant member of the species *homo* has not only the capacity for wisdom (as implied by *sapiens*), but also the capacity to act in the light of it (as implied by *agens*). First, 'acting man is eager to substitute a more satisfactory state of affairs for a less satisfactory. ... The incentive that impels man to act is always some uneasiness'. Secondly, the actor '*imagines conditions that suit him better*, and his action aims at bringing about this desired state' (p. 13, emphasis added). This was the most contentious step in relation to Mises's claim that all action is rational. For, by recognizing the future orientation of deliberations, together with the necessary resort to the creations of the imagination in the process, it introduced an extreme subjectivism into the idea of choice. The third condition then compounded the subjectivism further. It was that the actor formed 'the *expectation* that purposeful behavior has the power to remove or at least to alleviate the felt uneasiness' (p. 14, emphasis added). With the benefit of our hindsight, we can see that citing these agent characteristics posed a number of critical issues for Mises to address if a realist epistemology was to be pertinent to subjectivist economics.

One matter raised here was Mises's treatment of the ends that agents choose to pursue with the intention of mitigating their 'uneasiness'. He did not address the matter of how agents form the ends they deem to be realizable under a set of perceived circumstances. But, because the end state aimed at does not exist ex ante, and must therefore be a product of the individual's imagination, the choice of the end that drives any action is wholly subjective. The precise meaning to be attributed to the pure logic of choice and action in the face of such subjectivism was left unclear as a result. Mises sidestepped this difficulty and chose rather to regard praxeology as strictly unconcerned about the particular ends, purposes or goals that agents choose to pursue. As a libertarian, he saw these things as a subjective matter to be settled by private individual values and judgements. This meant that praxeology 'is subjectivistic and takes the value judgements of acting man as ultimate data not open to any further critical examination' (ibid., p. 22, cf. p. 95), Praxeology is also, then, 'neutral with regard to the ultimate ends that the individuals want to attain' (Mises, 1990, p. 42). Here Mises reasoned as a result that 'any examination of ultimate ends turns out to be purely subjective and therefore arbitrary' (Mises, 1966, p. 96). It is not the province of scientists to challenge the philosophies of eudaemonism, hedonism, utilitarianism or any other that are manifested in agents' choices of objectives. Rather it is their obligation to accept that all goals may exist and confine themselves to ensuring that actions are understood (see Mises, 1990, pp. 22f, cf. 1966, pp. 14f). Thus Mises wrote that 'ends are irrational, i.e., they neither require nor are capable of a rational justification' (Mises, 1960, p. 92f, cf. 1958, p. 267).[7]

The most general of the difficulties that Mises confronted with respect to human agency was *time as it is integral to reason and action*. He explicitly recognized that all actual human action takes place within the unceasing and irreversible efflux of time: 'It is acting that provides man with the notion of time and makes him aware of the flux of time. The idea of time is a praxeological category' (Mises, 1966, p. 100). This latter assertion is the challenging one. It poses the question of the sense in which Mises intended time to be involved in arguments about human reason and action. If praxeological arguments are a priori, the issue to be resolved is how time can enter the analysis. It could be as an a priori category in line with Kant's transcendental logic, but this does not appear to have been Mises's belief (cf. Parsons, 1990, pp. 309ff). His concern was with the pragmatics of time rather than its metaphysics, so he accepted that what really mattered was to understand agents' experience of time in relation to reason and action.

In accordance with this view, he wrote that 'the concepts of change and of time are inseparably linked together. Action aims at change and is therefore in the temporal order. Human reason is even incapable of conceiving the ideas of timeless existence and of timeless action' (Mises, 1966, p. 99).

Human agents must act from an ever-moving and changing location between an irrevocable and cumulative past and an unknowable and perfidious future. Thus 'he who acts distinguishes between the time before the action, the time absorbed by the action, and the time after the action has been finished. He cannot be neutral with regard to the lapse of time' (p. 99). In this respect, 'action is always directed toward the future; it is essentially and necessarily always a planning and acting for a better future'. The very driving force for action depends upon an agent's 'dissatisfaction with expected future conditions as they would probably develop if nothing were done to alter them' and the agent 'becomes conscious of time when he plans to convert a less satisfactory present state into a more satisfactory future state' (p. 100).

Planning for and choosing such teleological action requires agents to rely upon imagined future outcomes and expectations about the means for realizing them. Mises demonstrated his awareness that individual active agents must act in the face of time yet to come: 'No action can be planned and executed without understanding of the future. ... Every action is a speculation, i.e., guided by a definite opinion concerning the uncertain conditions of the future. Even in short-run activities this uncertainty prevails. Nobody can know whether some unexpected fact will not render vain all that he has provided for the next day or the next hour' (Mises, 1962, pp. 50f). This is because, in pursuing a chosen course of action, 'man is at the mercy of forces and powers beyond his control' (p. 65). As a consequence, the agent faces true uncertainty because it is 'one of the fundamental conditions of man's existence and action ... that he does not know what will happen in the future' (Mises, 1958, p. 180) and 'to acting man the future is hidden' (Mises, 1966, p. 105). Mises saw clearly that 'the uncertainty of the future is already implied in the very notion of action. That man acts and the future is uncertain are by no means two independent matters. They are only two different modes of establishing one thing' (p. 105). In particular, as Mises put it, the agent 'can never know beforehand to what extent his acting will attain the end sought and, if it attains it, whether this action will in retrospect appear – to himself or to the other people looking upon it – as the best choice among those that were open to him at the instant he embarked upon it' (Mises, 1962, p. 65).

The image of human agents portrayed by Mises in considering their problematic of action in the face of uncertainty exposed a high degree of potential contingency. Whatever it means to apply reason to such circumstances, the need to form expectations means that the results are unlikely to flow from the use of ratiocinative logic alone. Moreover, Mises was prepared to concede that active subjective agents, '*homo agens* as he really is', turn out to be 'often weak, stupid, inconsiderate, and badly instructed' (Mises, 1990, p. 24). Economics, in particular, must deal with 'real man, weak and subject to error as he is, not with ideal beings, omniscient and perfect as only gods could be' (Mises, 1966, p. 97, cf. pp. 92f, 651). Understanding and accounting for the realities of agents' economic conduct, and attempting to predict their responses to circumstances, quite apparently cannot flow from the rational action premises of praxeology alone.

3.7 CONCLUDING OBSERVATIONS

The exegetical revelations of the previous sections leave us with mixed results to apply in assessing Mises's most fundamental contributions to subjectivist economics. The intended nature and point of praxeology as the existential foundation for understanding observed economic actions and phenomena seem clear. The ontological and epistemological status to be ascribed to its logical arguments appear to be much less definite when the totality of Mises's thought is taken at its face value. There is no denying his ambivalence between the unreal conceptual forms of neoKantianism and the realism of Aristotelian epistemology. Consciously or unconsciously, he simply left in place an incompatible mix of arguments in which the concepts of praxeology were sometimes ontologically sterile and sometimes replications of living forms claimed to be actually discoverable in empirical phenomena. A reasonable response to this dilemma is to give priority to Mises's realist inclinations in understanding his ontology and epistemology. This would require us to agree that maximum sense of his praxeology is made if it is perceived as expressing a rationality that active agents actually can and do universally exercise, albeit always in some imperfect but purposeful empirically manifested form. But, as we have seen, Mises himself had a vision of human agents that included facets that negate any realistic ontology of rational action even at the most essential level.

In the end, the subjectivist metatheoretical insights that comprise his legacy, therefore, are confined to a compendium of pertinent observations concerning the problematic at issue. Beyond that, he left much unresolved and much to be done to provide a complete and cogent alternative to the well-established foundations of orthodox economics.

NOTES

1. Smith added some mitigation at this point, noting that 'this is hardly surprising, given that ... the special nature of Austrian Aristotelian apriorism was appreciated by very few at the time when Mises was working out the philosophical foundations of his praxeology' (1990a, pp. 279f).
2. Parsons's paper consists of a complex of philosophical inquiry that has relevance to our

understanding of Mises's and George Shackle's contribution to Austrian economic thought. I do not pretend to have dealt with the paper as a whole in any detail. My intention is only to nominate some key points where I think Parsons fails to pursue and interpret Mises's ideas completely.

3. The Kantian and neoKantian roots were also dominant in the foundations for human science developed by Max Weber, foundations which Mises found largely congenial. The merits of the neoKantian approach seem to have been confirmed to Mises through his study of Weber. There are good reasons, then, to agree with Ludwig Lachmann's assertion that, while 'Max Weber can hardly be called an Austrian economist, ... he made a contribution of fundamental significance to what in the hands of Mises became Austrian methodology' (Lachmann, 1976a, p. 56). Mises had met Weber when the German spent a semester at the University of Vienna in 1918–19 and was a critical admirer of his work. As Lachmann observed, 'Mises was struck by Weber's genius and admired his work' (Lachmann, 1982a, p. 35; and see Mises, 1960, p. 74; 1978, pp. 9, 69f, 104, 122f; 1990, pp. 39, 44). Although Weber's impact on intellectual life in Vienna was never great, his *verstehende Soziologie* did become a frequent topic of discussion in Mises's own *Privatseminar* from its inception in the early 1920s (Haberler, 1981, p. 123). When he reviewed Mises's magnum opus, *Human Action*, on an earlier occasion, Lachmann was one of the first to notice that 'it is the work of Max Weber that is being carried on here' (Lachmann, 1977, p. 95). On yet another occasion Lachmann observed that Weber's writings 'provided the main focus of orientation for the methodological essays Mises began to publish in the German journals in the second half of the 1920s'. And Lachmann went on significantly to add that 'even where he disagrees with Weber, ... it is clear that, throughout, his thought reflects the impact of Weber's work' (Lachmann, 1982a, p. 35). The crucial questions that these claims beg are the meanings to be given to 'carried on' and to 'reflects the impact of Weber's work'. These matters require more careful exegetical attention in the respective writings of these two authors than they have hitherto received. Richard Ebeling (1988) makes a cogent case for the Weber to Mises link, but he concentrates his extended discussion upon how far the connection allowed the latter to give due emphasis to the role of time, uncertainty and expectations in human action. Jeremy Shearmur finds a complementarity between the work of Weber and Mises that comprises a duality in the conception of subjectivism (Shearmur, 1992, pp. 104, 113). This involves setting the praxeological subjectivism of Mises, with its axiomatics of human action, against the historical or institutional subjectivism of Weber, with its depiction of human agency as ideal types tied to the historical situation. Parsons (1990) chooses to ignore the mediation of Weber in the neoKantian connection. Mises pursued his own critical connection with Weber in one of his earliest metatheoretical essays, 'Sociology and history', published in 1929 (1960, pp. 68ff). A more detailed treatment of Weberian influences on Mises can be found in Oakley (1997b, ch. 7).
4. Barry Smith (1990a) provides an extended and detailed listing of the theses that constitute Austrian Aristotelianism. I have emphasized here only those most pertinent to my understanding of Mises's metatheory.
5. This situation of Mises's praxeology in relation to empirical experience has been noted by Jochen Runde. He writes that, for Mises, 'observation alone is not enough. Explanation requires subjecting the observed data to praxeological reasoning, and this is independent of the "fact"' (Runde, 1988, p. 104). I thank Anthony Endres for this reference.
6. In spite of his focus on human action, with its necessarily mental origins, it is nonetheless certain that Mises intended to avoid any taint of psychologism. He took the trouble to separate two schools of psychology, distinguishing the naturalistic cum experimental orientation from one which pursues 'cognition of human emotions, motivations, ideas, judgements of value and volitions ' (Mises, 1958, p. 264). As far as the former was concerned, Mises remained adamant that nothing meaningful could be established about human action by observations or experiments that had become the methods of behaviourist psychologists (ibid., pp. 245ff, 1960, pp. 10f, 66, 131f). Similarly, he rejected the claims of 'instinct psychology' that action is not determined by reason, but rather by 'innate forces, impulses, instincts, and dispositions which are not open to any rational elucidation' (Mises, 1966, pp. 15f). To the latter, 'mundane and common-sense' version of psychological inquiry

Mises ascribed the distinctive name of 'thymology' (Mises, 1958, pp. 265ff, cf. 1962, pp. 46ff). Mises's belief was that, while psychology qua thymology dealt with 'the psychic events that result in action', this was of no concern in praxeology because its exclusive focus was 'action and what follows from action' (Mises, 1960, p. 3; cf. 1966, pp. 11f). He quite bluntly stated that 'thymology has no special relation to praxeology and economics' (Mises, 1958, p. 271). Therefore, he concluded, as a branch of praxeology, 'economics is distinguished from psychology by the fact that it considers action alone and that the psychic events that have led to an action are without importance for it' (Mises, 1960, p. 208) Praxeology acknowledges that the economizing choices made in action are conditioned by the antecedent psychological and physiological characteristics of agents. But it is not concerned, Mises emphasized, with the motivations that direct the choices made. It is psychology and not praxeology that 'deals with the internal processes determining the various choices in their concreteness' (Mises, 1990, p. 21).

7. Mises's lack of concern about the nature and choice of ends has elicited some negative comments in the secondary literature. Long ago, Alan Sweezy observed with some critical insight that, while it 'is no affair of the economist whether any particular individual prefers cigarettes to bread, or moving pictures to art galleries', this cannot absolve the economist from 'concrete investigation of the *structure* of the system of ends which the individual is supposed to possess'. In particular, it should be his direct concern to establish 'whether or not people in general act in accordance with deliberately prepared plans, and if so what sort of internal relationships these plans show, how they are adapted to meet changes in prices, etc.' (1933–4, p. 179, original emphasis). Taken at face value, such neglect reinforced Sweezy's view that it was merely a product of Mises's extreme a priorism and rationalism (ibid., pp. 179f); Mises was led to treat human action as tautologically rational because 'all behaviour must be taken as rational since only the person behaving can say whether it is rational or not' (p. 180, n2). Later critics were to suggest that, in this respect, Mises appeared to adopt a behaviourist escape from concern about the way agents choose their ends. Mark Addleson attributes this particular criticism to Ludwig Lachmann, but his own point is similar to Sweezy's: in cutting ourselves off from the selection of ends, we neglect a vital part of understanding the actions of agents (1984, p. 519). The same observation is made by Jochen Runde (1988, p. 108). I thank Anthony Endres for drawing these critical comments to my attention.

4. Hayek's early formalism and subjectivism

4.1 INTRODUCTION TO HAYEK

Hayek's work is chronologically complex, and it is characterized by the shifts of intellectual orientation and substance that would be expected during the many decades of his research. He made explicit references to these dynamics himself on a number of occasions (Hayek, 1967, pp. 91f; 1978, pp. 23ff *passim*; 1994, pp. 78ff).[1] It is not my intention to delve too much into Hayek's intellectual biography as such. Rather, my particular objective is to select and critically to assess those elements of its composition that have a continuing importance for the subjectivist endeavours of his neoAustrian followers. The selection of themes that will concern me are those which tell us something about the problematic of devising an economics that is grounded on a proper subjectivist understanding of the human ontology of its phenomena. Hayek made some particular contributions in this respect that need to be recognized and critically studied independently of his own patchwork mode of developing and presenting them. Discontinuities and limitations are readily shown to exist in Hayek's fragmented metatheory of economics. Nonetheless, his legacy contains many pertinent insights that require more development if the neoAustrians are to bring them to their full potential.

Although the matter cannot be pursued to any meaningful extent here, one important biographical factor is how Hayek saw his connections with the three generations of Austrians who were his antecedents. It was evidently Carl Menger's work, rather than his university lectures, that initially turned Hayek's attention to economics as a discipline worthy of serious pursuit in its own right: 'I really got hooked when I found Menger's *Grundsätze* such a fascinating book, so satisfying' (Hayek, 1994, p. 48). And as he put it also, 'I realize – I wouldn't have known it at the time – that the decisive influence was just reading Menger's *Grundsätze*' (ibid., p. 57; cf. 1934, pp. 533ff; 1973a, *passim*). While it was Menger who provided the intellectual foundations for Hayek's thought in economics, it was his contact with Wieser that exposed him initially to economics as an academic subject. As he recalled, 'I was a direct student of Wieser, and he originally had the greatest influence on me' (Hayek, 1994, p. 57). Somewhat ironically now, this influence came about to some extent because of Wieser's stand in defence of interventionism and against the extreme market liberalism being espoused by his mentor Ludwig von Mises at the time. It was the foundations of Hayek's vision of the human realm that were established initially by his finding in Wieser the endeavour 'to gain insight into the operations of the great impersonal forces in human society, forces to which every individual is subject and which with necessity bring about events desired or predicted by no one' (Hayek, 1926, p. 556). In the study of human economy and society, Wieser was aware, too, that the methodology required must effectively be the product of what dealing with the relevant phenomena demands. Most importantly, Hayek found him to give priority to ontological integrity as a principle of inquiry, for 'never could he be induced to do violence to [the] facts for the sake of greater elegance of the logical construction, and on occasion he was willing to sacrifice greater unity and consistence of thought for the sake of greater realism' (p. 565). This principle gave his substantive analyses the quality of realism which Hayek clearly found appealing.

Whatever Hayek had taken away from his exposure to the works of Menger and Wieser, his most obvious mentor was Mises. For there can be no doubt that much of Hayek's lasting intellectual development took place very much with Mises 'present', as it were. The two were in close contact in Vienna during Hayek's formative years after completing his university studies. He worked for Mises, as well as attending Mises's seminar series and presumably participating in the methodological debates that were so much a part of the sessions. Hayek has recalled that, during these first ten years of his career, the main guidance for his evolving ideas came from Mises. His summary assertion was that 'there is no single man to whom I owe more intellectually, even though he was never my teacher in the institutional sense of the word'. In spite of this, it was always to be a critically qualified influence that he retained (Hayek, 1983, pp. 17, 18; cf. p. 72). Nonetheless, Hayek mostly tried to cast the best light on his mentor's methodology. He noted how Mises had directed his efforts at a vindication of 'the autonomous character of the method of the social sciences by systematically building up a general theory of human action' (Hayek, 1992, p. 152). The effect was to have drawn attention to the ontologically distinct nature of phenomena generated by human action and thus to have suggested that the human sciences demand distinct metatheoretical treatment.

However, debates about these sometime connections with his early mentor, whether they be judged as for better or for worse, are of little pertinence to the form and treatment of his ultimate legacy. This is of course not to deny that there is an issue here to be addressed as an integral part of the doctrinal history of Austrian thought. In the debates about the periodization of Hayek's intellectual evolution, the evidence of his turning away from various key aspects Mises's principles has some role to play. But, as with the periodization debate more generally, it is not intended to try to do the controversy justice here. The main disputed ideas may be found in Caldwell (1988, pp. 528f; 1992a, pp. 37, 40) and Hutchison (1992, pp. 20ff, *passim*; 1994, pp. 212ff, *passim*).

Studying Hayek as a source of subjectivist metatheoretical ideas for economics reveals that he considered, in more or less depth and detail, a number of pertinent and significant themes that will be taken up in the chapters to follow. My arrangement of these themes is structured so as to give his contributions their maximum logical coherence in the light of my objectives, independently of their chronology. First, early on in his career as an academic economist, Hayek chose to set aside the pursuit of orthodox economic theory on subjectivist grounds. The central rationale for this abandonment was his concern about the legitimacy of the methodology that he had been attempting to apply as dominant and determinate in his own theories. Specifically, he came to recognize that neither substantively nor methodologically could orthodoxy capture and properly represent the human ontology of individual and collective economic action. In doing so, he set down the fundamental ground rule of his subsequent pursuit of a metatheory for economics as a human science: rather than being borrowed from the physical sciences, and rather than being set prior to scientific inquiry, his premise was that methodology should be a consequence of ensuring ontological integrity in the representation of phenomena.

Secondly, in order to set this emerging subjectivist consciousness in context, it is necessary to recognize that Hayek revised his vision of the economic problem very early in his career. He did so by critically reflecting upon some crucial facets of human agency that are involved in generating the phenomena concerned. In the first years of his contributions to economic thought, his fundamental concern was with accounting for the cyclically unstable, but equilibrium tending, nature of market capitalism. During this period of formalistic endeavour, we will find it is readily apparent that, from the outset, subjectivist elements were set to intrude into the analyses in spite of their abstract and formal nature. If we look ahead to the last major work of his life, *The Fatal Conceit* (1989), we find Hayek summing up this revised vision of economics in just the sort of subjectivist terms that he will be shown to have applied throughout much of his career. Because 'the activity that economics sets out to explain is not *about* physical phenomena but about people', it follows that we 'might describe economics ... as a *meta*theory, a *theory about* the theories people have developed to explain how most effectively to discover and use different means for diverse purposes' (p. 98, original emphasis). Such subjectivist intrusion had come much more to the fore by the mid-1930s, when he began to give primary and explicit emphasis to understanding the temporal processes of competition and coordination between individual economic agents in their market activities and the role of these processes in generating spontaneously ordered market outcomes.

Thirdly, as a consequence of his awareness of this 'deeper', subjectivist level of economic inquiry, Hayek undertook to develop his own psychological theory of the human agent. His focus in this endeavour was on agents whose actions constitute the 'underlying' ontological substance of human science phenomena in general, and those comprising the substance of the observed economic problem in particular. Active agents' objectives are to grasp and interpret the world around them in a continuing effort to resolve life's problems, large and small, by action responses. And, it should be emphasized in passing, his sole concern was with actions of interest in the non-clinical human sciences such as economics; that is, those actions that involve prior self-conscious, reasoned interpretations of, and deliberations about, agents' problem circumstances. Then, fourthly, in recognition of the fact that agents normally do not deal with their life circumstances in isolation, he went on to situate them in an inherited, but evolving, multidimensional environment within and through which they carry out their economic actions. That is, Hayek provided a situated human agent ontology as the foundation for his subjectivist vision of economics.

Fifthly, Hayek concerned himself with the methodological implications and epistemological consequences of making ontological consistency the essential criterion of theoretical analyses in economics. My aim in dealing with this aspect of his legacy will be to elicit his methodological response to the subjectivist ontology of economic phenomena. In this context, our main attention must shift to a different category of agents, those who are formal observers and analysts of other active agents and their deliberated agency and whose objective is formally to understand and represent what active agents do. In these respects, economic agents and actions, and their study by economists, are but a subset of human scientific inquiry more generally.

The theses argued within each of these themes appeared at various times throughout Hayek's life's work and were developed with varying degrees of detail and success. It is my intention to draw on the relevant sources as required critically to elaborate and reinforce, as well as to give coherence to, the ideas I find to have the most enduring legitimacy for the development of a neoAustrian subjectivist economics. Two summary questions concerning the pursuit of his subjectivist legacy are pertinent in directing my inquiries. First, to what extent can we find in his contributions a satisfying ontology of situated human agency as the origin of economic phenomena, making due allowance for the vision of the economic problem within which it was developed? Secondly, to what extent did he provide appropriate methodological guidance, and set legitimate epistemological limitations, when dealing with these phenomena of human agency in a manner that allows transparent formalized representation of that ontology?

4.2 FORMALISM AND SUBJECTIVIST INCLINATIONS

When Hayek went to London in the early 1930s and established his *bona fides* as a formal analyst, it was his initial adherence to an objectivist and formalist analysis that gained him an *entrée* to the world of English academia. In this early period of his work, he chose to give priority to matters other than subjectivism in his economic writings. Above all, as far as concerns the present inquiry, the general tenor of his economics then was identified with and bounded by the need to preserve some concept of equilibrium as the centrepiece of any theoretical analysis (cf. Caldwell, 1988, pp. 521ff; Hutchison, 1994, pp. 215f; Shackle, 1981). He thus started out as an equilibrium economic theorist, albeit one with some unorthodox ideas that the English 1930s establishment found peculiar and confronting (Caldwell, 1988, pp. 516ff).

While still working in Vienna in 1928, Hayek published the paper, 'Intertemporal price equilibrium and movements in the value of money', that set the direction of the theoretical inquiries he would pursue over the next few years. But it also contained a hint of misgiving about equilibrium that would resurface later. In it, he gave explicit recognition of the need to incorporate the *real time* dimension of economic action into any formal analysis that was to reach beyond a description of a static state in which action has ceased. Thus 'All economic activity is carried out through time. Every individual economic process occupies a certain time, and all linkages between economic processes necessarily involve longer or shorter periods of time' (1928, p. 71). Abstraction from the efflux of real time was more the norm than the exception in the assumptions of established economic analyses, but this constituted a fiction with the capacity to mislead unless duly qualified. For, 'as soon as these assumptions, oversimplified and all too contradictory of reality as they are, are replaced by ones corresponding more to the facts, it becomes evident that the customary abstraction from time does a degree of violence to the actual state of affairs which casts serious doubt upon the utility of the results thereby achieved' (pp. 71f). In this same period, Hayek's other main works, *Monetary Theory and the Trade Cycle*, published in German in 1929, and *Prices and Production*, his four debut lectures on the theory of the trade cycle at the London School of Economics published in 1931, were all but bereft of subjectivist concerns. Nevertheless, it would soon become apparent to Hayek that the mechanistic, equilibrium-centred approach he had adopted could not carry him very far in understanding the true origins and nature of economic instability. For this, the real-world character and effects of time, and a recognition of human agents' limitations and fallibility, had to be included. Subjective agents, acting in time in the face of uncertainty, must resort to expectations in order to make decisions about investment and production. Their decisions could turn out to be wrong and the consequent collective outcomes would involve disruptive, disequilibrium-inducing inconsistencies (cf. Shackle, 1981, pp. 240f).

The subjectivist views that initiated Hayek's misgivings about the nature of economic theory were first expressed most explicitly when he lectured in Copenhagen during December of 1933 on 'Price expectations, monetary disturbances and malinvestments'.[2] In the version of this lecture published in 1935 (Hayek, 1939a, pp. 135ff), he questioned the nature and role of the equilibrium concept as it might be applied to understanding economic fluctuations over time that are the consequence of the actions of particular strategic agents. The particular difficulty he emphasized was that of relating an individual agent's potential to achieve a subjective and personal equilibrium to the collectively coherent state that may result from the interactions of independent individuals. While we can 'speak of a necessary equilibrium between the decisions which a person will make at a given moment, it is much less clear in what sense we can apply the same concept to the actions of a great number of persons, whose successive responses to the actions of their fellow-beings necessarily take place in time'. Hayek continued: 'The main difficulty of the traditional approach is its complete abstraction from time', and thus from processes, whereas such collective outcomes can be represented 'as a timeless equilibrium relationship only by means of unrealistic special constructions'. Hence, reasoned Hayek, 'the realistic significance of tendencies towards a state of equilibrium ... can be shown only when we know what the conditions are under which it is at least conceivable that a position of equilibrium will actually be reached' (p. 139).

Notice that it was the subjectivist implications of the way agents cope with time that Hayek emphasized in this argument. As he indicated at the end of the lecture, the theme was intended as a defence against Gunnar Myrdal's implication that Hayek's theories left 'no room for the role played by expectations – to show how important a part they do play was in fact one of the purposes of this lecture' (ibid., p. 155).[3] Most especially, 'instead of completely disregarding the time element, we must make very definite assumptions about the attitude of persons towards the future' (p. 139). The usual procedure was to assume perfect foresight on the part of each individual agent concerning the objective data of the world around them, as well as with respect to 'the behaviour of all the other people with whom he expects to perform economic transactions' (p. 140). This he considered to be an unsatisfactory approach to the problem, for he now recognized that 'every explanation of economic crises must include the assumption that entrepreneurs have committed errors' as one of its endogenous contributing factors (p. 141). The errors stem from the fact that 'the various expectations on which different individuals base their decisions at a particular moment either will or will not be mutually compatible; and that if these expectations are not compatible those of some people at least must be disappointed' (p. 140). As a specific and crucial case, Hayek made reference to decisions about investment in means of production as where 'the outcome depends entirely on the correctness of the views *generally* held about future developments' (p. 142, original emphasis). But, as he realized, the missing link in his argument comprised 'the much more difficult and important question of what determines the expectations of entrepreneurs', for he was in no doubt that in 'the further development of the theory of industrial fluctuations ... the whole complex of the theory of uncertainty and risk ... will become increasingly important' (pp. 155f).

Some similar sensitivity to subjectivist contingencies remained evident in Hayek's last major theoretical work in economics, *The Pure Theory of Capital* of 1941 (cf. Shackle, 1981, pp. 242ff, Caldwell, 1988, pp. 531ff). Of particular concern here is that an integral part of his endeavours in this magnum opus turned out to be a continuation of the struggle to work around his subjectivist misgivings about equilibrium methodology. It was especially in Chapter II of the work that he made a determined effort to situate the problems of capital theory in an equilibrium analysis that made proper allowance for the exigencies of human agency. His subjectivist intention was to overcome the limitations of using orthodox equilibrium constructs in the context of capital and investment theory in two particular respects (Hayek, 1941, pp. 14f). First, he wanted to ensure that the equilibrium concept used was one in which interdependence between the actions of singular economic entities were included in the argument. Secondly, he required that the equilibrium state should not be stationary in the sense that relevant processes have ceased, for 'in the sphere of capital theory ... the construction of a stationary state is particularly useless because the main problem, that of investment, arises just because people intend to do in the future something different from what they are doing in the present'. This meant that 'to postulate a self-repeating stationary state is to abstract from the very phenomena that we want to study' (p. 22). In this respect, 'what we need is a theory which helps us to explain the interrelations between the *actions* of different members of the community during the period ... *before* the material structure of productive equipment has been brought to a state which will make an unchanging, self-repeating process possible' (p. 17, original emphasis). The subjectivist challenge was to design an equilibrium concept that 'refers to a certain type of relationship between the plans of different members of society'. That is, to devise the conditions under which agents' plans are 'fully adjusted to one another, so that it is possible for all of them to be carried out because the plans of any one member are based on the expectation of such actions on the part of the other members as are contained in the plans which those others are making at the same time' (p. 18). The maintenance of such consistency of plans depends upon agents meeting one or both of two conditions: continuing habitual repetition of relevant economic operations and/or correct anticipations of and responses to any changes in environmental circumstances or in the actions of others (pp. 18, 22). And, in this process, 'the direction in which an entrepreneur will have to revise his plans will depend on the direction in which events prove to differ from his expectations' (p. 23).

All of this left unasked and unanswered a number of decisive subjectivist questions about what active agents can 'know' concerning the present and future circumstances within which they must plan and act, and what economic analysts can 'know' about the deliberations and intentions of those agents. These are questions that Hayek chose not to confront. He hastened on with the assertion that, although a situation in which there is consistency of agents' plans is fictitious, 'it is only by contrast with this imaginary state, which serves as a kind of foil, that we are able to predict what will happen if entrepreneurs attempt to carry out any given set of plans' (ibid., pp. 22f, cf. pp. 18, 19, 21, 23, 26, 27). His often reiterated view was that the fact that 'it is probably impossible to formulate any conditions under which such a state would ever be fully realised does not destroy its value as an intellectual tool' because 'its function is simply to serve as a guide to the analysis of concrete situations, showing what their relations would be under "ideal" conditions' (p. 28).

It is evident that the vexed problem of the status to be given to equilibrium continued to trouble him in the remainder of this work, for subjectivist reasons. In Chapter XIX, entitled 'The general conditions of equilibrium', there was a shift of analysis from the 'simple' centrally directed model of investment in real capital to a 'competitive' one in which 'command over the existing resources is distributed between a multitude of independent persons, each of whom uses his share of them in the service of his individual system of ends and all of whom are in a position to exchange on a market'. He believed that this shift took the analysis 'one step nearer to reality' (ibid., p. 247). However, the strategy meant confronting again what to do about the involvement of equilibrium as the core of the analysis. He became very cautious about what he was doing and achieving in developing his theory, noting that 'this transition to a set of assumptions which are somewhat more closely related to real phenomena does not ... mean that we shall undertake to explain *the actual process on a competitive market*'. And, he hastened to add, 'the question of how and when such a state of competitive equilibrium will come about does not directly concern us here' (pp. 247f, emphasis added). By way of further explanation of his strategy here, he reminded his readers of the need to retreat to employing equilibrium only as a foil. He emphasized that 'we are here really not interested in the *process* which brings about equilibrium but merely in the *conditions* of a state of equilibrium, and when we are considering positions other than equilibrium positions it is merely to show why they are not equilibrium positions'. Thus the notion of equilibrium 'is not meant as a description of a process but merely as a conceptual tool which leads us, as it were, as spectators from positions which are more removed from equilibrium to positions which are closer to it, and finally to the equilibrium position itself' (p. 248, original emphasis). All in all, then, equilibrium remained a foil in the analysis of capital, with Hayek implicitly promising that somehow something would have to be done to move closer to economic reality than this technique would allow. As we are to see, he was soon to lose interest more or less completely in equilibrium as a formal technical problem in this sense and context.

Hayek recalled later in life, in one of the interviews he gave about his work, that he went to London as a theorist in the more or less orthodox sense: 'In my early years in London, my interest remained concentrated on the theory of money, capital, and industrial fluctuations, and my main goal became soon a restatement of the theory of capital as a foundation for a more satisfactory account of the dynamic phenomena' (Hayek, 1994, pp. 78f). More specifically, in the same context he expressed his feelings about the theory of capital as far as he had been able to take it: 'Like so many things, I am afraid, which I have attempted in economics, this capital-theory work more shows a barrier to how far we can get in efficient explanation than sets forth precise explanations. All these things I've stressed – the complexity of the phenomena in general, the unknown character of the data, and so on – really much more point out limits to our possible knowledge than our contributions that make specific predictions possible' (p. 142). One review of the achievements of *The Pure Theory of Capital*, that of George Shackle, reinforced this self-deprecating view. His opinion was that, in spite of the long struggle to write it and the detailed analyses it contained, Hayek was unable to satisfy the concurrent demands of maintaining any form of equilibrium methodology and of giving due recognition to the real-world problematic of conditioned and temporally situated human action (Shackle, 1981, pp. 248f). Bruce Caldwell reasonably concludes, too, that although Hayek 'viewed his new definition of non-stationary equilibrium (one based on compatibility of [individual] plans) as an advance over its stationary, full knowledge predecessor', he was left with the problem of 'answering the question of *how* such an equilibrium might be reached' (1988, pp. 532f, original emphasis). Shackle judged the notion more harshly:

> Such a conception has, perhaps, its greatest usefulness in compelling us to ask, in view of its evident utter unattainability, what in fact the process of history must be like. Individuals will not necessarily surrender the freedom of imagination, of enterprise, of attempted exploitation of the void of time-to-come, in order to try to reconcile their ambitions with those of all other individuals. The seething cauldron of history mocks such a notion. (Shackle, 1981, pp. 252f)

Shackle continued by observing that there is just no hope that individuals will plan consistently, given their differential characters, experiences, environments and time horizons. To all this, he might well have added the complicating conundrum of how individuals are to identify ex ante what the plans of others are so that they could, even if they so desired, make their own consistent with them. It was to this problem of inter-agent coordination, as the basis for the spontaneous socioeconomic order he claimed would emerge from free-market competition, that Hayek was to devote so much intellectual effort in the future.

As we have seen above, Hayek could not sustain his interest in economics through pure theory alone and he recalled that, 'though I tried hard to concentrate further on this subject, my interest began to wander to other topics' (Hayek, 1994, p. 79). These 'other topics' involved him in the pursuit of the metatheoretical foundations and processes of human science generally and economics in particular. Thus he wrote that 'I got increasingly interested in ... philosophical and methodological questions ... [and the] decisive step in this development of my thinking was the paper on "Economics and Knowledge" [1949, pp. 33ff] ... Together with some later related papers reprinted with it in *Individualism and Economic Order* [1949], this seems to me in retrospect the most original contribution I have made to the theory of economics' (p. 79). In the next chapter, I begin by seeking reasons for this assessment.

NOTES

1. The timing, nature and extent of these intellectual shifts, or 'transformations' as they have more boldly been called, have been the subjects of some, often vituperative, controversy and exchanges in the literature. These date from the time Terence Hutchison posited the existence of a Hayek I and a Hayek II (1981, pp. 210ff). The relevant contributions to pursue here are Caldwell (1988, 1992a, 1992b, 1994b); Fleetwood (1995); Foss (1995); Hutchison (1992, 1994, pp. 189ff and 212ff); Lawson (1994b, 1994d, 1997, ch. 10). I will avoid couching my critical interpretations in these terms. As far as I am concerned, ideas from all periods of Hayek's life warrant careful scrutiny to seek out their enduring legitimacy and relevance to the neoAustrian revival. They do so, too, irrespective of Hayek's own expressions and beliefs about them. Nevertheless, there can be no doubt that discontinuities exist in Hayek's treatment of the subjectivist metatheory for economics. What my approach has revealed in this respect is that, in some senses, the periodization of his thought has become too specific and precise, and that the profundity of its discontinuities

has been exaggerated. In the context of the controversy, there has also been an inclination to overemphasize specific *chronological* points of transition in the substance and methodology of his arguments. The result has been to neglect the core dimensions of subjectivist continuity that can be found from very early on in his writings. And, where there have been shifts, their compositions really matter more than the exact dates of their occurrence. Because of the overlapping and repetitious nature of much of Hayek's work, I find that Tony Lawson's idea of a 'continuing transformation' makes most sense (1994d).

2. Most recently, the matter of dating Hayek's earliest application of subjectivist ideas in his economic theory has been considered by Nicolai Juul Foss (1995). My analysis of this theme has benefited greatly from Foss's carefully researched contributions.
3. For more details of the nature of Myrdal's critique, see Foss (1995, pp. 354f).

5. Hayek and the vision of economic order

5.1 THE IDEA OF ECONOMIC ORDER

Soon after Hayek's move to London, he became involved in the socialist calculation debates, the substance of which was initially addressed in two of his papers from 1935 (1949, pp. 119ff and 148ff). It was to be this controversy that would induce him to modify his vision of the dominant economic problem and to change his attitude towards the nature and status of equilibrium as part of that problem. Accounting for and defending the capacity of free markets to deliver ordered outcomes by means of spontaneously coordinated agents' actions became the main substantive preoccupation with economics over the remainder of his life.

Hayek foreshadowed the nature of the coordination problem that is central to any emergence of economic order as early as March 1933, in his Inaugural Lecture on taking up the Tooke Chair in Economics. The lecture was published in *Economica* as 'The trend of economic thinking' (1933) and in it we find him engaged in a critical examination of the perceived imperative for economics to meet the practical challenges of guiding reform and policy, the 'intense urge to reconstruct a world which gives rise to profound dissatisfaction' (ibid., p. 122). This observation set the stage for the lecture in that it implicitly posed the primary issue of the extent to which self-conscious human reason had been and could be instrumental in generating and directing the advantages of economic order and change. Hayek expressed his misgivings about any argument that gave priority to such constructivist reasoning (p. 123). His view was that economic order and its dynamics could not be explained as the result of conscious construction, making the point that 'it is an error ... to assume that the existing economic system serves a definite function only in so far as its institutions have been deliberately willed by individuals' (p. 130). Analysts need to recognize that 'the spontaneous interplay of the actions of individuals may produce something which is not the deliberate object of their actions but an organism in which every part performs a necessary function for the continuance of the whole, without any human mind having devised it' (p. 130).

In a market economy, a proper understanding of events must be based on the premise that 'the co-ordination of individual efforts in society is not the product of deliberate planning, but has been brought about ... by means which nobody wanted or understood' (ibid., p. 129, cf. pp. 130f). Any attempt to replace the spontaneously coordinated outcomes of collective action by a rationally designed system of intervention would require that it fully emulate the spontaneous capacities of the free-market system (pp. 132f). That is, as Hayek put it, 'the best the [market] dictator could do ... would be to imitate as closely as possible what would happen under free competition' (p. 133). But, in the absence of a market-price system, the most intelligent planner 'would lack the most important guide to such action which the competitive system affords' (p. 132). But what was missing in this brief reference to the problem was any explication of the precise role that prices must play in the coordination process. The transformation of vision that Hayek experienced during the later debates about socialism shifted his attention to the connection between prices and agents' knowledge as subjectively conditioned, diverse and widely dispersed, along with their implications for the processes of achieving coordination through market exchanges. More generally, it directed his concerns towards the need to integrate his treatment of individual agents and their subjectivist decision processes and actions that he had emphasized in another lecture of 1933, given in Copenhagen (1939a, pp. 135ff), with the problem of accounting for coordinated collective outcomes of agents' concurrent decisions. In both dimensions, agents' given accumulations of individual knowledge and their market positions are of fundamental significance (cf. Caldwell, 1988, pp. 533, 536).

In Hayek's writings on socialist calculation in 1935 (1949, pp. 119ff), the immediate issue was the inclination of some economists to claim a legitimate role for economic engineering in constructing idealized, rationally designed market processes and outcomes. For these people, 'to apply reason to the organization of society, and to shape it deliberately in every detail according to human wishes and the common ideas of justice seemed the only course of action worthy of a rational being' (ibid., p. 119). The human dimension of this constructivist planning proposal was just assumed to be resolvable, with individual agents merely directed to conform to the demands of their positions in the plan (p. 120). Hayek attributed such naïveté on the part of socialists to a lack of appreciation of the true nature of the economic problem and its solution (pp. 120f). Indeed, it was the fact that the myth of a perfectly competitive market mechanism had been claimed by orthodox economists effectively to solve the pricing and resource allocation problems by invisible means that had resulted in the precise nature of the complex process involved not being the object of much direct inquiry. From the time of his earliest reflections on the economic problem, Hayek was conscious of a contrast between the subjectivist approach as he understood it and that of the neoclassical model with its pure logic of choice, its situational determinism and rationality principle, and its equilibrium framework (cf. Latsis 1972, 1983). This vision of the market economy represented the outcomes of production and exchange in a misleadingly rationalist and objective way. The price-theoretic notion of a stationary competitive equilibrium outcome was taken for granted as the appropriate focus for economic analysis and expression, with its actual *origins* in the processes of human agency of little concern. There was a minimal role for any subjectivist dimensions of the processes, with independent individual decisions presumed to be in accordance with the pure logic of maximizing choice under given and totally known circumstances, present and future. The key given and known elements were the atemporal relative prices of factors and commodities upon which agents presumed to base their market actions.

It followed from such analysis that, if the free-market 'invisible hand' failed to bring the desired socioeconomic results, the markets could be replaced by centrally planning and directing agents' responses to the imposition of properly calculated cost and pricing signals. It was simply a matter of bringing forward, in effect, the competitive market outcome of prices equal to marginal costs and transforming it into a short-run directive for socialist managers so as to set their prices. For Hayek, the lack of analytical endeavour to penetrate into the nature of production decisions and market processes, including their necessarily subjectivist dimensions, led to a failure to appreciate the nature and scale, as well as the ambiguity, of the prior calculation problems that central planners and their enterprise managers would confront (Hayek, 1949, pp. 152ff). Moreover, this lack of penetration meant a failure to understand the role that individually motivated agents with specialist situational knowledge play in generating the collective outcome. The idea that such a complex of knowledge could be replicated and applied by the directives of a single planning authority, and that directed agents would, as a matter of course, respond in accordance with the correct motivations and action directives, was naive in the extreme, according to Hayek. The importance of individual agent knowledge and its implications for action were soon to be taken up as a particular theme of his research.

5.2 KNOWLEDGE AND ECONOMIC ORDER

Overall, then, by the time he came to write and deliver the 'Economics and knowledge' lecture in 1936, subsequently published in 1937 (1949, pp. 33ff), Hayek had shown his preparedness to confront some dimensions of the metatheoretical impact of subjectivism in economics. However, the treatment of the fundamental subjectivism of individual agents' decision making and actions was now integrated with the role of subjectivist agency in understanding the collective, ordered outcomes of market processes. In this 1936–7 paper and beyond, it was to be the latter problematic that would form the focus of so much of his attention.

He began by emphasizing his critique of the orthodox treatment of economic phenomena on the ontological grounds that it failed to give any serious attention to the real-world nature of human agents and agency. As he put it so pointedly, 'I am certain that there are many who regard with impatience and distrust the whole tendency, which is inherent in all modern equilibrium analysis, to turn economics into a branch of pure logic, a set of self-evident propositions which, like mathematics or geometry, are subject to no other test but internal consistency' (ibid., p. 35). And if such purely logical theory was to have any significance in economics it must be unequivocally isolated from any immediate empirical claims to relevance, for 'the tautological propositions of pure equilibrium analysis as such are not directly applicable to the explanation of social relations' (p. 35). More specifically, now, his focus was on the significance of recognizing knowledge that economic agents can be claimed to possess and use in determining the economic actions that are the origin of such phenomena. Here Hayek had the insight to see that 'the tautologies, of which formal equilibrium analysis in economics essentially consists, can be turned into propositions which tell us anything about causation in the real world only in so far as we are able to fill those formal propositions with definite statements about how knowledge is acquired and communicated' (p. 33). The implication of this claim was that equilibrium outcomes could have real-world relevance if their origins in coordinated agents' actions could be accounted for in terms of their forming and applying consistent patterns of knowledge in working up their plans of action. In doing so, the 'actions of a person can be said to be in equilibrium in so far as they can be understood as part of one plan'. For 'only if this is the case, only if all these actions have been decided upon at one and the same moment, and in consideration of the same set of circumstances, have our statements about their interconnections, which we deduce from our assumptions about the knowledge and the preferences of the person, any application' (p. 36).

One crucial issue raised by these arguments was the question of what individual agents can actually be said to 'know' about their 'circumstances'. Hayek showed that he was at least conscious of the most intractable problem concerning individual agents' knowledge: the need for 'foresight and "anticipations"' when they are deliberating and deciding upon actions that will have results in the future. As economic analysts, 'we cannot escape the vexed problem of the exact position which assumptions about foresight are to have in our reasoning'. Here he wrote the now well-known aphorism that, 'before we can explain why people commit mistakes, we must first explain why they should ever be right' (ibid., p. 34). What he did not pursue was whether and how analysts could ever provide an answer to the latter question.

In this same direction of inquiry, Hayek also gave some renewed attention to the issue of the role of real time in the conception of an individual's equilibrium state. He reasoned that, 'since equilibrium is a relationship between actions, and since the actions of one person must necessarily take place successively in time, it is obvious that the passage of time is essential to give the concept of equilibrium any meaning' (ibid., p. 37). His efforts to come to grips with the import of real time here centred around the evolving dynamics of agents' knowledge. Any equilibrium of *successive* actions by an individual within some time horizon is only possible if they are elements in the execution of a single and consistent plan. It followed that 'any change in the relevant knowledge of the person, that is, any change which leads him to alter his plan, disrupts the equilibrium relation between his actions taken before and those taken after the change in his knowledge. In other words, the equilibrium relationship comprises only his actions during the period in which his anticipations prove correct' (p. 36). Such correct anticipations were unlikely to be realized, as Hayek must have been aware, thus giving the associated individual equilibrium idea a rather tenuous relevance for modelling the real world of human agency.

So it was that he presented agents as having the capacity *as acting individuals* to establish for themselves a personal equilibrium state in their life-world. He was prepared to go so far as to write that 'I have long felt that the concept of equilibrium itself and the methods which we employ in pure analysis have a clear meaning only when confined to the analysis of the action of a single person'. But, with some subtle but powerful insight, the ultimate significance of which he did not pursue at the time, he observed that 'we are really passing into a different sphere and silently introducing a new element of altogether different character when we apply ... [equilibrium arguments] to the explanation of the interactions of a number of different individuals' (ibid., p. 35). That is, in any attempt to extend the notion of individual equilibrium to the collective results of agents' actions, where inevitably their plans will include some pattern of interdependence between the individuals, Hayek was aware of additional complications (pp. 37ff). Such an outcome, he argued, would depend upon all agents acting consistently in the sense of basing their plans on a *common and correct* set of subjective expectations about relevant external events yet to occur. It followed that 'the concept of equilibrium merely means that the foresight of the different members of society is in a special sense correct. It must be correct in the sense that every person's plan is based on the expectation of just those actions of other people which those other people intend to perform and that all these plans are based on the expectation of the same set of external facts, so that under certain conditions nobody will have any reason to change his plans'. On this basis, Hayek concluded that 'correct foresight is then not ... a precondition which must exist in order that equilibrium may be arrived at. *It is rather the defining characteristic of a state of equilibrium*' (p. 42, emphasis added). Any conflicting expectations would mean that no outturn of events would enable all plans to be realized.

It is apparent that, by this stage of his career, Hayek was very wary of attributing any self-evident *existential* status to economic equilibrium as the outcome of agents' actions. Whatever may be the links between the formation of individuals' perceptions of the relevant 'subjective data' and their experience of 'objective data', he realized that the existence of an equilibrium will require the *assumption* that their actions are to be based on a common and mutually compatible relationship between these 'data'. As he put it, 'equilibrium relationships cannot be deduced merely from the objective facts, since the analysis of what people will do can start only from *what is known to them*' (ibid., p. 44, emphasis added). An endogenously generated tendency toward collective equilibrium consequent upon individual actions as 'an empirical proposition', Hayek noted, would require that 'the knowledge and intentions of the different members of society ... come more and more into agreement ... [and] the expectations of the people and particularly of the entrepreneurs ... become more and more correct' (p. 45). But he was quick to point out the realities of the state of economic understanding of such matters: 'The only trouble is that we are still pretty much in the dark about (*a*) the *conditions* under which this tendency is supposed to exist and (*b*) the nature of the *process* by which individual knowledge is changed' (p. 45, original emphasis). He took these issues very seriously and attempted critically to assess their implications. In particular, he posed some pertinent questions about the knowledge that agents can be expected to possess, how they acquire and change it and how they apply it in their choices and actions.

Hayek showed an acute awareness of the essential problem posed by making claims that agents know things about their life-world conditions (ibid., pp. 48ff). It is inevitable that these conditions will be in a continuous and never-ending state of temporal flux that defies any assumptions about 'constancy of data' and poses immediate difficulties for making claims that active agents are able progressively to learn by experience about those conditions. The immediate import for agents situated in a changing environment is that they must form expectations about the future states of relevant conditions. At this point, he made the realist ontological observation in connection with expectations that 'there must be some discernible regularity in the world which makes it possible to predict events correctly. But, while this is clearly not sufficient to prove that people will learn to foresee events correctly, the same is true to a hardly less degree even about constancy of data in an absolute sense' (p. 49). So, sorting out 'how much knowledge and what sort of knowledge the different individuals must possess in order that we may be able to speak of equilibrium' (p. 50) became a profound challenge for analysts. It meant confronting the fact about equilibrium that, 'if the concept is to have any empirical significance, it cannot presuppose that everybody knows everything'. The issue is, then, one of understanding the '*division of knowledge*'. As far as Hayek was concerned, this 'seems to me to be the really central problem of economics as a social science' that is analogous to, and warrants as much attention as has been received by the concept of the division of labour (p. 50, original emphasis).

In a paper published in 1945, 'The use of knowledge in society' (1949, pp. 77ff), Hayek's opening gambit was to reinforce his rejection of orthodox presumptions about human agency in economics. As he put it, 'any approach, such as that of much of mathematical economics with its simultaneous equations, which in effect starts from the assumption that people's *knowledge* corresponds with the objective *facts* of the situation, systematically leaves out what is our main task to explain' (ibid., p. 91, original emphasis). His critical challenge here was that 'there is something fundamentally wrong with an approach [to economic theory] which habitually disregards an essential part of the phenomena with which we have to deal: the unavoidable imperfection of man's knowledge and the consequent need for a process by which knowledge is constantly communicated and acquired' (p. 91). The consequent implication concerning such a presumption about the human agent was that, 'when it comes to the point where it misleads some of our leading thinkers into believing that the situation which it describes has direct relevance to the solution of practical problems, it is high time to remember that it *does not deal with the social process at all*' (p. 91, emphasis added).

Here again the primary issue was that of the nature and role of knowledge in coordinating agents' actions in the competitive process. Hayek noted that 'the economic problem of society is mainly one of rapid adaptation to changes in the particular circumstances of time and place'and concluded that the market can handle such changes effectively because 'the ultimate decisions must be left to the people who are familiar with these circumstances, who know directly of the relevant changes and of the resources immediately available to meet them' (ibid., pp. 83f). Then, however, he went on to add the rider that 'the "man on the spot" cannot decide solely on the basis of his limited but intimate knowledge of the facts of his immediate surroundings. There still remains the problem of communicating to him such further information as he needs to fit his decisions into the whole pattern of changes of the larger economic system' (p. 84). But even here, Hayek failed fully to express the subjectivist problematic of how agents cope with uncertainty, with the need to claim 'knowledge' about the future that is, as a matter of epistemological fact, not available to anyone.

Some two decades on, in the late 1960s, Hayek further reiterated the themes of agents' ignorance and knowledge found in his writings of the 1930s and 1940s. As its title, 'Competition as a discovery procedure' (1978, pp. 179ff) suggests, his intention in this paper was to amplify his understanding of markets as processes crucially involving the exigencies of agents' knowledge. What he emphasized again in this context was the 'absurdity' of any analysis that attempts to comprehend markets by simply making assumptions about the information used by agents in the market process. All that can follow from this 'is a *state* of affairs which economic theory curiously calls "perfect competition". It leaves no room whatever for the *activity* called competition, which is presumed to have already done its task' (ibid., p. 182, original emphasis). The challenge is rather to establish the information they can actually have and to explicate how it is acquired. Missing from such a presumption, that is, are the emergent effects of the acquisition and application of the dispersed and varied subjective knowledge and objectives held by individual agents who participate in the market process. These data are known to no one collectively and it is this fact that Hayek cited as the rationale for using the market. For 'if anyone really knew all about what economic theory calls the *data*, competition would indeed be a very wasteful method of securing adjustment to these facts'. On the contrary, '*wherever* the use of competition can be rationally justified, it is on the ground that we do *not* know in advance the facts that determine the actions of competitors' (p. 179, original emphasis).

For Hayek, operational significance of this premise in actual market processes was that the results of competition 'are unpredictable and on the whole different from those which anyone has, or could have, deliberately aimed at. Further, that the generally beneficial effects of competition must include disappointing or defeating some particular expectations or intentions' (ibid., p. 180). In the latter circumstances, the 'beneficial effects' referred to can only emerge if human agents have the knowledge and capacity to adjust ex post in the appropriate manner. Whatever may be the nature of this knowledge, Hayek's contribution is limited to the claim that some 'self-organizing' feedback is inherent in the market process, and that this is merely a consequence of price adjustments: 'Prices direct their [agents'] attention to what is worth finding out about market offers for various things and services'. The result is that 'a high degree of coincidence of expectations is brought about by the systematic disappointment of some kind of expectations' (p. 185). This less than satisfying assertion suggests a naive form of adaptive expectations based on learning-by-doing in some sense and allows minimal insight into the subjectively determined market conduct of agents forced to contend with true uncertainty about an ever-changing set of circumstances. In the next section, agents' dependence on prices as the crucial means of sharing knowledge will be more fully situated in Hayek's evolving theory of competition.

5.3 COMPETITION AND ECONOMIC ORDER

It was during the 1940s that Hayek was most concerned with the development of his theory of competition as central to economics. The first indications of this concern came in *The Road to Serfdom* (1944), where he effectively built onto his earlier contributions to the socialist calculation debate by examining, albeit briefly, the conditions under which a free-market economy could function as a means of coordinating individual economic actions. It was perhaps the most fundamental of his beliefs that 'the very complexity of the division of labour under modern conditions ... makes competition the only method by which ... co-ordination can be adequately brought about'. And if economic freedom is to be ensured, this coordination must involve a process which 'leaves the separate agencies free to adjust their activities to the facts which only they can know, and yet brings about a mutual adjustment of their respective plans'. By keeping his focus on the needs of competing agents for knowledge, the problem was that 'the co-ordination can clearly not be effected by "conscious control", but only by arrangements which convey to each agent the information he must possess in order effectively to adjust his decisions to those of others' (ibid., p. 36).

In Hayek's vision, such 'arrangements' could only be made by means of a market-price system. As he went on to argue the situation, 'what is required is some apparatus of registration which automatically records all the relevant effects of individual actions, and whose indications are at the same time the resultant of, and the guide for, all the individual decisions' (ibid., p. 36). And, he asserted, 'this is precisely what the price system does under competition' in that 'it enables entrepreneurs, by watching the movement of comparatively few prices, as an engineer watches the hands of a few dials, to adjust their activities to those of their fellows'. But he added the essential rider that rules out any monopoly power over prices: 'The important point here is that the price system will fulfil this function only if competition prevails, that is, if the individual producer has to adapt himself to price changes and cannot control them' (p. 36). Of course, this brief exposition of the principles of free-market coordination could hardly be expected to provide a full account of the processes involved. However, as we are to see below, this outline of Hayek's superficial analytical vision of competition was to comprise the form in which he argued the matter throughout his lifetime. Most of the lacunae evident in the argument above were never to be properly filled.

This minimalist analytical content was again evident in the 1946 lecture entitled 'The meaning of competition' (1949, pp. 92ff). Here Hayek set out to make more of his view that what had always been missing from the orthodox theory of competition was a consciousness of the *process* by which any equilibrium outcome or tendency is realized. He noted that the mainstream equilibrium concept defies the realities of the economic adjustments 'in which we have to deal with a social process in which the decisions of many individuals influence one another and necessarily succeed one another in time'. When the focus is on competitive equilibrium as an *assumed outcome*, the 'moving force of economic life is left almost altogether undiscussed' (ibid., p. 93) and 'the neglect of the time element makes the theoretical picture of perfect competition so entirely remote from all that is relevant to an understanding of the process of competition' (p. 102).

It is, then, sharply contrary to the presumptions of orthodoxy for analysts to recognize that the real-time dimension is ever-present once markets are represented as processes. For Hayek, the substance of competition as a process had to focus on the optimal acquisition and application of knowledge to circumstances by economic agents. In understanding the operations involved in the competitive process, analysts must give attention to 'how it can be brought about that as much of the available knowledge as possible is used'. The effect was to raise 'for a competitive society the question, not how we can "find" the people who know best, but rather what institutional arrangements are necessary in order that the unknown persons who have knowledge specially suited to a particular task are most likely to be attracted to that task' (p. 95). Informational signals which form the basis for agents' application of their knowledge to their circumstances in forming actions were confined at this stage to the relevant relative prices available in the market. In this regard, Hayek made reference to the assumed 'insurmountable difficulties of discovering ... such a system of prices by any other method except that of trial and error in the market, with the individual participants gradually learning the relevant circumstances' (p. 100). However, in this reference, the real problematic that agents confront when the learning process has an ever-changing body of 'relevant circumstances' to cope with was not evident. Common sense would suggest, rather, that the 'learning' required of agents is more an open-ended and continuing process of incomplete adaptations to an ever changing world than an incremental approach to some finite and fixed body of knowledge.

Hayek's concerns were to become more directly focused upon developing a subjectively grounded understanding of the socioeconomic order spontaneously generated by free markets in his three-volume work, *Law, Legislation and Liberty* (1973b, 1976, 1979). The archetypical example of spontaneous order as he had considered it in general terms was that which he claimed would be delivered by an 'invisible hand' directing the operations of individuals under the implicit rules of free market competition. His intention in the 1970s work was to provide a deeper understanding of '*how* that coincidence of expectations and plans is produced which characterizes the market order and the nature of the benefits we derive from it' (1973b, p. 38, emphasis added, cf. 1976, pp. 107ff). In specifically addressing the 'how' of this process, Hayek really set himself a challenge that would prove impossible to meet.

A primary distinction drawn in Volume 2 of the work was that between constructed organizations of the '*economy*' and the broader vision of competitive order that is generated by the forces of the free market. That is, 'an economy, in the strict sense of the word in which a household, a farm, or an enterprise can be called economies, consists of a complex of activities by which a given set of means is allocated in accordance with a unitary plan among the competing ends according to their relative importance' (Hayek, 1976, p. 107). In this sense, both organizations and individual agents are 'economies'. By contrast, 'the *cosmos* of the market neither is nor could be governed by such a single scale of ends; it serves the multiplicity of separate and incommensurable ends of all its separate members' (ibid., p. 108, emphasis added). Hayek highlighted the distinction by applying Mises's name *catallaxy* to the market order. In defining such an order, though, he continued to pose more questions than answers in his attempt to say what the concept means explicitly. A catallaxy, he suggested, describes 'the order brought about by the mutual adjustment of many individual economies in a market. A catallaxy is thus the special kind of spontaneous order produced by the market through people acting within the rules of the law of property, tort and contract' (pp. 108f). Without supporting argument, this is mere assertion and tells us nothing about a number of key matters raised. For instance, 'mutual adjustment' of what particular dimensions of agents' plans; in what ways do the specific bodies of law cited set up rules which agents choose to follow in devising their actions; and how can we be sure that a spontaneous order will be the result of actions coordinated by these implied plans and rules, given the highly subjectivist nature of human actions? Moreover, satisfactory answers to these questions must be premised on an answer to the key situational question: how is the 'market' referred to defined in terms of the many and various structural and operational qualities that can characterize it?

In the present context, though, Hayek did mount a more analytical defence of his assertions about free market efficacy and order by means of what he called the 'game of catallaxy" (ibid., pp. 115ff). He started out with just the right insight that, viewed as an interaction of agents, 'the outcome of this game for each will, because of its very character, necessarily be determined by a mixture of skill and chance' (p. 115). After this, however, the argument piles assertion upon assertion, with minimal effort to establish any precise analytical defence for the conclusions reached. He reiterated his claim that available prices act as crucial signals to convey collected information of use to individual producing agents in making plans and decisions to act. A number of further assertions about prices in this respect were then added: that 'current prices ... serve ... as indicators of what ought to be done in the present circumstances' (p. 116); that 'prices will spread the knowledge that some technical possibilities exist to produce a commodity more efficiently'; that prices indicate 'which of the available technical methods is the most economical in the given circumstances '; and that prices indicate 'changes in the relative scarcities of the different materials and other factors, which alter the relative advantages of the different methods' (pp. 117f). The idea that prices are instrumental in agents' decisions about participation in production was amplified further in the argument that, 'for the same reason that the prices which guide the direction of the different efforts reflect events which the producer does not know, the return from his efforts will frequently be different from what he expected, and must be so if they are to guide production appropriately'. As a result, 'the remunerations which the market determines are ... incentives which as a rule guide people to success, but will produce a viable order only because they often disappoint the expectations they have caused when relevant circumstances have unexpectedly changed. It is one of the chief tasks of competition to show which plans are false' (pp. 116f).

Notice how Hayek believed that he must argue agents to be purely market price takers if the outcomes are to be optimal. The matter of *price determination* itself, under the conditions of monopoly power in real-world markets, was not a topic that he was anxious to broach. Agents were simply assumed to take extant commodity and factor prices as guides to future rewards from production decisions. Then it was possible to argue that their expected pattern of returns will prove to be incorrect if the circumstances of the production vary unexpectedly. Such variation calls for some correction to future directions of resource use that will, it must be presumed, be signalled by relevant price changes. The spontaneous order emerges only when all such false expectations are expunged from the market process, whatever its implicit form may be in reality. Hayek suggested an iterative, learning-by-doing procedure that may well leave spontaneous order as no more than a tendency if circumstances continue to change unexpectedly. The disappointments stimulate a 'process of adaptation' that operates by means of agents' 'responses to the differences between the expected and the actual results of actions so that these differences will be reduced'. Very specifically defined price signal dynamics are critical in facilitating this process of adjustment, for agents' adaptations 'will produce an increased correspondence of expectations of the different persons [only] so long as current prices provide some indications of what future prices will be ' (ibid., p. 125). This will depend upon two conditions applying in the markets concerned: first, 'so long as, in a fairly constant framework of known facts, always only a few of them change'; second, 'so long as the price mechanism operates as a medium of communicating knowledge which brings it about that the facts which become known to some, through the effects of their actions on prices, are made to influence the decision of others' (p. 125). Both of these conditions pose and leave unanswered questions of their relevance for agents in practice.

A concern of fundamental and crucial significance, to which we have seen Hayek only make some passing reference, is the implied *process* by which, and on which criteria, the commodity and factor prices referred to are determined. The assertion that 'the sum of information reflected or precipitated in the prices is wholly the product of competition, or at least of the openness of the market to anyone who has relevant information about some source of demand or supply for the good in question' (ibid., p. 117) most often is taken to mean that prices result from a competitive auction. This is, of course, a myth deriving from the assumed presence of an auctioneer, an assumption that is irrelevant for most modern markets, whatever the degree of abstraction of the analysis. To the extent that agents' self-conscious discretion and fiat are involved in setting prices that reflect some calculation of costs and a degree of monopoly power, another subjective source of expectation failure is introduced by virtue of the incomplete pooling of knowledge that is the basis of such prices. Moreover, as he was well aware, 'though to some extent past prices will serve as the chief basis for forming expectations about future prices, they will do so only where a large part of the conditions have remained unchanged, but not where extensive changes have occurred' (p. 121). Although there may well be an element of practical truth in this assertion, it does not address the questions of how active agents gain access to, and form expectations about, the appropriate pattern of prices for making current decisions, and where the so-called present prices come from, if not from the past. No argument was given to overcome this fudging of a very problematical part of subjectivist economic agency in the market process.

In Volume 3 of *Law, Legislation and Liberty* (1979), Hayek again touched on his vision of the competitive process in a chapter dealing with government policy and the market (pp. 65ff). The chapter began by reiterating the most fundamental of his beliefs about the benefits of competition: that it has little to do with notions of 'perfect competition'. The required conditions for such 'perfection' are simply not available, nor could they ever be created, in real-world markets. On this premise, the issue became: what is the nature and extent of the 'imperfection' of markets that can be accepted without destroying their superiority over any other system of resource allocation? What was primarily at issue for Hayek in addressing this question was that markets should enable agents to be free to apply their inherited resource positions in a manner that depends on their discovering and making the best use possible of the accumulated totality of knowledge, even though it is widely dispersed amongst them as individuals and incomplete for any one agent. His vision of competition was a functionalist one in which the ends, consisting of the most efficient and effective use of resources, were more important than the means, consisting of the precise forms of market structures and operations. Competition is a process that must deliver three things: first, that 'everything will be produced which somebody knows how to produce and which he can sell profitably at a price which buyers will prefer to the available alternatives'; secondly, that 'everything that is being produced is produced by persons who can do so at least as cheaply as anybody else who in fact is not producing it'; thirdly, that 'everything will be sold at prices lower than, or at least as low as, those at which it could be sold by anybody who in fact does not do so' (p. 74). Implicit in these sorts of arguments about the benefits of market competition was the suggestion that participating agents should accept the outcomes without question because, whatever its limitations, no alternative system can deliver more. In the next section, I examine more fully this 'market fatalism' as a dimension of Hayek's analyses.

5.4 FATALISM AND ECONOMIC ORDER

For Hayek, his often sanguine attitude towards markets resulted in his conveying a rather fatalistic vision of the competitive process and its outcomes. He based this on the notions that 'competition must be seen as a process in which people acquire and communicate knowledge', and that it is 'nonsensical to judge the concrete results of competition by some preconception of the products it "ought" to bring forth' (Hayek, 1979, p. 68). As a consequence, 'it cannot be said of competition ... that it leads to a maximization of any measurable results. It merely leads, under favourable conditions, to the use of more skill and knowledge than any other known procedure' (ibid., p. 68).

It was in the 1976 lecture on 'The ativism of social justice' that Hayek elaborated most fully his implied philosophy of market fatalism (Hayek, 1978, pp. 57ff). As far as he was concerned, the free and competitive market is a wholly impersonal system of allocating resources to the creation of wealth and of distributing the proceeds of that creation. Participation in the process of production would bring via the market just the rewards to agents that are warranted by their respective contributions to the creation of wealth, with some allowance made for chance. The market distribution process was presented as amoral and neutral as between agents in the sense that its ideal design is such as to allow no ex ante constructivist, and hence particular interest-biased, vision of a proper distribution to have any effect whatsoever. Hayek argued the case again by envisaging the market process as a 'game': thus 'the market process ... is "a contest played according to rules and decided by superior skill, strength or good fortune". It is in this respect both a game of skill as well as a game of chance' (ibid., p. 60). And having said this, he compounded the fatalism involved by arguing that 'it is not a valid objection to such a game ... that the initial prospects for different individuals, although they are all improved by playing that game, are very far from being the same'. He saw the answer to 'such an objection ... [as] precisely that one of the purposes of the game is to make the fullest possible use of the inevitably different skills, knowledge and environment of different individuals' (p. 64). That is, this is a 'game which serves to elicit from each player the highest worthwhile contribution to the common pool from which each will win an uncertain share' (p. 60) and in which 'an order results from individuals observing the same abstract rules of the game while using their own knowledge in the pursuit of their own ends' (p. 61). Indeed, because it 'disregards human conceptions of what is due to each [agent], and rewards according to success in playing the game under the same formal rules, ... it produces a more efficient allocation of resources than any design could achieve' (pp. 63f). The only moral attitude which such an order demands of agents 'is that they compete honestly according to the rules of the game, guided only by the abstract signals of prices and giving no preferences because of their sympathies or views on the merits or needs of those with whom they deal' (pp. 65f).

Part and parcel of this same market fatalism was for Hayek an acceptance of the potential for monopoly power to emerge. He put the point quite explicitly in Volume 3 of *Law, Legislation and Liberty* (1979) that 'sometimes ... the appearance of a monopoly (or of an oligopoly) may even be a desirable result of competition, that is, competition will have done its best when, for the time being, it has led to a monopoly' (p. 73). Any attempt to rule out monopoly power per se by means of government edict certainly could not be justified. Indeed, he took the contrary view that, as regards enterprises, 'neither size in itself, nor ability to determine prices at which all can buy their product is a measure of their harmful power. More important still, there is no possible measure or standard by which we can decide whether a particular enterprise is too large' (p. 77). The ideal size of an enterprise will 'depend on the ever-changing technological and economic conditions' that it must confront and make best use of. Thus 'the most effective size of the individual firm is as much one of the unknowns to be discovered by the market process as the prices, quantities or qualities of the goods to be produced and sold' (p. 78).

On the basis of this functionalist vision of competition, Hayek granted that enterprises may need to be of a size and have a market share that gives them monopoly power by virtue of the requirements for efficient production (ibid., pp. 66f). This will enable enterprises to set prices above marginal cost if the agents involved choose to do so. Their potential exploitation of such opportunities, and the consequences for supply conditions and such issues as consumer welfare, are, however, to be thought of as secondary to the fundamental requirement that producing agents are free to exercise their self-interest. It was Hayek's belief that 'we rely on self-interest because only through it can we induce producers to use knowledge which we do not possess, and take actions the effects of which only they can determine' (p. 70). The capacity for individual agents to make the best use of their resources on the basis of their situations as they subjectively perceive them to be is the fundamental principle of competition as he envisaged it. Integral to this principle is that any emergence of monopoly power rests on the subjectivist fact that 'men and things are not perfectly alike and that often few or even only one of them will possess certain advantages over all others' (p. 73). He used the maximum efficiency argument to defend, though *not* to advocate encouragement or protection for, monopoly power: it is 'desirable not only to tolerate monopolies but even to allow them to exploit their monopolistic positions – so long as they maintain them solely by serving their customers better than anyone else' and so long as the monopolist 'can produce at costs lower than anybody else can, and sells at prices which are lower than those which anybody else can sell' (p. 73). And more explicitly: 'so long as aggregations of material resources make it possible to achieve better results in terms of improved or cheaper products or more desirable services than smaller organizations provide, every extension of this kind of power must be regarded as in itself beneficial' (p. 80). Even collusive practices were not ruled out as a mode of monopoly power operation, for there is, he argued, 'much reason to believe that some wholly voluntary organizations of firms that do not rely on compulsion are not only not harmful but actually beneficial' (p. 86).

Nonetheless, a number of caveats about monopoly power warranted attention in Hayek's view. First, although 'we know how to induce such individuals or organizations to serve their fellows better than anyone else can do ... we have no means of always making them serve the public as well as they could' (ibid., pp. 73f). Secondly, the use of monopoly power as a means to raise *artificial* barriers to competitive market entry by others is to be resisted (pp. 72f). In this respect, the barriers he was concerned about were not those arising from economic efficiency advantages developed by enterprises. Monopoly 'that rests entirely on superior performance is wholly praiseworthy', and this remains so 'even if such a monopolist keeps prices at a level at which he makes large profits and only just low enough to make it impossible for others to compete with him successfully, because he still uses a smaller amount of resources than others would do if they produced the same quantity of the product' (p. 83). Thirdly, although genuine economic efficiency advantages may be at the root of an enterprise acquiring monopoly power, once this justification has been eroded it may contrive to retain its power. Any such artificially protected and prolonged monopoly is no longer legitimate (p. 84). Fourthly, monopoly power is market power that can be used as a means of discrimination in the treatment of all agents who must deal with the enterprise, sellers and buyers alike (pp. 84f). This capacity to discriminate may allow the enterprise to exercise coercion in such dealings. It also links back to the potential for the enterprise to create artificial barriers to prevent competition by means of preferential supply agreements with certain customers and/or preferential purchasing agreements with certain suppliers, including workers. Fifthly, there are dangers associated with allowing groups of economic entities to organize and through collusive practices amplify their monopoly power. Here Hayek was concerned about what he called 'group selfishness', for 'the selfishness of a closed group, or the desire of its members to become a closed group, will always be in opposition to the true common interest' (p. 90). It is a force, too, that may extend to lobbying governments for market regulations that serve their sectional interests. In particular, what is pursued as 'freedom of organization' is not to be 'interpreted to mean that the activities of organizations must not be subject to rules restricting their methods, or even that the collective action of organizations should not be restricted by rules which do not apply to individuals' (pp. 89f).

But in spite of all these negative potentials arising from monopoly power, the one thing Hayek was unequivocal about was that any interventions by governments that aim to modify the 'natural' emergence and form of this power require careful design if the merits of such market conditions are to be preserved. For, in the end, he believed that 'it is not monopoly as such but only the prevention of competition which is harmful' (p. 83).

5.5 CONCLUDING NOTE

What has been made apparent in this chapter and the previous one is that, from the outset and throughout his intellectual life, Hayek's vision of the economic problem was firmly grounded in a subjectivist understanding of how economic phenomena are generated. That is, he was continuously conscious that the problem he was formulating has its origins in the deliberated actions of human agents. Markets are, indeed, constituted by the actions of individual agents engaging in the process of competition. The collective outcomes of such actions, whatever their degree of coordination and order, must ultimately be the product of what individuals decide to do in pursuit of their objectives. The fact that the results will always comprise both intended and unintended elements does not change this fact. Properly defining and addressing the economic problem by understanding these processes and their consequences required a deep insight into the subjective nature of human agents and the actions that comprise their agency. In Hayek's writings, this explicit concern was constantly juxtaposed to the contributions examined above. The next chapter focuses upon and critically assesses the specific insights he was able to formulate about the ontological origins of economic phenomena in human action.

6. Hayek and subjectivist human agency

6.1 HUMAN COGNITION AS THE FOUNDATION FOR SUBJECTIVISM

In order fully to understand the nature and significance of the subjectivist vision of human agency as Hayek depicted it, we need to inquire more deeply into his treatment of the concept of the human agent per se. According to his own testament on a number of occasions, his awareness of the subjectivist dimension of human science had one of its foundations in the strong affinity for psychology that he developed during his student years in Vienna. Mostly by means of private study, he was able during this period to reach a degree of proficiency in the subject sufficient to draft a paper on an alternative theory of cognition, although he modestly ruled out any claims to originality (Hayek, 1952, pp. vi, vii). The paper languished unpublished, he told us later, because 'though I felt that I had found the answer to an important problem, I could not explain precisely what the problem was' (ibid., p. v, cf. 1994, p. 62). Nevertheless, the ideas would always remain with him as implicit background to the wide-ranging human studies that he undertook. For, as Hayek informed us, although he found himself unable formally to pursue his interest in psychology, 'the basic idea then conceived has continued to occupy me; its outlines have gradually developed, and it has often proved helpful in dealing with the problems of the methods of the social sciences' (1952, p. v).

In the years after the 1920s, when his focus was on devising economic theories and then on the critical metatheoretical issues that such theories raised, he believed he had 'learnt at least to state the nature of the problem … [he] had been trying to answer'. And as things turned out, 'in the end it was concern with the logical character of social [and economic] theory which forced me to re-examine systematically my ideas on theoretical psychology' (ibid.). Similarly, he recalled much later that this effort 'helped me greatly to clear my mind on much that is very relevant to social theory', making specific reference to his recognition of the 'limits of our endeavours to explain complex phenomena'. And at this time, too, he went on to indicate that the inquiries were mutually beneficial, for 'as I was using the work I had done in my student days on theoretical psychology in forming my views on the methodology of the social science, so the working out of my earlier ideas on psychology with the help of what I had learnt in the social science helped me greatly in all my later scientific development' (Hayek, 1979, pp. 199f, n26). Still later, Hayek responded to an interviewer's specific suggestion that his psychology and his economics were interdependent that 'one sees this in retrospect rather than while one is doing it. I must say that the insights I gained ... both from the first stage in 1920 or later in the 1940s, were probably the most exciting events that ever occurred to me, which shaped my [economic] thinking' (Hayek, 1994, p. 153).

The eventual result of these early psychological investigations, along with the metatheoretical research in the interim, was the writing of *The Sensory Order* (1952), a work that he later looked back upon as 'one of my more important contributions to knowledge' (Hayek, 1994, p. 138).[1] An objective of the book was to redirect psychology away from the rising dominance of empiricism and behaviourism as a response to his belief at the time that 'the different attributes of mental entities – conscious or not – could be reduced to differences in effects as guides to human action. But the crudities of behaviorism ... had too much repelled me ... to make the effect on observable conduct more than a final visible outcome of a complex process we had to reconstruct' (Hayek, 1982, p. 289). Behaviourism had 'treated the problem of mind as if it were a problem of the responses of the individual to an independently or objectively given phenomenal world; while in fact it is the existence of a phenomenal world which is different from the physical world which constitutes the main problem' (Hayek, 1952, p. 28). It was his conviction, in making this contrast, that agents develop a subjective mental capacity which puts the cognitive processes that drive action beyond any immediate, exclusive and unique links to physicosensory stimuli. That is, the implied challenge here was to understand cognition phenomenologically. He realized that the object phenomena of human science could be linked to their origins in the deliberations, choices and actions of individual human agents. With such ideas behind him, it was to be expected that his treatment of economics would, eventually, include an awareness of its subjectivist and individualist dimensions. The image of the mind that he depicted was one in which its functions are to generate human action in response to the perceived situations and problems agents confront in their dealings with the real world. In these functions, the mind operates as the mediation between agents and their given conditions in the determination of these actions.

The nature of the theory of the subjective mind that Hayek developed was unashamedly physiological. In this sense, it represented an unavoidable continuity between physical scientific arguments and the roots of human agency in the mental processes of agents. The inference was that human action has a physiological source and could not be *fully* accounted for, with no unexplained remainder, without an understanding of that source. The theory was couched in terms of hypotheses about a system of neurological connections that he ascribed to the structure of the brain, and he made reference to mental processes as manifested in physiological structures and events. The mind comprises a 'system of connexions ... acquired in the course of the development of the species and the individual by a kind of "experience" or "learning"; and ... it reproduces therefore at every stage of its development certain relationships existing in the physical environment between the stimuli evoking the impulses' that it receives as its primary activating input (ibid., p. 53). To reinforce this hypothesis, Hayek quoted a piece from his original drafting of the ideas in 1920: 'we do not first have sensations which are then preserved by memory, but it is as a result of physiological memory that the physiological impulses are converted into sensations. The connexions between the physiological elements are thus the primary phenomenon which creates the mental phenomena' (ibid.).

As is apparent in the above passages, the origin of the physiological structure on which the processes of the mind depend was not envisaged by Hayek as comprising a set of innate and given mental categories in the Kantian manner.[2] Rather, '*mind and consciousness are ... products of experience*' (ibid., p. 166, emphasis added) in the sense that each agent possesses an inherited physiologically based response pattern at any point in time, part of which is human species-specific and part of which is genetico-physiologically and biographically specific to the individual. Depending upon the time perspective adopted, some degrees of change to this response pattern are always in progress as a consequence of continuing engagements by agents with their environmental situations, for 'the apparatus by means of which we learn about the external world is itself the product of a kind of experience'. Specifically, 'it is shaped by the conditions prevailing in the environment in which we live, and it represents a kind of generic reproduction of the relations between the elements of this environment which we have experienced in the past; and we interpret any new event in the environment in the light of that experience' (p. 165). The actual dynamics involved here were explained by Hayek as comprising incongruities between the pre-existing mental apparatus and the sensory experiences with which it is confronted. The cognitive system possessed by agents will undergo a reclassification process affecting the linkages that handle sensory inputs 'whenever the expectations resulting from the existing classification are disappointed, or when beliefs so far held are disproved by new experiences. The immediate effects of such conflicting experiences will be to introduce inconsistent elements into the model of the external world' (p. 169).

For Hayek, it followed that the human mind is to be depicted as providing an *active and substantive* mediation in the process by means of which human agents perceive and understand their environment, and in the consequent process in which they decide to act. That is, the mediation Hayek envisaged was one in which the perceived 'facts' of existentially independent reality that agents confront are in part products of the mind itself. They are incompletely given in sensory form and cannot be fully experienced or known in any other way than by means of the active processing of the mind, for 'every sensation, even the "purest", must ... be regarded as an interpretation of an event in the light of the past experience of the individual or the species', and 'the process of experience thus does not begin with sensations or perceptions, but necessarily precedes them'. 'We may express this', he went on, 'by stating that experience is not a function of mind or consciousness, but that mind and consciousness are rather products of experience' (p. 166).

As we have seen in the previous chapter, Hayek ascribed a profoundly significant role to agents' environmental knowledge in any attempt to understand their individual actions and consequent collective outcomes. It is now apparent from his theory of mind that the acquisition of knowledge as he envisaged it transcends the limits of immediate sensory experience: 'it is ... clearly not true that all that we know is due to such experience' (p. 167). Indeed, sense experience itself 'presupposes the existence of a sort of accumulated "knowledge", of an acquired order of the sensory impulses based on their past co-occurrence', with the result that 'a certain part at least of what we know at any moment about the external world is ... not learnt by sensory experience, but is rather implicit in the means through which we can obtain such experience' (ibid.). Thus '*what we call "mind" is ... a particular order of a set of events taking place in some organism [human agent] and in some manner related to but not identical with, the physical order of events in the environment*' (p. 16, original emphasis).

The key difficulty implied in such claims is 'deciding what part of our knowledge can properly be described as knowledge of mental events as distinguished from our knowledge of physical events' (ibid., p. 1). That is, 'the existence of mental phenomena' raises the problem of how they 'may be said to reflect some features of the physical order as a whole, and which thereby enables the organism [human agent] which contains such a partial reproduction of the environmental order to behave appropriately towards its surroundings' (p. 16). In this sense, all perception is interpretation and all knowledge is in the form of some abstract theory about external physical or other realities. The phenomenologically devised depictions of reality include mediated reflections of its existential features, for agents 'are able within themselves to reproduce (or "build models of") some of the relations which exist between the events in their environment' (p. 7). So, because the realm of external reality and its reflection in the mental realm are separate, albeit related, entities, the problem of the mind cannot legitimately be represented as merely 'the responses of the individual to an independently or objectively given phenomenal world'. Rather, it is 'in fact ... the existence of a phenomenal world which is different from the physical world which constitutes the main problem' (p. 28).

Hayek argued further in this vein that 'psychology must take the physical world ... as given and try to reconstruct the process by which the organism [human agent] classifies the physical events in the manner which is familiar to us as the order of sensory qualities' (ibid., p. 7). In this respect, 'every sensory experience of an event in the external world is ... likely to possess "attributes" ... to which no similar attributes of the external events correspond. These "attributes" are the significance which the organism [human agent] has learnt to assign to a class of events on the basis of the past associations of events of this class with certain other classes of events' (p. 166). In attempting to grasp slices of external reality cognitively, agents generate subjective conceptual forms which can never have a one-to-one correspondence with the objective physical things and relations in focus (p. 14). Understanding the external world is more than replicating its characteristics mentally, so that the challenge for theoretical psychology, and for the human sciences grounded upon it, is to account for the generation of cognitive phenomena that transcend their physical counterparts. The realism and existential independence of the world outside of the agent is not denied, because the cognitive products are mental reflections of an object world that is *there* whether agents choose to pay attention to it or not. But human access to any knowledge of it through cognition is necessarily an interpretive process that is mind-dependent. For, once in focus, physical descriptions of an object or event, however perfect, can 'give us only a partial explanation of the world as we know it through our senses and must always leave an unexplained residue' (p. 7). That is, 'by saying that there "exists" an "objective" world different from the phenomenal world we are merely stating that it is possible to construct an order or classification of events which is different from that which our senses show us and which enables us to give a more consistent account of the behaviour of the different events in that world'. It is this achievement, he added, which 'underlies all our efforts at a scientific explanation of the world' (p. 173).

It was apparent to Hayek, too, that the environment in which agents are situated, and to which they respond through the mediation of the mind, must include the formal and informal relationships that have been established with other agents. Clearly, the viable existence of such a social dimension depended upon agents including in their cognitive capacities the ability to understand the mental make-up of others. On this issue, Hayek expressed his belief that 'it would ... not be possible to discuss the phenomenal world with other people if they did not perceive this world in terms of the same, or at least of a very similar, order of qualities as we do'. Or, put another way, 'although the system of sensory qualities is "subjective" in the sense of belonging to the perceiving subject as distinguished from "objective" (belonging to the perceived objects) – a distinction which is the same as that between the phenomenal and the physical order – it is yet interpersonal and not (or at least not entirely) peculiar to the individual' (p. 23; cf. 1967, pp. 45f, 54ff).

Access to the way the minds of other agents function, especially as these others become increasingly remote in the sense of intersubjective intimacy, must be derived from personal introspection and extrapolation. Such insight may be reinforced by discursively available scientific and lay reports on the matter at issue that are consistent with what we 'know' of ourselves. As Hayek saw the problematic, 'we can ... use our direct ("introspective") knowledge of mental events in order to "understand", and in some measure even to predict, the results to which mental processes will lead in certain conditions. But this introspective psychology ... will always have to take our direct knowledge of the human mind for its starting point' (Hayek, 1952, p. 192). And, more than this, he continued, 'for our understanding of human action familiar mental entities must always remain the last determinants to which we can penetrate ' (ibid., p. 193). He concluded, therefore, that what he referred to as 'a *verstehende* psychology, which starts from our given knowledge of mental processes, will ... never be able to explain why we must think thus and not otherwise, why we arrive at particular conclusions' (p. 192). That is, in all endeavours to account for individual human action, there will always be an unpredictable, contingent remainder with which observers must contend. In particular, the links between situations and action responses cannot be completely grasped: 'Even though we may know the general principle by which all human action is causally determined by physical processes, this would not mean that to us a particular human action can ever be recognized as the necessary result of a particular set of physical circumstances' (p. 193). This is because 'human decisions must always appear as the result of the whole of a human personality – that means the whole of a person's mind' to which we simply can never have access (ibid.). This same problem confronts both active lay agents and scientific analysts as far as their activities involve observing and understanding the conduct of other agents.

It is apparent, then, that Hayek's venture into psychology brought him to a quite deep understanding of the nature of human agents and their actions. In particular, he had set out a clear image of agents as living their lives as situated in and conditioned by an existentially independent external environment. The implication was that, whatever their innate cognitive qualities as individuals, the activities of agents could not be understood without giving due recognition to the influence of their cumulative experiences on their mental make-up and of their immediate situations in this socially structured external environment. And, in some of his later writings, he remained intent upon reinforcing these insights into the nature of human agency.

For example, Hayek further reinforced his ideas about the influences and capacities that control human action in a 1971 paper entitled 'Nature v. nurture once again' (1978, pp. 290ff). His opening gambit was the assertion that 'the old controversy between "Nature" and "Nurture" ought to be allowed to die' (ibid., p. 294), from where he proceeded to negate the whole idea behind the implied dichotomy. Especially did he emphasize that a 'true appreciation of the genetic factor is hardly assisted by ascribing to it more than it is really capable of explaining adequately', and he objected to the claim that 'all actions that are not guided by conscious reason must be genetically determined' (pp. 290, 291). His argument here was that it is simply not realistic even to consider the nature of human beings in isolation from their situational conditioning: that is, to recognize 'the simple dichotomy between, on the one hand, the genetically determined, innate, instinctive, or unconscious capacities ... and, on the other hand, rational or learned activities' (p. 291). In understanding human agency, therefore, the joint consequences of the genetics of nature and of the nurture of society must be given due weight, for 'the processes of cultural and of genetic evolution will ... constantly interact, and their respective influence will be very difficult to distinguish' (p. 292). More strongly put, 'to exclude the *cultural* aspect of evolution and claim almost everything for *genetic* transmission is surely doing violence to the subject' (p. 293, original emphasis). Recognizing the nurture dimension enables the analyst of human phenomena to give proper attention to the fact that 'cultural transmission has ... [the] great advantage over the genetic ... [that] it includes the transmission of acquired characters' (p. 292). Most individuals grow to maturity in intimate social contact with their parents. Therefore 'there is no ground for supposing that those attributes which are normally transmitted only from parents are all transmitted genetically'. Indeed, Hayek continued, 'most of an individual's aptitudes, propensities and skills are probably acquired in early infancy, and firmly entrenched by the time he becomes capable of rational thought. These learned action patterns are not tools which he consciously selects, but rather properties in accordance with which he will be selected by a process which nobody controls' (p. 291).

Even in his last magnum opus, *The Fatal Conceit* (1989), among many other things, Hayek reinforced this subjectivist depiction of situated and conditioned human agents for whom the capacity to reason is a dimension of mind that is a product of the dual effects of innate mental character or instinct and a process of learning. He reiterated this point in unequivocal terms: 'What we call mind is not something that the individual is born with, as he is born with his brain, or something the brain produces, but something that his genetic equipment … helps him to acquire, as he grows up, from his family and adult fellows by absorbing the results of a tradition that is not genetically transmitted'. In this sense, he continued, the mind consists 'in the capacity to restrain instincts'. Moreover, as it is 'shaped by the environment in which individuals grow up, mind in turn conditions the preservation, development, richness and variety of traditions on which the individuals draw' (ibid., pp. 22f). The practical meaning of this origin of mind in influencing the nature of human agency is that it gives a dominant role to cumulative and contemporaneous external conditioning. Under these conditions, 'learning how to behave is more the *source* than the *result* of insight, reason and understanding. Humankind, he believed, 'is not born wise, rational and good, but has to be taught to become so', for it is 'not our intellect that created our morals; rather, human interactions governed by our morals make possible the growth of reason and those capabilities associated with it. Man became intelligent because there was *tradition* … for him to learn' (p. 21, original emphasis). Here the crucial point is that the shape of civilized human agency is formed by the intervention of 'custom and tradition [that] stand *between* instinct and reason – logically, psychologically, temporally' (p. 23, original emphasis).

Hayek meant by this that, whereas humankind in its hypothetical 'state of nature' would only have animal instincts to draw upon, the capacities of civilized agents are enhanced by having available the situational conditions through which they operate. So it was, he argued, that the 'decisive change from animal to man was due to … culturally-determined restraints on innate responses' (p. 17). He went on to amplify this assertion by giving emphasis to the consequences of living within an established order. The point is that 'learnt moral rules, customs, progressively displaced innate responses, not because men recognised by reason that they were better but because they made possible the growth of an extended order exceeding anyone's vision, in which more effective collaboration enabled its members, however blindly, to maintain more people and to displace other groups' (p. 23). The penalty for accepting the demands of a situationally conditioned existence is that choices and conduct must be delimited. But although 'rules of conduct necessarily constrain … order is their product; and … these rules, precisely by limiting the range of means that each individual may use for his purposes, greatly extend the range of ends each can successfully pursue' (p. 49). So, even though modern agents really have little choice but to operate within and through the dictates of their situational environment if they want to satisfy their life-world outcomes, the result is one that they could not achieve without the constraints imposed. The next section shows how Hayek's psychological investigations led him to espouse an understanding of situated human agency as influenced by the directing and shaping effects of rules.

6.2 INDIVIDUALISM AND THE NEED FOR RULES

The principles of conditioned agent conduct elicited above were already clearly expounded in a paper published by Hayek in 1938 and reprinted in expanded form a year later as the pamphlet entitled 'Freedom and the economic system' (1939b). There we find him explaining the virtues of any *constructed* economic and social system that preserves the essentials of freedom on the basis of a belief that the situation in which agents are placed conditions and directs their actions. As agents, 'we can "plan" a system of general rules, equally applicable to all people and intended to be permanent (even if subject to revision with the growth of knowledge), which provides an institutional framework within which the decisions as to what to do and how to earn a living are left to the individuals'. 'In other words,' he continued, 'we can plan a system in which individual initiative is given the widest possible scope and the best opportunity to bring about effective co-ordination of individual effort' (ibid., pp. 8f). At this time, Hayek was rather less reserved about the potential of constructivist planning than he would become later on. The main criterion for planning for freedom was that the system operate as if it were a free-market system. Planning in this sense 'means that the direction of production is brought about by the free combination of the knowledge of all participants, with prices conveying to each the information which helps him to bring his actions in relation to those of others' (p. 9). However, rather than rely upon the 'invisible hand' alone, the idea was to provide some more 'visible' rules of individual conduct so as to ensure an efficient and properly coordinated market outcome. The essence of such rules is that they are to be 'general not only in the sense that they apply equally to all people, but also in the sense that they are instrumental in helping people to achieve their various individual ends, so that in the long run everybody has a chance to profit from their existence' (p. 10).

But it was to be in a 1945 lecture entitled 'Individualism: *true and false*' (1949, pp. 1ff), that Hayek developed a more intensive theory of individual agency that depicted agents as far from acting in isolation. Most importantly, it was here that he posited more detailed argument about the social and structural conditioning of the actions of rationally limited individual human agents in confronting their life-world problems. It seems to have been clear to him very early on that individual agents always act in situ. Therefore any analysis of the nature of human agency must be properly integrated with a representation of the multidimensional situations within and through which they operate as individuals with collective consequences.[3]

As a fundamental corollary of subjectivism, he argued that what he called true individualism means 'there is no other way toward an understanding of social phenomena but through our understanding of individual actions directed toward other people and guided by their expected behavior'. Individualism, he stressed, is a means of understanding society from the perspective of 'an attempt to understand the forces which determine the social life of man' (ibid., p. 6). It is based on the belief that 'by tracing the combined effects of individual actions, we discover that many of the institutions on which human achievements rest have arisen and are functioning without a designing and directing mind ...; and that the spontaneous collaboration of free men often creates things which are greater than their individual minds can ever comprehend' (pp. 6f). Here he expressed an idea that was to become one of his trade marks: human institutions are 'the result of human action but not the result of human design' (p. 7). One outcome of such an intersubjective and conditioned vision of individualism was that it effectively recognizes and embraces all agents as they *are* existentially. It makes no special assumptions about their natures or capacities in placing them each as integral parts of a properly functioning social and economic order. In Hayek's view, the spontaneously coherent order to which he referred 'does not depend for its functioning on our finding good men for running it, or on men becoming better than they now are, but ... *makes use of men in all their given variety and complexity*, sometimes good and sometimes bad, sometimes intelligent and more often stupid' (p. 12, emphasis added). He explicitly rejected the ostensible 'individualist' notion that all human achievement could be comprehended through its links to and control by the exercise of individual human reason. Instead, his premise was that social and economic analysts should rate 'rather low the place which reason plays in human affairs'. They should accept that 'man has achieved what he has in spite of the fact that he is only partly guided by reason, and that his individual reason is very limited and imperfect' (p. 8).

Hayek thus adopted what he referred to at the time as an 'antirationalistic approach' to individualism 'which regards man not as a highly rational and intelligent but as a very irrational and fallible being, whose individual errors are corrected only in the course of a social process, and which aims at making the best of a very imperfect material' (ibid., pp. 8f). Here he cited claims about Adam Smith inventing the 'bogey of the "economic man"', with its readily falsified 'assumption of a strictly rational behavior or generally ... rationalistic psychology'. He took the position that, on the contrary, Smith's vision was of a man 'by nature lazy and indolent, improvident and wasteful, and that it was only by the force of circumstances that he could be made to behave economically or carefully adjust his means to his ends' (p. 11; cf. Oakley, 1994, Part I, *passim*). Such an approach, Hayek asserted, constitutes 'the only theory which can claim to make the formation of spontaneous social products intelligible' on the basis of a belief that, 'if left free, men will often achieve more than individual human reason could design or foresee' (Hayek, 1949, pp. 10f). This is because, given 'the unlimited variety of human gifts and skills and the consequent ignorance of any single individual of most of what is known to all the other members of society taken together', the full benefits of collective human reason can only be tapped 'as an interpersonal process in which everyone's contribution is tested and corrected by others' (ibid., p. 15). Nor did the existence of such 'social products' need any assumptions about innate harmony of interests between individuals in order to account for collective outcomes that serve the constrained maximization of the interests of all constituent individuals. He emphasized as integral to an individualist understanding of agents that the 'conflicts of individual interests' gave rise to 'the necessity of "well-constructed institutions" where the "rules and principles of contending interests and compromised advantages" would reconcile conflicting interests without giving any one group power to make their views and interests always prevail over those of all others' (p. 13).

In this argument about potentially unfettered but always contained human agency, Hayek was very sensitive to the negative implications of the idea of individualism as necessarily identified with egoism on the part of human agents. As far as he was concerned, although there was no escaping the self-centredness of an individualist depiction of agents, this was not a moral or ethical matter when argued as part of a social theory. Individualism allows that 'people are and ought to be guided in their actions by *their* interests and desires' in the sense that they 'ought to be allowed to strive for whatever *they* think desirable' (ibid., p. 15, original emphasis). To do so, given their limited mental capacities, they will each develop a 'clearly delimited area of responsibility' on the premise that, 'if a man is to exercise his own gifts, it must be as a result of his activities and planning that this sphere of responsibility is determined' (pp. 17f). That is, Hayek recognized that in any society there will evolve some principles and rules that impinge on and shape individuals' self-centred actions. These will refer to 'typical situations, defined in terms of what can be known to the acting persons' (p. 18) and serve to situate individuals relative to each other and facilitate the cooperative use of their respective knowledge and talents. Quite explicitly, the social purpose of rules was stated as 'to inform the individual what is his sphere of responsibility within which he must shape his own life'. Indeed, 'the most general principle on which an individualist system is based is that it uses the universal acceptance of general principles as the means to create order in social affairs' (pp. 18f). The expressed reason for this was that 'our submission to general principles is necessary because we cannot be guided in our practical action by full knowledge and evaluation of all the consequences. So long as men are not omniscient, the only way in which freedom can be given to the individual is by such general rules to delimit the sphere in which the decision is his' (p. 19). This sphere will be defined for individuals within a range of evolved 'traditions and conventions' which 'establish flexible but normally observed rules that make the behavior of other people predictable in a high degree' (p. 23)

Hayek also emphasized that agents will find it advantageous to pursue their individual interests in a context that involves them in existentially volitional associations with others. With specific reference to the necessarily social conditioning of individuals that is an integral part of any functioning collective order, he made the point that 'the individual, in participating in the social processes, must be ready and willing to adjust himself to changes and to submit to conventions which are not the result of intelligent design, whose justification in the particular instance may not be recognizable, and which to him will often appear unintelligible and irrational' (ibid., p. 22). For this reason, 'the case of the individualist ... rests on the contention that much of what in the opinion of many can be brought about only by conscious direction, can be better achieved by the voluntary and spontaneous collaboration of individuals' (p. 16). The crucial qualification stressed at the same time was that associations must not be a means for the exercise of coercive power except under circumstances where such powers are needed to prevent or minimize coercion itself. This brought Hayek face-to-face with the problematic of what constitutes the appropriate role for a government and for any legal system within and through which it operates. He referred to those desirable interventions which give 'assistance in the spread of information and in the elimination of genuinely avoidable uncertainty, by which the government might greatly increase the efficiency of individual action' (p. 21). But in all of such ideas which relate to 'constructing a suitable legal framework and ... improving the institutions which have grown up spontaneously', there must be a limit to the extent of interventions. Any state apparatus, 'the embodiment of deliberately organized and consciously directed power', must be limited to being 'only a small part of the much richer organism which we call "society", and ... the former ought to provide merely a framework within which free ... collaboration of men has the maximum of scope' (p. 22). Most significantly, Hayek noted that the core of such a concept of 'society' is to be found in the 'common conventions and traditions among a group of people [that] will enable them to work together smoothly and efficiently' (p. 23). He claimed as a consequence that any need for coercive interventions 'can probably only be kept to a minimum in a society where [these] conventions and tradition have made the behavior of man to a large extent predictable' (p. 24).

By 1945, then, Hayek's thought about subjectivist human agency had enabled him to see that individual agents are always situated in an inherited environment that exists independently of them and has evolved by means of collective human actions largely unaided by any conscious design. Agents operate within and through the structures, institutions and social relations of this situational environment as mediations in and means of achieving their objectives by individual action. That is, he saw how situations condition and direct voluntary actions in ways that give subjective individualist interpretations of what people are observed to do a dimension of commonality. Quite clearly, his major concern in defining the conditioning of agents' actions was the origin and nature of the rules that they are induced consciously or otherwise to follow. These theses require special attention in Hayek's thought and are the subject of the next section.

6.3 RULES AND THE NEED FOR REASON

In his writings of the 1960s and beyond, Hayek took a stance against the necessary presumption of rationalism in understanding the origin or application of the rules that govern the nature of human affairs. One of his objectives in his magnum opus on liberal political ideals, *The Constitution of Liberty* (1960), was to explain the functional purpose of the structured situation within and through which free human agents carry on the various facets of their life. This purpose was to secure a feeling of increased certainty about the expected actions of others and about the anticipated results of their own actions. Stability and viability of social life itself, he thought, depends upon voluntary conformity to the demands of situational conditions: 'Life of man in society ... is made possible by individuals acting according to certain rules' (ibid., p. 148). Moreover, he thought most generally that 'submission to undesigned rules and conventions whose significance and importance we largely do not understand ... is indispensable for the working of a free society' (p. 63). The issues that are posed by such claims concern the origin and form of the 'rules' that manifest the demands of situational conditioning to which agents respond with varying degrees of conscious conformity.

Hayek introduced this matter by means of the evolutionary claim that 'with the growth of [human] intelligence, these rules tend to develop from unconscious habits into explicit and articulated statements and at the same time to become more abstract and general' (ibid., p. 148). In the exposition that follows this claim (pp. 148ff), he espoused a version of rule-following conduct that is dominated by the criterion of voluntarism, as befits the theme of liberty more generally. Emphasis was given, that is, to the functioning of rules that are predominantly abstract in their status and obeyed in a manner that is largely less than fully conscious. The effect claimed is that individuals live in and conduct themselves in accordance with the rule of law without any necessary requirement that they can articulate all the rules involved, or even that they be consciously aware of them. So it is that 'the appropriateness of our conduct is not necessarily dependent on our knowing why it is so. Such understanding is one way of making our conduct appropriate, but not the only one' (p. 64). In a society ordered by rules, this subconscious conformity comes from 'our familiarity with the institutions of law [that] prevents us from seeing how subtle and complex a device the delimitation of individual spheres by abstract rules is' (p. 148). Thus 'that such abstract rules are regularly observed in action does not mean that they are known to the individual in the sense that it [*sic*] could communicate them' (p. 149).

In his 'Rules, perception and intelligibility' from 1963 (Hayek, 1967, pp. 43ff), he dealt further with the origin and dynamics of the mental rules formed by agents as the basis for engaging their environment. The point was re-emphasized quite explicitly that such rules were not a priori in the Kantian sense of being innately present as generic qualities of the human mind. Instead, they had to be acquired by cumulative experiences: 'In the course of its development any organism will acquire a large repertoire of ... perceptual patterns to which it can specifically respond' (ibid., p. 51). While 'we ought to regard what we call mind as a system of abstract rules of action (each "rule" defining a class of actions) which determines each action by a combination of several such rules', these rules themselves are not exclusively internally generated or reflexively modified. On the contrary, as he would write somewhat later, in the 1968–9 piece, 'The primacy of the abstract' (1978, pp. 35ff), 'the formation of abstractions ought to be regarded not as actions of the human mind but rather as *something which happens to the mind*, or that alters that structure of relationships which we call the mind, and which consists of the system of abstract rules which govern its operation' (ibid., p. 43, emphasis added).

Here Hayek reiterated the argument from *The Sensory Order* that 'all the conscious experience that we regard as relatively concrete and primary, in particular all sensations, perceptions and images are the product of a superimposition of many "classifications" of the events perceived according to their significance in many respects' (p. 36). All concrete experience is formed as the product of previously held abstractions, so that for the mind, there can be no experience without the imposition of some established abstract schemata. As he put it, 'subjectively, we live in a concrete world and ... when we want to explain what makes us tick, we must start with the abstract relations governing the order which, as a whole, gives particulars their distinct place', for 'in one way or another ... our perception of the external world is made possible by the mind possessing an organizing capacity' (pp. 37, 38). If such an idea is accepted, it means, as Hayek realized, that action becomes in part the product of prior mental rules held by the agent concerned and learnt by experience (pp. 38f). Thus 'particular actions are determined by the superimposition of various instructions concerning the several attributes of the action to be taken' (pp. 39f). An abstraction then becomes 'a disposition towards certain ranges of actions', and such dispositions to act in certain ways 'can be regarded as adaptations to typical features of the environment, and the "recognition" of such features as the activation of the kind of disposition adapted to them' (pp. 40, 41). So it is that 'what we call knowledge is primarily a system of rules of action assisted and modified by rules indicating equivalences or differences or various combinations of stimuli' (p. 41). As human agents, we have a primary capacity to 'govern ... actions by rules which determine the properties of ... particular movements', and in this sense our actions are 'governed by abstract categories ... and ... what we call mind is essentially a system of such rules conjointly determining particular actions' (p. 42).

But, in a lecture delivered in 1964 on 'Kinds of rationalism' (Hayek, 1967, pp. 82ff) and in one delivered in 1970 on 'The errors of constructivism' (Hayek, 1978, pp. 3ff), he made more of the above point that situational guidance by means of rules *consciously* accepted and applied by agents could not be the full story behind their actions. Because he believed that the rational capacities of agents to operate in practical situations are limited, the essential principle that he espoused was that human agents 'are in their conduct *never* guided *exclusively* by their understanding of the causal connections between particular known means and certain desired ends, but always also by rules of conduct of which they are rarely aware, which they certainly have not consciously invented' (1978, p. 7, original emphasis). He rejected what he called the naive principles of constructivist rationalism that presumed 'to regard as truly rational only behaviour such as is based on decisions which judge each particular situation "on its merits", and chooses between alternatives in concrete evaluation of the known consequences of the various possibilities' (1967, p. 89). This, he thought, represented 'a colossal presumption concerning our intellectual powers ... [and] a complete misconception of the kind of world in which we live' (ibid., p. 90). For, on the contrary, he argued, 'human intelligence is quite insufficient to comprehend all the details of the complex human society, and it is this inadequacy of our reason to arrange such an order in detail which forces us to be content with abstract rules' (p. 88). He expressed the idea, then, that conscious reason requires supplementation by a non-discursive supraconsciousness: 'in all our thinking we are guided (or even operated) by rules of which we are not aware, and ... our conscious reason can therefore always take account only of some of the circumstances which determine our actions' (p. 87; cf. 1978, pp. 8f). Thus, in recognizing the 'limits of the powers of reason [we] want to use abstraction to extend it by achieving at least some degree of order in the complex of human affairs' (Hayek, 1967, p. 89). Even more strongly put: 'a true insight into the significance of behaviour according to rules demands much more rigid adherence to them than would be conceded by the constructivist rationalists who would accept abstract rules at best as a substitute for a decision in full evaluation of all of the particular circumstances' (ibid., p. 91).

Hayek later questioned in more detail the extent to which agents are and need to be conscious of rules when applying them in formulating their individual actions. In a lecture published as 'The confusion of language in political thought' in 1968 (1978, pp. 71ff), he further emphasizes the need to make due allowance for the fact that a part of successful human conduct is rule-dependent in a manner that does not require the rules to be consciously articulated. He expressed his belief that 'a rule may effectively govern action in the sense that from knowing it we can predict how people will act, without it being known as a verbal formula to the actors'. Given this, it follows that agents 'may "know how" to act, and the manner of their action may be correctly described by an articulated rule, without their explicitly "knowing that" the rule is such and such; that is, they need not be able to state the rule in words in order to be able to conform to it in their actions, or to recognise whether others have or have not done so' (ibid., p. 81). It followed as a consequence, too, that agents must be represented as having a 'capacity to act, and to recognise whether others act, in accordance with non-articulated rules', where such capacity 'probably always exists before attempts are made to articulate such rules'. As it turns out, then, 'most articulated rules are merely more or less successful attempts to put into words what has been acted upon before, and will continue to form the basis for judging the results of the application of the articulated rules' (p. 81). On this basis, there exists for human agents a 'governing influence of a background of unarticulated rules' and 'it seems probable that no system of articulated rules can exist or be fully understood without [this] ... background of unarticulated rules which will be drawn upon when gaps are discovered in the system of articulated rules' (pp. 81f). Moreover, Hayek made the point that human action may at times be 'guided by rules which limit it to permissible kinds of actions – rules which generally preclude certain *kinds* of action irrespective of their foreseeable particular results'. This means that, as agents, 'our capacity to act successfully in our natural and social environment rests as much on such knowledge of what *not* to do ... as on our knowledge of the particular effects of what we do' (pp. 83f, original emphasis).

Similar themes relating to the notion of rules and their place in the situational conditioning of human agents were accorded prominent attention again in Volume 1 of *Law, Legislation and Liberty*, written in the early 1970s (1973b, pp. 5ff, 20ff). There Hayek argued out further the balance between the roles of reason and situations in human agency as these contribute to the understanding of spontaneous social and economic order. In dealing with this matter. Hayek's claim was that he should not be read as *anti*-rationalist, for his concern was only to expose 'the limitations of the powers of conscious reason' (ibid., p. 29). As he explained his position, 'if the desire to make reason as effective as possible is what is meant by rationalism, I am myself a rationalist. If, however, the term means that conscious reason ought to determine every particular action, I am not a rationalist, and such rationalism seems to me to be very unreasonable' (p. 29). More specifically, he believed that 'it is always only in combination with particular, non-rational impulses that reason can determine what to do, and its function is essentially to act as a restraint on emotion, or to steer action impelled by other forces'. From this perspective, reason is 'merely a discipline, an insight into the limitations of the possibilities of successful action, which often will tell us only what not to do. This discipline is necessary precisely because our intellect is not capable of grasping reality in all its complexity' (p. 32).

In confronting their life-world problems, then, agents apply their personal capacities to reason to a delimited knowledge of their individual circumstances, but always as these circumstances comprise relevant parts of an inherited situation within and through which their current action responses must be undertaken. Agents' conduct is contained and constrained within the framework of rules that are the manifested appearance of the various structures that constitute their situation. The return for acceptance of such constraint is the capacity of agents to draw upon the accumulated collective wisdom imbedded in these rules. In this sense, 'knowledge of the world is knowledge of what one must do or not do in certain kinds of circumstances' (ibid., p. 18). Such knowledge is available by virtue of the evolutionary selection of the structures and institutions with which the rules are associated, given the implicit continuing 'testing' of their efficacy that such selection involves. Thus 'the cultural heritage into which man is born consists of a complex of practices or rules of conduct which have prevailed because they made a group of men successful' (p. 17).

The point that Hayek was ultimately intent upon making was that those phenomena of evolutionary human origin, those products of human action that were not the products of human design, comprise the very substance of human science. For, because their generation transcends any rational account, 'these were the phenomena which required for their explanation a distinct body of theory and which came to provide the object of the theoretical social sciences' (ibid., p. 20). That is, it was 'the formation of regular patterns in human relations that were not the conscious aim of human actions [that] raised a problem which required the development of a systematic social theory' (p. 22; cf. p. 37). He rejected constructivist notions of the origin of social and economic institutions and rules because the argument that the conditions of human order are the product of human design 'can be shown to be false both in its factual and in its normative conclusions' (p. 5). Most importantly for the present purpose, the constructivist 'way of looking at the pattern of human activities' (p. 8) involves what he thought to be a 'false conception of the human mind as an entity standing outside the cosmos of nature and society, rather than being itself the product of the same process of evolution to which the institutions of society are due' (p. 5). That is, 'mind is as much the product of the social environment in which it has grown up and which it has not made as something that has in turn acted upon and altered these institutions' (p. 17). Even more precisely put, 'the mind does not so much make rules as consist of rules of action, a complex of rules that is, which it has not made, but which have come to govern the actions of the individuals because actions in accordance with them have proved more successful than those of competing individuals or groups' (p. 18).

But what went straight to the heart of the subjectivist theory of human agency that Hayek had spent half of his life developing was his continuing concern about the nature and function of rules. He repeated once more his fundamental depiction of agents and their actions as crucially dependent upon the existence of external rules: 'Man is as much a rule-following animal as a purpose-seeking one. And he is successful ... because his thinking and acting are governed by rules which have by a process of selection been evolved in the society in which he lives, and which are thus the product of the experience of generations.' It follows that, as active human agents, 'we live in a society in which we can successfully orientate ourselves, and in which our actions have a good chance of achieving their aims ... because our fellows are governed by known aims or known connections between means and ends' (ibid., p. 11).

More specifically, within a spontaneous order, rules, and the dimensions of agents' situations which they reflect, condition what agents acting interdependently do in response to the problems they confront in two particular ways. First, the rules enable agents to act with reason, to the limit of their capacities, in a world that is far too complex and extensive for them fully to comprehend. In Hayek's argument, 'complete rationality of action in the Cartesian sense demands complete knowledge of all the relevant facts. ... But the success of action in society depends on more particular facts than anyone can possibly know' (p. 12). It followed that 'the problem of conducting himself successfully in a world only partially known to man was thus solved by adhering to rules which had served him well but which he did not and could not *know* to be true in the Cartesian sense'. The point is that there exists as a result of cumulative human experience a wealth of communal knowledge that 'although it can be described in terms of rules, the individual cannot state in words but is merely able to honour in practice' (p. 18, original emphasis). So it is that 'the utilization of much more knowledge than anyone can possess, and therefore the fact that each moves within a coherent structure most of whose determinants are unknown to him, that constitutes the distinctive feature of all advanced civilizations' (p. 14).

Secondly, rules enable agents to mitigate the uncertainties that flow from inter-agent relations that may be integral to the success of their own actions.

As agents living in a social situation, where our individual actions have results that depend upon our cooperation with, and upon cooperation from, relevant others around us, 'we depend for the effective pursuit of our aims clearly on the correspondence of the expectations concerning the actions of others on which our plans are based with what they will really do' (ibid., p. 36). It is 'this matching of the intentions and expectations that determine the actions of different individuals [that] is the form in which order manifests itself in social life' (p. 36). In the presence of commonly understood and accepted rules, agents can act in social situations with more or less of an expectation that their own introspection and interpolation will reveal what other agents like themselves will do in the current circumstances. As Hayek put the point, 'every man growing up in a given culture will find in himself rules, or may discover that he acts in accordance with rules – and will similarly recognize the actions of others as conforming or not conforming to various rules' (p. 19).

In the present context, Hayek was especially anxious again to stress agents' conformity to rules at the non-conscious level as giving them the capacity to act so as to serve their needs, for 'man certainly does not know all the rules which guide his actions in the sense that he is able to state them in words' (ibid., p. 43). These rules, then, 'will manifest themselves in regularity of action which can be explicitly described, but this regularity of action is not the result of the acting persons being capable of stating them' (p. 19). Nor are such rules 'known to those who are guided by them ... [or] observed with the intention of producing those consequences' (p. 19). He granted that 'in advanced society only some rules will be of this kind; what we want to emphasize is merely that even such advanced societies will in part owe their order to some such rules' (p. 19). In this his intention was to distance himself from the rationalist view of the conscious construction and application of rules in human conduct, thereby leaving the door open for human agency to generate spontaneous orders by otherwise purely volitional and uncoordinated individual actions.

At a deeper level of ontological inquiry, Hayek adopted the position that the capacity of human agents that enables them to cope with complex situations about which their knowledge is incomplete and uncompletable, and for which their cognitive equipment is to some degree inadequate, is manifested in the process of forming abstractions. He reiterated that 'reliance on the abstract' results from 'an insight into the limited powers of our reason' as active agents and reflects the notion that 'when we say that what all men have in common is their reason we mean their common capacity for abstract thought' (ibid., p. 33). Such abstractions are 'the indispensable means of the mind which enable it to deal with a reality it cannot fully comprehend ... – an adaptation to ... [man's] ignorance of most of the particular facts of his surroundings'. More than this, abstraction is 'a property of the categories with which ... [the mind] operates – not a product of the mind but rather what constitutes the mind'. Indeed, 'the main purpose of our stress on the rules which govern our actions is to bring out the central importance of the abstract character of all mental processes'. So, as agents, 'we never act, and could never act, in full consideration of all the facts of a particular situation, but always by singling out as relevant only some aspects of it' (p. 30). In this respect, it is 'the use of abstraction [that] extends the scope of phenomena which we can master intellectually'. This is made possible by 'limiting the degree to which we can foresee the effects of our actions' in specific terms (p. 32). The consequence for understanding observed human agency is that it will be 'a *type* of situation [that] evokes in an individual a *disposition* towards a certain *pattern* of response' (p. 30, original emphasis). It is the individual particulars of the results of agents' actions that can thus no longer be predicted by them, leaving all action with potentially significant unintended outcomes. By following rules, agents mitigate the uncertainties of their actions, but in a manner that demands that they individually forgo any guarantee of a specific outcome. The collective result is ostensibly a spontaneous order planned by no agent as an individual but available to all by conforming to the evolved general rules of their situations.

Later, in Volume 3 of *Law, Legislation and Liberty* (1979, pp. 155ff), Hayek shifted his emphasis to the nature and influence of the rules imbedded in the broader cultural situation of human agents, especially with respect to their juxtaposed independent and limited capacity to reason. The definition he proposed for culture asserted that it '*is neither natural nor artificial, neither genetically transmitted nor rationally designed.* It is a tradition of learnt rules of conduct which have never been "invented" and whose functions the acting individuals usually do not understand' (ibid., p. 155, original emphasis). Culturally situated human agents retain their rationalist competence, but in a very particular form, for 'culture and reason developed concurrently' and it is therefore '*probably no more justified to claim that thinking man has created his culture than that culture created his reason*' (p. 155, original emphasis). In terms recalling his *Sensory Order* work, he saw the human mind as 'embedded in a traditional impersonal structure of learnt rules, and its capacity to order experience is an acquired replica of [the] cultural pattern which every individual finds given. *The brain is an organ enabling us to absorb, but not to design culture*' (p. 157, original emphasis). Indeed, because of this holistic containment of agents within their culture, Hayek was inclined to attribute a superior role to rules over reason in the determination of rational conduct. As he put it with emphasis regarding the shaping of human action, there is '*probably much more "intelligence" incorporated in the system of rules of conduct than in man's thoughts about his surroundings*' (p. 157, original emphasis). The agent is thus 'often served better by custom than understanding', for 'it was a repertoire of learnt rules which told him what was the right and what was the wrong way of acting in different circumstances that gave him his increasing capacity to adapt to changing conditions – and particularly to co-operate with the other members of his group'. It thus became the norm for 'a tradition of rules of conduct, existing apart from any one individual who had learnt them ... [to] govern human life'. From the point of view of understanding human actions, the point was that rules enabled agents to establish relevant 'classifications of different kinds of objects' they are likely to confront and to formulate 'a sort of model of the environment that enabled ... [them] to predict and anticipate in action external events' pertinent to devising apt responses (p. 157).

Of continuing concern here is the fact that the argument above brings into focus Hayek's awareness of the need for analysts to get beyond mere tenets of reason if economic phenomena are to be properly understood as the products of deliberated and conscious human action. To achieve this objective, analysts must give due recognition to the notion of a mutually interactive involvement of rational, but cognitively limited, human agents with their situational environment in its several dimensions. This is the theme dealt with at length in the next chapter.

NOTES

1. It will not be possible, nor is it necessary, in the present context to pursue the origins and substance of Hayek's theory of the mind and cognition as it was argued in *The Sensory Order*. Some recent interest has been taken in investigating his psychology per se, but that is not my objective here (cf. Weimer, 1982; de Vries, 1994; Smith, 1995). I will accept the work more or less uncritically at its face value and thus ignore the caveats implicit in the author's own reports that his 'colleagues in the social sciences generally find my study ... uninteresting or indigestible', while the ideas 'received a respectful but not very comprehending welcome by the psychologists' (1979, pp. 199f, n26).
2. It is worth noting that one Hayek scholar, John Gray (1984), has made a point of arguing out the Kantian content of Hayek's theory of mind. I do not intend to pursue this issue here, except to note that the notion ultimately had Hayek's indirect acceptance. In an interview dating from the 1980s, he recalled concerning Gray that 'of course he interprets me as a Kantian. I first was inclined to say, "You exaggerate the influence. I've never studied Kant very carefully." But the fact is that at the crucial age of, say, twenty or twenty-one, I got very fascinated by the works of a Kantian contemporary named Alois Riehl, who wrote a great work on criticism and two semi-popular introductions'. So, he added, 'I suppose what I know about Kantian philosophy comes largely from a Kantian ... [from whom] I had to admit that indirectly I got a good deal' (1994, pp. 139f).
3. With respect to this aspect of Hayek's thought, Tony Lawson (1994d) and Steve Fleetwood (1995) have given key status to the 1960 work, *The Constitution of Liberty* (1960), in what they argue to be the transformation process that characterizes Hayek's thought. Within Fleetwood's 'three Hayeks', designated I, II and III, the crucial transition between the latter two stages came with the emergence of Hayek's consciousness that human agents operate within an inherited situational structure that conditions and shapes their deliberations,

decisions and actions. The association of this transition with the 1960 work is excessively precise because this in situ status of active agents was already apparent much earlier in his writings. The 1939 pamphlet and the 1945 lecture cited here both contain explicit discussion of the idea. And, as will be shown in the next chapter, the 1944 book, *The Road to Serfdom*, also included much pertinent argument concerning this theme. But what is required here is no more than a tempering of Fleetwood's exact dating of Hayek's transformation from 'II' to 'III', for it must be granted, nonetheless, that agents interacting with external rules and social structures feature much more prominently in *The Constitution of Liberty* and beyond. The deepening of his insight in this matter enabled Hayek to develop an increasingly sophisticated theory of human agency.

7. Hayek's situated human agency

7.1 DEFINING SITUATED HUMAN ACTION

When Hayek turned his attention to drafting *The Constitution of Liberty* (1960), it was evident that economics was still on his mind. But now, the subject concerned him in so far as it dealt with just one among many of the dimensions of the human life-world to be addressed through a formalized philosophy of freedom. The work comprised essentially a comprehensive statement of liberal social and political philosophy, and Hayek informed his readers that 'the chief aim of this book… [is] the interweaving of the philosophy, jurisprudence, and economics of freedom which is still needed' (ibid., p. 6). In this respect, it broadened considerably the reach of the 'economic problem' with which he was now prepared to deal. He introduced the intentions involved by noting that 'though I still regard myself as mainly an economist, I have come to feel more and more that the answers to many of the pressing social questions of our time are to be found ultimately in the recognition of principles that lie outside the scope of technical economics' (p. 3; cf. p. 6). He went on to explain further that, 'though it was from an original concern with problems of economic policy that I started, I have been slowly led to the ambitious and perhaps presumptuous task of approaching them through a comprehensive restatement of the basic principles of a philosophy of freedom' (p. 3). Moreover, one part of the work had as its objective to test the principles he had 'enunciated by the application of them to some of today's critical economic and social issues' (p. 5).

Economic agency, as with any other facet of subjectively determined human action, took on a very particular form under the conditions of freedom as these were defined by Hayek. Without delving too deeply into his discussion of the problematics of the idea of freedom (ibid., pp. 11ff), we may accept that the central concept on which he intended to focus was one in which freedom to act is contained within some imposed limits. It comprised the free capacity to devise individual plans of action that address individual economic goals, and to act on those plans consequently, given a voluntary acceptance of the constraints of the inherited structural and institutional order within which the agents live (pp. 12, 20f, 35). The necessary coercive effects that remain were envisaged as minimized and mitigated by the fact of their being generally and impersonally applied through the existence of abstract rules that are independent of the designs of any other person. Specifically put, 'coercion according to known rules, which is generally the result of circumstances in which the person to be coerced has placed himself, then becomes an instrument assisting the individuals in the pursuit of their own ends and not a means to be used for the ends of others' (p. 21; cf. pp. 133ff).

The ultimately voluntaristic orientation of Hayek's ideas was made clear in his expression that 'the conception of freedom under the law that is the chief concern of this book rests on the contention that when we obey laws, in the sense of general abstract rules laid down irrespective of their application to us, we are not subject to another man's will and therefore free' (ibid., p. 153). Under these conditions, freedom 'does not assure us of any particular opportunities, but leaves it to us to decide what use we shall make of the circumstances in which we find ourselves' (p. 19). Also it demands a measure of faith in the capacity of these inherited circumstances to enable the results agents want from their actions to be delivered with some degree of assurance. That is, 'freedom necessarily means that many things will be done which we do not like. Our faith in freedom does not rest on the foreseeable results in particular circumstances but on the belief that it will, on balance, release more forces for the good than for the bad' (p. 31). It is the nature of these situational 'circumstances', and their influence on agents' economic conduct, that will mainly be at issue here.

The primary ontological message conveyed by Hayek was that, at any stage of its history, humankind inherits an ordered civilization comprising institutions and social structures that embody values, ends and means, all of which are their own, albeit unconscious and unintended, products (ibid., p. 63). In any era, the mediation of such situational conditions influences agents' cognitive patterns and the actions they take in a way that transcends the pure application of reason to circumstances. Thus 'Man did not simply impose upon the world a pattern created by his mind. His mind is itself a system that constantly changes as a result of his endeavor to adapt himself to his surroundings' (p. 23). It is, he reiterated, 'erroneous intellectualism' to regard 'human reason as something standing outside nature and possessed of knowledge and reasoning capacity independent of experience' (p. 24). So it was that, for Hayek, conscious knowledge of circumstances and the application of reason to them, on the part of active agents, is a necessary but by no means sufficient means of accounting for their actions. Such actions are the compounded consequence of this knowledge and reason, together with the biographical cum experiential dimensions of their mental make-up and their tacit use of the collective knowledge that has gone into the structuring of the various entities comprising their situations (pp. 24ff).

Hayek's position in this issue of situating individual human agents in order to understand their actions was further clarified when he examined the contrasts between determinist and voluntarist ideas about agency (ibid., pp. 72ff). His critique of both positions as extremes concluded with the need to recognize the sort of balance between the two that is implicit in all of the argument above. In terms of their actions, agents are neither passive victims of their circumstances, 'a bogey of an automaton' (p. 74), nor free-willed and arbitrary, 'a metaphysical "self" that stands outside the whole chain of cause and effect' (p. 73). The former vision of the human agent 'seemed to eliminate the spontaneity of human action' and its implication that 'the working of man's mind must be believed ... to obey uniform laws appeared to eliminate the role of an individual personality which is essential to the conception of freedom and responsibility' (p. 72). An image of agents as automata, however, included a number of elements about their conduct that Hayek did not want entirely to eliminate. He noted that what we might interpret as a 'softer' form of determinism meant that 'the conduct of a person at any moment, his response to any set of external circumstances, will be determined by the joint effects of his inherited constitution and all his accumulated experience, with each new experience being interpreted in the light of earlier individual experience'. The latter is a 'cumulative process which in each instance produces a unique and distinct personality' (p. 74).

Such a position on situated human agency appears unexceptional as far as it goes. But Hayek was concerned to ensure that determined actions were tempered by the existence of a voluntarist dimension of the individual psyche encompassing a 'self' or an 'I' whose 'disposition cannot be affected by external or material influences' (ibid.). This dimension is what potentially gives conduct some ethical and sociomoral content and makes it possible for individuals to take responsibility for the consequences of their actions by closing off the determinist retreat. For this potential to be realized, 'the assigning of responsibility ... presupposes the capacity on men's part for rational action, and it aims at making them act more rationally than they otherwise would. It presupposes a certain minimum capacity in them for learning and foresight, for being guided by a knowledge of the consequences of their action' (p. 76).

Hayek summarized this conditioned situation of human agents by referring to the fact that, by virtue of our total evolution, 'we command many tools – in the widest sense of that word – which the human race has evolved and which enable us to deal with our environment' (ibid., p. 27). To a large extent unconsciously, we use these inherited 'tools', including material implements and virtual traditions and institutions, for our own purposes. And we do so to the best of our ability, limited as it is, given our innate and learned cognitive and other capacities. Conforming to the demands of such impersonally derived and applied conditions could not impede freedom in Hayek's sense, for they involve a voluntary conformity by individuals that serves directly to benefit nobody but themselves. The effect of conformity is felt by most agents as a positive return for living in an ordered environment. For 'on the whole, those conventions and norms of social intercourse and individual conduct do not constitute a serious infringement of individual liberty but secure a certain minimum of uniformity of conduct that assists individual efforts more than it impedes them' (p. 147). Indeed, his general position was that 'there has certainly been no successful attempt to operate a free society, without a genuine reverence for grown institutions, for customs and habits' (p. 61). This is because 'coercion can be reduced to a minimum only where individuals can be expected as a rule to conform voluntarily to certain principles' (p. 62). Individual agents are effectively assigned a responsibility for appropriate actions by virtue of their taking their place in a free social or economic order: 'Liberty and responsibility are inseparable. A free society will not function or maintain itself unless its members regard it as right that each individual occupy the position that results from his action and accept it as due to his own action' (p. 71).

When agents as carriers of a set of ends and preferences confront particular problems, their deliberations, plans and actions are delimited by the situational conditions within which they find themselves. But, as already suggested, the return for agents' acceptance of such voluntary delimitation is an improved efficacy of and certainty about the success of their own actions. But the success of individuals in this sense depends upon their living in a mutually compatible state with others around them. Thus 'the rules under which the citizens act constitute an adaptation of the whole society to its environment and to the general characteristics of its members. They serve, or should serve, to assist the individuals in forming plans of action that they will have a good chance of carrying through' (ibid., p. 157). More specifically put, 'the orderliness of social [and economic] activity shows itself in the fact that the individual can carry out a consistent plan of action that, at almost every stage, rests on the expectation of certain contributions from his fellows'. On this basis, the order requires 'essentially that individual action is guided by successful foresight, that people not only make effective use of their knowledge but can foresee with a high degree of confidence what collaboration they can expect from others' (pp. 159f).

However, the uncertainties of such expectations about others cannot be so readily countervailed as was suggested in this piece. Here Hayek showed his willingness to leave aside any investigation of the full implications of subjectivism as it involves agents acting in the face of uncertainty. This inclination remained throughout *The Constitution of Liberty*, for his other references to the matter of uncertainty and expectations were similarly made *en passant*.

Earlier in the work he had made the point that 'man learns by the disappointment of expectations' and went on to refer to the potential of institutions to 'increase the chances of correct foresight' (ibid., p. 30). Just what these assertions meant for situated human agency was not pursued. Beyond this, he made another passing reference to the matter, again without further development: 'Most human aims can be achieved only by a chain of connected actions, decided upon as a coherent whole and based on the assumption that the facts will be what they are expected to be. It is because, and insofar as, we can predict events, or at least know probabilities, that we can achieve anything' (p. 134). Here Hayek chose not to pursue the important subjectivist issues of how such future, so-called 'facts' are devised by agents and the ambiguity of applying the idea of probability in the realm of predicting human actions and their consequences.

In his 'Notes on the evolution of systems of rules of conduct', circa 1966 (1967, pp. 66ff), Hayek had much more to say about the nature of individual agent conduct in group situations and the orders of regularized action that may emerge as a consequence. As he put it there, 'the whole task of social theory consists of little else but an effort to reconstruct the overall orders' which are formed as a result of 'the interplay of the rules of conduct of ... individuals with the actions of other individuals and the external circumstances'. The complexity of the task is then the result of 'that special apparatus of conceptual construction' required by such theory (ibid., p. 71). Such complexity was attributed by Hayek to an explicitly ontological quality of the object of analysis: 'Societies differ from simpler complex structures by the fact that their elements are themselves complex structures' in the form of individual human agents. The result is a phenomenon in which an 'individual with a particular structure and behaviour owes its [*sic*] existence in this form to a society of a particular structure, because only within such a society has it been advantageous to develop some of its particular characteristics' (p. 76). At the same time, 'the order of society ... is a result of these regularities of conduct which the individuals have developed in society ... [and] the structures possessing a kind of order will exist because the elements do what is necessary to secure the persistence of that order' (pp. 76f).

An added complexity that confronts social theorists is to allow for the dynamics of such orders. The key requirement for the continuing viability of the order over time as 'a steady structure (showing "homeostatic" control)' is that its agents are called upon only to operate in 'an environment in which there prevails a certain probability of encountering the sort of circumstances to which the rules of conduct are adapted' (ibid., p. 71). Given this, orders of action have an inertia of purpose that agents are prepared to conform to and are reluctant to alter. That is, 'the knowledge of some regularities of the environment will create a preference for those kinds of conduct which produce a confident expectation of certain consequences, and an aversion to doing something unfamiliar'. For this reason, there emerges 'a sort of connection between the knowledge that rules exist in the objective world and a disinclination to deviate from the rules commonly followed in action, and therefore also between the belief that events follow rules and the feeling that one "ought" to observe rules in one's conduct' (p. 79).

In Hayek's view, though, it must be accepted that, in these circumstances, individuals' conduct is not necessarily consciously linked to the collective purpose and consequences that follow their combined situated actions. That is, 'the order which will form as the result of these actions is of course in no sense "part of the purpose" or of the motive of the acting individuals. The immediate cause, the impulse which drives them to act, will be something affecting them only; and it is merely because in doing so they are restrained by rules that an overall order results' (ibid., p. 77). In addition to the restraint factor cited here, it is also the case that individuals' purposes will be facilitated to the extent that they come to know of and act within the rules. It is 'our knowledge of fact (and especially of that complex order of society within which we move as much as within the order of nature) [that] tells us mainly what will be the consequences of our actions in some circumstances'. And agents 'do not so much choose between alternative actions according to their known consequences as prefer those the consequences of which are predictable over those the consequences of which are unknown' (pp. 79f). To this idea Hayek added the qualification that, 'while this will help us to decide what to do if we want to obtain a particular result, or are driven by a particular impulse, it needs to be supplemented in a largely unknown world by some principle which inhibits actions to which our internal drives might lead us but which are inappropriate to the circumstances' (p. 80). It is socialization into normative beliefs about acceptance of the factual rules that inclines agents appropriately to delimit their conduct.

One of the most important pieces written by Hayek on the theme of understanding subjective human agency through its situational conditions of deliberation and action was published as 'The confusion of language in political thought' in 1968 (1978, pp. 71ff). The ideas had been presented a year earlier as a lecture to the Walter Eucken institute in Freiburg. What the paper provided was a detailed exposition of the origin, nature and role of the situations which all agents find themselves confronting and through which they must conduct their life-world activities. The background to the ideas presented was his denial of 'the rationalistic prejudice that intelligent behaviour is governed exclusively by a knowledge of the relations between cause and effect, and by the associated belief that "reason" manifests itself only in deductions derived from such knowledge. The only kind of rational action [this] constructivistic rationalism recognises is action guided by such considerations as "If I want X then I must do Y"' (ibid., p. 83). Giving a proper account of agents' conduct must probe deeper than this sort of superficial logic.

In this context, Hayek was concerned to identify and separate aspects of situations and rules that are the result of conscious human construction from those that have evolved without any conscious effort. But the crucial point for the development of subjectivism is that, whatever their origins, the environmental conditions in which agents are situated are to be understood as contributing to the characteristics of their actions, individually and collectively. And, in understanding the nature of any human order, analysts must proceed on the basis that, 'while the order of the physical environment is given to us independently of human will, the order of our social environment is partly, but only partly, the result of human design' (ibid., p. 73). Most importantly, he warned, 'the temptation to regard it *all* as the intended product of human action is one of the main sources of error' in formulating the human sciences. Indeed, he consequently expressed 'the insight that *not all order that results from the interplay of human actions is the result of design* is ... the beginning of social theory' (p. 73, original emphasis). This conclusion reflected his belief that the demand for understanding individual and collective human agency stems from the fact that a significant part of it cannot be attributed to deliberate and self-conscious action, so that 'it is not the purposive but the rule-governed aspect of individual actions which integrates them into the order on which civilisation rests' (p. 85).

As far as the actual forms taken by situational entities are concerned, Hayek distinguished those collective orders in which agents participate in order to realize common purposes with others from those in which participation is intended exclusively as a means of realizing individual ends. This implies alternative origins of the social orders that agents confront. There are 'anthropomorphic or personalised explanations of social institutions ... [which] interpret the general rules which guide action [as] directed at particular purposes'. But there are also 'institutions [which] are successful adaptations to the irremediable limitations of our knowledge, adaptations which have prevailed over alternative forms of order because they proved more effective methods for dealing with that incomplete, dispersed knowledge which is man's unalterable lot' (ibid., p. 72). Social orders as active agents experience and use them and, as analysts attempt to account for them, may be designated as what Hayek called 'taxis' in the former case and 'cosmos' in the latter. And, he argued, 'the first important difference between a spontaneous order or *cosmos* and an organisation (arrangement) or *taxis* is that, not having been deliberately made by men, a *cosmos* has no purpose' (pp. 73f). Thus 'every *taxis* (arrangement, organisation) presupposes a particular end, men forming such an organisation must serve the same purposes' and comprises a constructed system of relationships that are 'determined by an agency which stands outside the order and is in the same sense exogenous or imposed' (p. 74, cf. pp. 75f). By contrast, a '*cosmos* will result from regularities of the behaviour of the elements which it comprises. It is in this sense endogenous, intrinsic or ... a "self- regulating" or "self-organising" system' (p. 74). This gives the cosmos some particular characteristics that will be 'determined by the facts and aims which guide the actions of individual elements, though they are confined by the general rules within a certain permissible range. In consequence, the concrete content of such an order will always be unpredictable' (p. 75).

What this distinction means for understanding the processes of human agency in an operational sense is that 'in a *cosmos* knowledge of the facts and purposes which will guide individual action will be those of the acting individuals, while in a *taxis* the knowledge and purposes of the organiser will determine the resulting order' (ibid., p. 75). The result is that an analogous distinction also needs to be drawn between the kind of rules and norms to which participating agents are expected to conform. Here Hayek's categories were 'nomos' for the cosmos and 'thesis' for the taxis. In the former case, he argued that 'the sense of *nomos* ... [is] of an abstract rule not due to anybody's concrete will, applicable in particular cases irrespective of the consequences, a law which could be 'found' and was not made for particular foreseeable purposes' (p. 79). It is thus 'a universal rule of just conduct applying to an unknown number of future instances and equally to all persons in the objective circumstances described by the rule, irrespective of the effects which observance of the rule will produce in a particular situation'. In contrast to this, 'we shall use *thesis* to mean any rule which is applicable only to particular people or in the service of the ends of rulers. ... They are the necessary instrument of running an organisation or *taxis*' (p. 77). More specifically, such 'rules for an organisation presuppose the assignment of particular tasks, targets or functions to individual people by commands; and most of the rules of an organisation will apply only to the persons charged with particular responsibilities' (p. 78).

In the early 1970s, Hayek included in Volume 1 of *Law, Legislation and Liberty* (1973b) a further intensive analysis of the situational entities in which human agents participate. Relatively simple orders, *taxis*, often functional organizations created by specific individuals, comprise rules with a degree of concreteness and specificity. They may be understood as a conceptual whole by reference to the particular purposes they serve and the decisions and actions that generated them (ibid., p. 38). Moreover, 'what distinguishes the rules which will govern action within an organization is that they must be rules for the performance of assigned tasks'. That is, 'they presuppose that the place of each individual in a fixed structure is determined by command

and that the rules each individual must obey depend upon the place which he has been assigned and on the particular ends which have been indicated for him by the commanding authority' (p. 49). By contrast with concrete organizations, spontaneous orders, *cosmos*, 'not having been made ... *cannot* legitimately be said to *have a particular purpose*' (p. 38, original emphasis). Rather, what the analyst must investigate is the senses in which for individual active agents, an 'awareness of its existence may be extremely important for ... [their] successful pursuit of a great variety of different purposes' (p. 38). One of the key purposes served by the regularized individual actions within an order, albeit non-consciously, is the reproduction and preservation of the order itself, perhaps in some changing form. And 'the fact is ... that we can preserve an order of such complexity, not by the method of directing the members, but only indirectly by enforcing and improving the rules conducive to the formation of a spontaneous order' (p. 51).

Hayek went on to make a great deal of this idea of spontaneous order flowing from rule-directed, independent and volitional human actions, actions that have their origin in some mix of the non-conscious and conscious mental processes of agents. It was a fundamental characteristic of liberalism itself that it 'restricts deliberate control of the overall order of society to the enforcement of such general rules as are necessary for the formation of a spontaneous order' (ibid., p. 32). Individual agents both produce such orders as an evolutionary outcome of their collective conduct and employ them as a continuing in forming their purposive action responses to life-world problems. It was from this latter perspective of the situated agent that the basic concept of any order envisaged by Hayek was defined as '*a state of affairs in which a multiplicity of elements of various kinds are so related to each other that we may learn from our acquaintance with some spatial or temporal part of the whole to form correct expectations concerning the rest, or at least expectations which have a good chance of proving correct*' (p. 36, original emphasis). That is, an order in human society is a facilitating mediation that allows agents to come to grips with their situations and to use them to guide their actions in the face of lack of complete knowledge and, with respect to time, to mitigate their uncertainty about the future.

It was Hayek's subjectivist view that agents volitionally choose to comply with and rely on the constraints of various kinds that they find built into the structures that comprise their situations. They do so for pragmatic reasons that he linked to their incomplete knowledge of the conditions that affect the outcomes of life-world decisions they must make. The existence of institutions, organizations and other social relationships, together with the rules and norms they establish, enable agents to deliberate, choose and act in ways that have more chance of success than if they attempted to operate with complete independence and in total isolation. Having so depicted these subjectivist complexities of situated human agency, Hayek faced an implicit methodological challenge to which he chose not to respond in the present context. This was to establish a mode of representing the associated phenomena of the human realm in a way that preserves the ontological integrity of their origins. Elsewhere he had worked on this challenge, and his results are taken up in the next chapter.

7.2 INTERVENTIONISM AND ECONOMIC ORDER

We have already encountered Hayek's rejection of constructivism and rationalism in favour of an apparent evolutionary fatalism in summing up the structures, processes and outcomes of free markets as they affect the material well-being of participating agents. However, no study of his subjectivism would be complete without some reference to his sustained concern that unfettered evolution of its structures and processes could not deliver the maximum benefits available from a market system. There remained a sense in which he could never bring himself to rule out any need for intervention and planning by some central authority, albeit with severe and stringent limitations imposed.

This concern was evident even in the most popular of all of Hayek's writings promoting liberalism and free-market capitalism, *The Road to Serfdom* (1944). The work was dedicated to negating any inclinations to replace such a system with one in which central planning and collective ownership of resources would dominate. But it also carried an additional thesis which he summed up retrospectively in the Preface to its 1976 edition: 'And the discussion of the consequences of socialist policies which the book attempts is of course not complete without an adequate account of what an appropriately run market order requires and can achieve. It was to the latter problem that the further work I have since done in the field was mainly devoted' (ibid., pp. viif). It was this need to ensure the *proper running of a market order* that required him to sustain the principle that agents need to be provided with appropriate conditioning and rules if they are to act freely and competitively in such a way as to ensure collective economic efficacy and stability. For, as he put it, 'there is, in particular, all the difference between deliberately creating a system within which competition will work as beneficially as possible, and passively accepting institutions as they are' (p. 13). In this respect, the key idea was to tap into the inherent desire and capacity of individuals to plan which 'owes its popularity largely to the fact that everybody desires, of course, that we should handle our common problems as rationally as possible, and that in so doing we should use as much foresight as we can command. In this sense everybody who is not a complete fatalist is a planner'. To this assertion he added the rider that 'an economist, whose whole task is the study of how men actually do and how they might plan their affairs, is the last person who could object to planning in this general sense' (p. 26).

What such 'planning in this general sense' amounted to was a very definite intention to intervene in order to provide the conditions appropriate to directing individual agents' competitive conduct towards actions that are coordinating. In this respect, 'the liberal argument is in favour of making the best possible use of the forces of competition as a means of co-ordinating human efforts, not an argument for leaving things just as they are' (ibid., p. 27). All the subsequent argument leads us to conclude that optimum free-market competition demands the support of rules that contain economic agents within certain bounds with a minimum of coercion. Such a system 'is based on the conviction that, where effective competition can be *created*, it is a better way of guiding individual efforts than any other'. Hayek reasoned that 'in order that competition should work beneficially, a carefully thought-out legal framework is required', together with 'other methods of guiding economic activity'. So it is, he concluded, that 'the successful use of competition as the principle of social organisation precludes certain types of coercive interference with economic life, but it admits of others which sometimes may very considerably assist its work and even requires certain kinds of government action' (p. 27, emphasis added). Quite clearly, the role of the government here is to construct the required institutional and other conditions for free-market success, because it will always be that '*some ... can never be adequately provided by private enterprise*' (p. 28, emphasis added).

A most important condition for the design and application of all rules was that they conform to what Hayek called 'the Rule of Law', which 'means that government in all its actions is bound by rules fixed and announced beforehand – rules which make it possible to foresee with fair certainty how the authority will use its coercive powers in given circumstances, and to plan one's individual affairs on the basis of this knowledge' (ibid., p. 54). That is, the crucial concern is that 'the individual can foresee the action of the state and make use of this knowledge as a datum in forming his own plans' (p. 60). The import of this condition is that agents can act independently with more certainty concerning the outcome of their actions to the extent that this depends upon the actions of relevant others within the same situation. Ultimately, in this context, he concluded that 'to create conditions in which competition will be as effective as possible, to supplement it where it cannot be made effective ..., these tasks provide indeed a wide and unquestioned field for state activity. In no system that could be rationally defended would the state just do nothing' (p. 29). It is worth reiterating that such argument as that just traversed indicates that, very early on, Hayek had adopted the principle of understanding human agency as the joint product of individual character and situational conditioning. He clearly believed that there was enough in common in the former to make viable the consciously devised and effected direction of conduct by means of the latter.

When interpreting Hayek in such later works as *The Constitution of Liberty* (1960) and beyond, what should not be neglected is his preparedness to get involved in concerns of *applied economics and economic policy*. Even more pronounced was his concern to deal instrumentally with institutions: 'My emphasis is on the *positive task of improving our institutions*'; to which he added that he hoped to 'indicate *desirable directions of development*' of such improvements (Hayek, 1960, p. 5, emphasis added). This was a repetition of the apparently rationalist and constructivist side of Hayek that we saw above emerged in 1944. It requires careful assessment if we are not to conclude that he had deserted his evolutionist and fatalistic principles of institutional development (cf. ibid., pp. 54ff).

He argued quite explicitly that the situational conditions confronted by agents could be the objects of conscious manipulation. As a matter of principle, 'though we leave people to decide for themselves because they are, as a rule, in the best position to know the circumstances surrounding their action, we are also concerned that conditions should permit them to use their knowledge to the best effect' (ibid., p. 76). For, as he went on to assert, 'there can be no doubt that the discovery of a better use of things or of one's own capacities is one of the greatest contributions that an individual can make in our society to the welfare of his fellows'. Moreover, 'it is by providing the maximum opportunity for this that a free society can become so much more prosperous than others' (p. 81). From a practical perspective, the way was open for some consciously constructed assistance from redesigning agents' situations: 'So far as possible, *our aim should be to improve human institutions* so as to increase the chances of correct foresight. Above all, however, we should provide the maximum of opportunity for unknown individuals to learn of facts that we ourselves are yet unaware of and to make use of this knowledge in their actions' (p. 30, emphasis added).

For Hayek, the important issue to be addressed in such argument was that of the role and limits of individual reason in effecting and affecting the social and economic order delivered by institutions. Most importantly, his intention was to emphasize that, although the use of reason must be explicitly recognized as delimited, its role remains significant and positive in the operation and development of social affairs and institutions. For, although 'reason undoubtedly is man's most precious possession', it remains the case that 'it is not all-powerful and ... the belief that it can become its own master and control its own development may ... destroy it' (ibid., p. 69). His point ultimately was to bring the use of reason to its optimum by situating its application within 'that indispensable matrix of the uncontrolled and non-rational which is the only environment wherein reason can grow and operate effectively'. In this respect, 'the first condition for such an intelligent use of reason in the ordering of human affairs is that we learn to understand what role it does in fact play and can play in the working of any society based on the co-operation of many separate minds' (p. 69). The purpose of such an endeavour by concerned agents was seen as a means of constructively acting to improve the functioning of the situational conditions they confront. Such a strategy requires that, 'before we can *try to remold society intelligently*, we must understand its functioning'. That is, we have to confront and grasp 'a self-maintaining whole which is kept going by forces which we cannot replace and which we must therefore use in all we try to achieve. *What can be done to improve it* must be done by working with these forces rather than against them' (pp. 69f, emphasis added).

It was to be in the case of economic policy that these constructivist directions were followed most specifically. Hayek devoted a chapter to this topic (ibid., pp. 220ff) and gave it the telling title, 'Economic policy and the rule of law'. His intention was to draw the general boundaries for the *design* of economic interventions in terms of their consistency with the rule of law. The chapter set out to delineate the principles of economic interventionism on the premise that 'the range and variety of government action that is, at least in principle, reconcilable with a free system is ... considerable' (p. 231). Specifically, 'it is the purpose of this chapter to show that the rule of law provides the criterion which enables us to distinguish between those measures which are and those which are not compatible with a free system' (p. 222). As far as he was concerned, the issue had been clouded by the misrepresentation of the benefits and disbenefits of such interventions without due attention to their specific forms. In particular, 'the habitual appeal to the principle of non-interference in the fight against all ill-considered and harmful measures has had the effect of blurring the fundamental distinction between the kinds of measures which are and those which are not compatible with a free system' (p. 221). Moreover, 'the old formulae of laissez faire or non-intervention do not provide us with an adequate criterion for distinguishing between what is and what is not admissible in a free system' (p. 231).

The design of legitimate interventions, Hayek believed, should avoid two joint characteristics. Measures should be confined to consistency with the 'rule of law' principle and the general body of laws and thus avoid the inclination to pursue ad hoc and expedient fulfilment of specific economic objectives, orders and prohibitions. So, 'in other words, it is the character rather than the volume of government activity that is important', and the 'coercive powers of government ... [should] serve general and timeless purposes, not specific ends' (ibid., pp. 222, 226). It should likewise avoid 'arbitrary discrimination between persons' and avoid any policy measure that 'determines for what specific purposes particular means are to be used (pp. 227, 231). Ultimately, 'the important point is that all coercive action of government must be unambiguously determined by a permanent legal framework which enables the individual to plan with a degree of confidence and which reduces human uncertainty as much as possible' (p. 222). In all these directions, the subjectivist, agent-centred rationale for intervention can be seen. He emphasized such an orientation by his assertion that all legitimate 'activities of government are part of its effort to provide a favorable framework for individual decisions; they supply means which individuals can use for their own purposes' (p. 223).

Nonetheless, Hayek was adamant that, in this respect, any such interventions should have no individual economic welfare objectives. His claim was that policies which 'determine the material position of particular people or enforce distributive or "social" justice' are such that they 'cannot be achieved within the limits of the rule of law' (ibid., p. 231). Advocates of such objectives, contrary to the principles he espoused, must 'favor discriminatory and discretionary action' that will inevitably conflict with, and thus need to be designed so as to bypass, the most fundamental tenets of the rule of law. Thus 'the restrictions which the rule of law imposes upon government ... preclude all those measures which would be necessary to insure that individuals will be rewarded according to another's conception of merit or desert rather than according to the value that their services have for their fellows' (p. 232). On the basis of such assertions, the apocalyptic fear he expressed for his readers to reflect on here was that the ultimate result of welfare interventions 'will necessarily be, not a modification of the existing order, but its complete abandonment and its replacement by an altogether different system – the command economy' (p. 232). Such unsubstantiated posturing really was unworthy of a scholar of Hayek's standing.

7.3 CONCLUDING REMARKS

In an endeavour to understand Hayek's critique of methodology in the human sciences that is the subject of the next chapter, it has been important to identify precisely what it is about the subjective nature of their objects of inquiry that sets them apart from those of the non-human world. It was to be this separate identity that rendered them as potentially unsuited to the application of established scientific principles of inquiry and representation. Exposing these ontological distinctions that flow from the origin of human phenomena in the actions of situated agents, as Hayek argued them in his writings, has been the objective of this and the previous chapters. What is now to be made apparent is that it was his realization of this distinctive ontological nature of human science phenomena, because of their origin in situated human deliberation and action, that gave the original impetus to his critique of scientism. Unfortunately, this ontological foundation of the critique was not to be carried forward into the 1960s ruminations on human science methodology. Somehow Hayek came to believe that, in spite of all the subjectivist insights he had achieved in discussing the nature of human agency in economics, and in spite of his erstwhile rejection of scientism, the methodology required for explanations of the complex phenomena agents generate was but a version of that which applied to natural phenomena of like, but always lesser, complexity. More on this in the next chapter.

8. Hayek's methodology of subjectivist economics

8.1 INTRODUCTION

Previous chapters have made it apparent that, from very early on in his career, Hayek was not prepared to accept the emerging orthodoxy of neoclassical microeconomics. Specifically, he objected to varying degrees to its substantive content, to its methodological premises and procedures, and to its epistemological claims. The general source of this dissatisfaction was his vision of the economy as comprising phenomena generated by independent subjective human agents whose separate actions are more or less coordinated by the situational structures and conditions within which they act. Orthodox economists had not, he believed, properly understood and represented the complexity that human exigencies bring to this generation process.

For Hayek, such understanding meant grasping the intricate composition of knowledge and ignorance, capacities and incapacities, that characterize agents in their real-life market activities. For instance, in the paper 'Coping with ignorance' from 1978, he put it that 'our problem is that, even if we have thought out a beautiful and possibly correct theory of the complex phenomena with which we have to deal, we can never ascertain all the concrete specific data of a particular position, simply because we do not know all that which the acting people know. But it is the joint results of those actions which we want to predict' (Hayek, 1983, pp. 20f). And in 'Science and socialism', a paper also written in 1978, he made the point critically by arguing against the neoclassicals that they have 'proceeded on the assumption of "given data" and produced a beautiful, aesthetically satisfying theory to show how these data determined the resulting order, but one forgot that, these data were purely fictitious; the data were not given to anybody ... [and] the economists merely succeeded in demonstrating that if they knew all the facts, they could determine the results' (ibid., p. 36). Orthodox economists had been able to bypass such complexities by setting prior scientific standards of methodology and forcing the analyses to conform to them by means of mandatory assumptions and abstractions concerning the nature and operations of human agents. It was these assumptions and abstractions that Hayek found to distort the representation of real economic phenomena and thus to render orthodox accounts of them misleading at best. As we are to see, this was not to deny the need for and legitimacy of assumption and abstraction in the metatheory of economics. What he intended was that these procedures and all others involved in designing a methodology for the discipline should give priority to maintaining human ontological integrity to the maximum extent possible.

In the entry that he had partly drafted for the *New Palgrave* dictionary towards the end of his life, Hayek wrote that, in their endeavours to reform economic methodology in such a direction, 'the main achievement of the Austrian school's theory ... became that it decidedly helped to clear up the differences that must inevitably exist among disciplines'. This applied especially between those that 'deal with relatively simple phenomena, like mechanics, which necessarily were the first to be very successful and which for this reason came to be regarded as paradigms that other disciplines ought to imitate' and those that comprise 'the sciences of highly complex phenomena, or of structures determined by a greater number of particular facts than could ever be concretely ascertained by scientific observers and containing objects of theoretical (rather than physically observable) thought – i.e., *the thoughts of other persons*' (1992, p. 56, emphasis added).

In his last major work, *The Fatal Conceit*, he made it clear that this same issue was still much on his mind: 'Mechanical methods and models of simple causal explanation are increasingly inapplicable as we advance to ... complex phenomena'. He referred here in particular to 'the crucial phenomena determining the formation of many highly complex structures of human interaction, i.e., economic values or prices, [that] cannot be interpreted by simple causal or "homothetic" theories'. They require instead 'explanation in terms of the joint effects of a larger number of distinct elements than we can ever hope individually to observe or manipulate' (Hayek, 1989, p. 148).

These summary statements set the stage for the chapter ahead, in that they point up the crucial metatheoretical issues, as well as the ambiguity, with which Hayek struggled during much of his life. In all his subjectivist writings, it was the distinct ontological nature of the phenomena confronted in the human sciences that he emphasized in his inquiries. To this end, he devoted much juxtaposed attention to three entailed metatheoretical matters, especially as they involve economics: first, how exactly to define the distinction of objects between the physical and human sciences; secondly, how to deal methodologically with theoretical analysis in the case of economic phenomena as objects thus defined; and thirdly, what epistemological claims could be defended concerning the explanations comprising, and predictions implied by, the resulting analyses.

My findings here are argued in two stages. First, it is shown that Hayek began his critique and research in these directions with much promise, focusing on the problem as one of human ontological veracity as the crucial precondition for methodological design. Secondly, it is argued that, for reasons that remain less than fully clear, he was induced to retreat from a position of defending a subjectivist ontology as the irreducible conditioning factor in economic theory construction. The emergent and inherently confusing alternative was one of compromise that made the object distinction in economics merely a matter of greater complexity in comparison with the simple world of mechanical things. In the above reflection on what he was doing, '*the thoughts of other persons*' as the most essential ontological element underpinning economic phenomena simply cannot be reduced with any legitimacy to a distinction of greater complexity alone. That Hayek reached a point where he seemed unaware of this is mystifying. I conclude that, ultimately, his struggle with these matters was inconclusive in its outcome and that his subjectivist legacy for the neoAustrians is, as a result, ambiguous with respect to some of its most vital dimensions.

8.2 SUBJECTIVISM AND SCIENTISM

To begin again at the beginning. Even in his Inaugural Lecture, 'The trend of economic thinking', delivered in London in 1933, Hayek was prepared to hint that there existed methodological problems with orthodoxy about which established economists should be concerned. He was, he told his audience by way of explanation, conscious of an 'attack on economics [that] sprang ... from a dislike of the application of scientific methods to the investigation of social problems' (1933, p. 124). But it was to be into the early 1940s before he wrote a number of papers in which he was directly and explicitly concerned with the specific substance of the methodological and epistemological difficulties of dealing formally with the subjectivist phenomena of the human sciences (see Hayek, 1949, pp. 57ff; 1955, pp. 11ff). As was discussed in the previous chapters, even at that stage of his inquiries he had shown how conscious he was of the need to identify subjective human agency as providing the ontological essence of these phenomena. In the papers of the 1940s, he made the point that, since the first half of the nineteenth century, there had been a marked and enduring shift towards the pretence that the study of economy and society could be scientific in the same sense as applied to the study of the physical world. As he was so well aware, one of the first casualties of such a contrived and formalistic endeavour had to be the proper subjectivist representation of human agents.

For Hayek, the object of all economic and social inquiry was the collective outcome of conditioned and situated human agency and its phenomenal manifestations. It is an object that has *existentially*, and thus irreducibly, a subjectivist dimension in its origins and character. The metatheoretical principles applied in understanding and analytically representing such an object demand careful design if they are to ensure that preserving its ontological integrity is given primacy in formulating the required argument. Hayek had much to say on this topic in a remarkable series of papers published in *Economica* during 1942–3 and collected under the title 'Scientism and the study of society' in the 1955 book, *The Counter-Revolution of Science* (pp. 11ff). Hayek set down the problematic with which he would be concerned by claiming that there is an 'element of truth in the ... contention that we can understand and explain human action in a way we cannot with physical phenomena' (1955, p. 18). Thus, 'with events other than human actions ... [an observer] could not expect the same kind of "explanation" as he can hope to obtain in the case of human behavior' (p. 19). Sorting out the implications of these fundamental beliefs would occupy much of his intellectual endeavour over the remainder of his life.

Hayek was here reflecting explicitly upon the primacy of subjectivist ontology in any study of human action as the foundation for understanding economy and society. His metatheoretical position was an immediately ontologically driven one, for he referred to the 'peculiar object and the methods of the social studies' in comparison with those found in studying the physical world. His vision could not be more clearly stated than in his assertion that social and economic studies '*deal, not with the relations between things, but with the relations between men and things or the relations between man and man. They are concerned with man's actions, and their aim is to explain the unintended or undesigned results of the actions of many men*' (ibid., p. 25, emphasis added). More specifically, these studies are not concerned with actions that have their source in unconscious physical reflexes. Rather, their focus is on 'man's conscious or reflected action, actions where a person can be said to choose between various courses open to him' (p. 26) and they recognize that 'only what people know or believe can enter as a motive into their conscious action' (p. 35).

At this point, he went on to open a 'Pandora's box' of ontological and epistemological puzzles by ruling out any unique correspondence between the characteristics of agents' given physical situations and their consequent conscious actions. His idea of subjectivism, with its realist overtones arising from the recognition of an objective world independent of agents' conceptions, led him to reason that, in such situations, we need to consider a relationship between three dimensions: 'the acting or thinking person,... some desired or imagined effect, and ... a [physical] thing in the ordinary sense' (ibid., p. 27). That is, the essence of action is to be found in the combination of the agent's characteristics and the intended effect of using the pre-existing physical conditions on the basis of plans formed ex ante to action. Such plans can only be formed through expectations manifested in imagined alternative outcomes. For Hayek, the physical forms per se were not of direct relevance because 'things *are* what the acting people think they are' and they act accordingly (p. 27, original emphasis). He believed that 'our senses make things appear to us alike or different which prove to be alike or different in none of their relations between themselves, but only in the way in which they affect our senses' (p. 29). This means that, in a science of human action, 'qualities disappear from our scientific picture of the external world ... [and] when we study qualities we study not the physical world but the mind of men' (p. 29). So it was that there must exist a substantial contingent remainder in any attempt to understand individual human action on the basis of the inherent characteristics of external and independent physical conditions.

As Hayek argued the point, 'we know that people will react in the same way to external stimuli which according to all objective tests are different, and perhaps also that they will react in a completely different manner to a physically identical stimulus if it affects their bodies in different circumstances or at a different point' (ibid., p. 26). For the sciences of human action, then, 'unless we can understand what the acting people mean by their actions any attempt to explain them, i.e., to subsume them under rules which connect similar situations with similar actions, are bound to fail' (p. 31). This conclusion, of course, leaves hanging the questions: what does it mean to 'understand' the actions of agents, and by what procedures do we as interacting agents or as analysts so 'understand'?

For any definition of understanding, the potential problems of applying it to situated human action are compounded by recognizing, in Hayek's words, that 'what is true about the relations of men to things is, of course, even more true [*sic*] of the relations between men, which for the purposes of social study cannot be defined in the objective terms of the physical sciences but only in terms of human beliefs' (ibid., p. 31). Consequently, he emphasized that 'not only man's action towards external objects but also all the relations between men and all the social institutions can be understood only in terms of what men think about them. Society as we know it is, as it were, built up from the concepts and ideas held by the people; social phenomena can be recognized by us and have meaning to us only as they are reflected in the minds of men' (pp. 33f). All this was consistent with what would be argued about the theory of mind in *The Sensory Order* some time later. There existed for agents an independent world of things and social relations. In confronting and participating in this world, they have no option but to form conceptual understandings of its features. There can be no guarantee of any unique correspondence between the concepts formed and the realities of the objects concerned. But what is evident is that, by the 1940s at the latest, Hayek avoided any taint of idealism in which that world had no existence for agents beyond their individual conceptions of it.[1]

For interdependently acting agents, and for observing analysts, these considerations leave a margin of contingency in understanding the actions of others that can only be overcome by means of introspective extrapolation of their own particular experiences and psychic orientations towards similar physical and social conditions. Hayek observed that this endeavour is facilitated by the presumption that there is sufficient common psychic ground between individuals, along with a generally understood system of typified categories and references to the real world that agents have in common, to give the extrapolation a chance of successfully facilitating a grasp of another agent's interpretations and intentions. As he put it, 'the structure of men's minds, the common principle on which they classify external events, provide us with the knowledge of the recurrent elements of which different social structures are built up and in terms of which we can alone describe and explain them' (ibid., p. 34). Thus 'it would be impossible to explain or understand human action without making use of this knowledge' (p. 26).

Hayek elaborated his ontological insight by arguing that 'the facts of the social sciences are merely opinions, views held by the people whose actions we study'. This means that 'they differ from the facts of the physical sciences in being beliefs or opinions held by particular people, beliefs which as such are our data, irrespective of whether they are true or false'. And, he went on, 'we cannot directly observe [these beliefs] in the minds of people but ... we can recognize [them] from what they do and say merely because we have ourselves a mind similar to theirs' (ibid., p. 28). In this sense, the social sciences 'deal in the first instance with the phenomena of individual minds, or mental phenomena, and not directly with material phenomena. They deal with phenomena which can be understood only because the object of our study has a mind of a structure similar to our own. That this is so is no less an empirical fact than our knowledge of the external world' (p. 28).

So, in all our attempts to understand the human world around us, Hayek wrote, 'we must start from what men think and what men do' and from 'the fact that the individuals which [*sic*] compose society are guided in their actions by a classification of things or events according to a system of sense qualities and of concepts which has a common structure'. So, as observers, we can recognize these action-inducing factors because 'we, too are men'. To this Hayek added the final rider that 'the concrete knowledge which different individuals possess will differ in important respects' (ibid., p. 33). In doing so, he was drawing attention to one of his key subjectivist theses. His view was that, because of the infinity of variations of potential and actual accumulated knowledge held by agents and upon which their action decisions are based, the collective results of individual actions contain unintended dimensions the precise origins of which cannot be accounted for or replicated by any single-minded endeavour. However, he was inclined to qualify this claim as a pragmatic matter, for agents of all sorts must comprehend enough of the collective functioning of their economy and society to get on effectively in what they need to do. The means for achieving this are supplied by the inherited structures and functions into which agents can install themselves.

> If the social structure can remain the same although different individuals succeed each other at particular points, this is not because the individuals which [*sic*] succeed each other are completely identical, but because they succeed each other in particular relations, in particular attitudes they take towards other people and as the objects of particular views held by other people about them.

The result is that 'individuals are merely the *foci* in the network of relationships and it is the various attitudes of the individuals towards each other (or their similar or different attitudes towards physical objects) which form the recurrent, recognizable and familiar elements of the structure' (p. 34, original emphasis). Hayek focused here on his understanding that categories of agents' deliberated conduct can be interpreted as strongly influenced and shaped by their cumulative biographies of experiences, by their socialization and by their inherited situational conditions. It was also emphasized that these situational conditions are existentially independent of and prior to the agents' involvement with them.

The definition of the 'scientism' that was the target of his critique exactly expressed its consequences in ontological terms consistent with the subjectivist premises just outlined. It is 'a mechanical and uncritical application of habits of thought to fields different from those in which they have been formed', with the resulting metatheory comprising 'a very prejudiced approach which, *before it has considered its subject, claims to know what is the most appropriate way of investigating it*' (ibid., p. 16, emphasis added). Of fundamental concern in the critique of scientism, then, was to say something specific about the particular ontology of the 'subject' of human science.

In a lecture delivered in 1942 and published in 1943, Hayek confronted the issue of 'The facts of the social sciences' head on (Hayek, 1949, pp. 57ff). The crucial issue was immediately ontological: '*with what kind of facts [do] we have to deal in the social sciences?*' (p. 58, emphasis added). We have seen in previous chapters that he was working up to a clearly subjectivist perception of these 'facts'. The importance of the line of attack here is that it posed the question about the nature of human science phenomena before any mention was made of potential methodologies. He went on in this same essential vein: 'Now the social sciences are without exception concerned with the way in which men behave toward their environment – other men or things' (ibid., p. 59). This premise led him to pose the question: 'How must we define or classify the objects of their activity if we want to explain or understand their actions?' (p. 59). Hayek the subjectivist was bound to respond that we can gain little insight here by means of physical and behavioural attributes alone, if such attributes exist at all. As he put it, 'such things as tools, food, medicine, weapons, words, sentences, communications and acts of production ... [are] fair samples of the kind of objects of human activity which constantly occur in the social sciences' (p. 59). From the perspective of human agency, there are no adequate definitions of these things in physical terms, for they are 'all instances of what are sometimes called "teleological concepts", that is, they can be defined only by indicating relations between three terms: a purpose, somebody who holds that purpose, and an object which the person thinks to be a suitable means for that purpose' (pp. 59f). This means that 'these objects are defined not in terms of their "real" properties but in terms of opinions people hold about them. In short, in the social sciences the things are what people think they are'. As observer-analysts, therefore, we must seek to classify and understand the objects of human activity 'not according to what we ... know about the objects, but according to what we think the observed person knows about it [*sic*]' (p. 60). That is, we are required to 'impute knowledge to the observed person' (p. 61). In these methodological arguments, Hayek's subjectivist premises were quite apparent, along with his realist vision of the existential independence of the world confronted by acting agents.

Similar reasoning must apply to analysts' subjectivist understanding of human actions themselves. These, too, are not appropriately classified and understood by means of any isolated physical criteria. The essential element here is the intention or purpose of the action, even though physical exigencies may be involved in directing and shaping its observed form. Thus, 'whenever we interpret human action as in a sense purposive or meaningful, whether we do so in ordinary life or for the purposes of the social sciences, we have to define both the objects of human activity and the different kinds of actions themselves, not in physical terms but in terms of the opinions or intentions of the acting persons' (ibid., p. 62). Hayek repeated his examples of 'words, sentences, communications and acts of production' as being linked to purposeful human action and whose meaning is so defined. That is, the physical manifestations, are not the point: 'It is not because of any objective or physical similarity but because of the (imputed) intention of the acting person that I regard the various ways in which in different circumstances he may make, say, a spindle, as instances of the same act of production' (p. 61).

The nature of the imputation process that must be part of understanding the observed actions of others was of explicit concern to Hayek. Physical identification and classification of an action may be necessary to make it meaningful to us as observers, but it cannot be sufficient. As he put it, 'do we not always when we say we "understand" a person's action, when we talk about "why" he is doing this or that, impute to him something beyond what we can observe – at least what we can observe in the particular case?' The necessary response must be that we as observers, 'in discussing what we regard as other people's conscious actions, ... invariably interpret their action on the analogy of our own mind' (ibid., p. 63). We are confronted, then, with a dual interpretation process, a 'double hermeneutic', in which an action induced by the interpretations of one individual is interpreted on the basis of the observer's own experiences extrapolated to the observed case. That is, 'I know the meaning of this action because I know what I would or might have done in similar circumstances' (p. 64). As a means of understanding what others do, Hayek stressed that, in using what amounted to a hermeneutical approach, we can never be sure of what we conclude, but 'that in the great majority of instances this procedure *works* ... [because] my conclusion will be sufficiently certain for practical purposes (p. 64, original emphasis). Epistemologically, it is clear that this situation for a formal analyst is a rather different problematic from that of determining, for example, the chemical composition of a sample of igneous rock. In this respect, he made the important observation that 'while at the world of nature we look from the outside, we look at the world of society from the inside; while, as far as nature is concerned, our concepts are about the facts and have to be adapted to the facts, in the world of society at least some of the most familiar concepts are the stuff from which that world is made' (p. 76).

More particularly, it can be questioned whether or not 'it is legitimate to employ in scientific analysis such concepts as these, which refer to a state of affairs which we all recognize "intuitively" and which we not only unhesitatingly use in daily life but on which all social intercourse, all communication between men, is based' (ibid., p. 64). Evidently, Hayek was troubled by this question of the essential metatheoretical demands of doing subjectivist human science. From the above perspectives, it was apparent to him that, as analysts, we are required to attribute to the minds of other agents our own cognitive capacities, characteristics and experiences. This poses potential difficulties, for it implies that 'we can understand less and less as we turn to beings more and more different from ourselves'. What must be meant when we claim to know about another's mind 'is that we can connect what we observe because the things we observe fit into the way of our own thinking'. Ultimately, it 'follows that it is not only impossible to recognize, but meaningless to speak of, a mind different from our own ... [and] where this possibility of interpreting in terms of analogies from our own mind ceases, ... we can no longer "understand"' (p. 66).

Hayek satisfied himself that this potential difficulty could be avoided by taking two crucial steps. First, by emphasizing that human sciences such as economics do not intend to explain *individual agents'* actions in their unique form, he was able to hive off this more clinically oriented problem onto psychology as, per se, a special and separate discipline. Secondly, and consequently, he was left to make the problematical claim that in the human sciences 'what we do is merely to classify types of individual behavior which we can understand, to develop their classification – in short, to provide an orderly arrangement of the material which we have to use in our further task' (ibid., p. 67). Looked at specifically, his envisaged strategy was that 'we can derive from the knowledge of our own mind in an "a priori" or "deductive" or "analytic" fashion, an (at least in principle) *exhaustive* classification of all the possible forms of intelligible behavior' (pp. 67f, original emphasis). In spite of the difficulties inherent in the consequent typological mode of inquiry and formal representation in relation to human actions and phenomena, Hayek proceeded to espouse it as a uniquely valid approach.

Hayek's belief was that we can make use of typical concepts as elementary parts of a larger formal construction: 'we use the different kinds of individual behavior thus classified as elements from which we construct hypothetical models in an attempt to reproduce the patterns of social relationships which we know in the world around us' (ibid., p. 68). He called the results of this approach 'compositive' theory (p. 73). In this move towards situating typical individuals and their actions into collectives, he raised the issue of why we cannot simply observe the quantitative phenomena that result and devise our analytical representations by direct induction. That is, 'should we not ... derive all our knowledge by observing and experiencing, instead of by "constructing models" from the elements found in our own thought?' (p. 69). He responded in the negative, for the reason that in the human realm the 'facts' themselves have to be constituted at both the individual agent and the collective level. When we study conceptually the manifestations of collective actions such as 'states or governments, battles or commercial activities ... we always refer to a scheme which connects individual activities by intelligible relations; that is, we use a theory which tells us what is and what is not part of our subject' (p. 71). Hayek concluded, therefore, that from a subjectivist perspective 'this is all the theories of the social sciences aim to do. They are not *about* the social wholes as wholes; they do not pretend to discover by empirical observation laws of behavior or change of these wholes'. Rather, he went on, 'their task is ... to *constitute* these wholes, to provide schemes of structural relationships which the historian [and the human scientist generally] can use when he has to attempt to fit together into a meaningful whole the elements which he actually finds' (p. 72, original emphasis).

In the later context of his theoretical analysis of agent psychology in *The Sensory Order*, Hayek again took the opportunity to make some critical comment on the problem of 'scientism' in human inquiry. He recognized that realist scientific investigations in general must confront the challenge of giving due recognition to the assumed 'existence of an objective world (or better, of an objective order of the events which we experience in their phenomenal order) towards the recognition of which the phenomenal order is merely a first approximation'. It is then the objective of realism in science 'to try and approach ever more closely towards a reproduction of this objective order' (Hayek, 1952, p. 173). And he went on to add that, as a practical matter, 'we shall never be able to bridge the gap between physical and mental phenomena; and for practical purposes, including in this the procedure appropriate to the different sciences, we shall permanently have to contend with a dualistic view of the world' (ibid., p. 179). At this point, Hayek made his realist inclinations plain, for 'by destroying the conception of elementary and constant sensations as ultimate constituents of the world', this methodological position 'restores the necessity of a belief in an objective physical world which is different from that presented to us by our senses' (p. 176).[2] It was here, then, that Hayek's confrontation with the problematic of contending with object complexity emerged.

We have seen in the first section of Chapter 6 that Hayek treated the mind as ultimately a physically constructed entity in which physical processes generate what we perceive as phenomenal events. But in any endeavour to understand these mental processes, and the phenomenal reproduction of real world events, as these are undertaken by other subjective agents, human scientists must reckon with an ever-present epistemological barrier of sheer complexity that precludes physicalist explanations. So it is that 'not only [the] mind as a whole but also all individual mental processes must forever remain phenomena of a special kind which, although produced by the same principles which we know to operate in the physical world, we shall never be able to explain in terms of physical laws' (ibid., p. 191). This outcome is, Hayek believed, a consequence of cognitive limitations of analysts' minds. So, as human scientists grappling with human as distinct from physical phenomena, 'we shall have permanently to be content with a practical dualism, a dualism based *not on any assertion of an objective difference between the two classes of events, but on the demonstrable limitations of the powers of our own mind fully to comprehend the unitary order to which they belong*' (p. 191, emphasis added). For this reason, he continued, 'we shall never achieve a complete "unification" of all science in the sense that all phenomena of which it treats can be described in physical terms' (p. 191).

In the present context, then, Hayek saw the practical differences between the two realms of reality as existential and deep-seated, thereby rendering human scientific inquiry as at least de facto methodologically distinct from its physical counterpart. The barrier to physicalist explanations in the human realm did not preclude explanations altogether. Rather, it made them rely on methodologically different arguments and led to epistemologically different knowledge outcomes. In short, 'the type of explanations at which we aim in the physical sciences is not applicable to mental events' (ibid., p. 192). The nature of the distinction was further explained by noting that 'in the study of human action ... our starting point will always have to be our direct knowledge of the different kinds of mental events, which to us must remain irreducible entities' and 'in discussing mental processes we will never be able to dispense with the use of mental terms' (p. 191). This fact of life for human scientists 'means, in particular, that the devices developed by the natural sciences for the special purpose of replacing the description of the world in sensory or phenomenal terms by one in physical terms lose their *raison d'être* in the study of intelligible human action' (p. 193). And, of especial relevance to representations of economic phenomena, he observed that 'this applies particularly to the endeavour to replace all qualitative statements by quantitative expressions, or by descriptions which run exclusively in terms of explicit relations' (p. 193). The challenge thus posed was to specify the precise meaning for the 'doing' of human science of this de facto distinction.

In all this, there are indications that the idea of degrees of complexity afflicting different fields of inquiry was beginning to intrude. This was a distinction that could be ascribed to a continuity of physicalist qualities rather than to any shift in quality at the border between physical and human science. Such a view meant that, ontologically, mental phenomena are interpreted to be ultimately of the same quality as those of the physical world. From this essentialist perspective, the challenge of accounting for the complexities of the weather and tidal patterns is qualitatively identical to that of accounting for human action, for they are all the manifestations of some particular arrangement of a purely physical environment. Such a notion was soon to resurface as the basis for Hayek's retreat from the full methodological import of subjectivism in the human sciences.

8.3 COMPLEXITY CONTRA SUBJECTIVISM

Hayek returned to the specific problem of explanations and their legitimation in the human sciences in his 'Degrees of explanation' from 1955 (Hayek, 1967, pp. 3ff) and in his 'The theory of complex phenomena' from 1961 (ibid., pp. 22ff). He commented in a note introducing the former that the two papers 'are closely connected, so closely indeed that they might be regarded as treatments of the same subject at an interval of about eight years' (p. 3, n). What follows here and further below will, therefore, treat them as a single and continuous exposition of what amounts to a plea for the recognition of a science as methodologically 'soft', perhaps 'inexact', where the ontology of the objects in terms of their extensive and/or intensive complexity requires it. His premise about methodology in writing these papers remained just as it had been earlier: 'some of the characteristic procedures of physics', the generally accepted epitome of a 'hard' and 'exact' science, 'may not be of universal applicability, and ... the procedure of some of the other sciences, "natural" or "social", may differ from that of physics ... because the *situation in their fields* differs in significant respects from that of physics' (p. 3, emphasis added). The specific rationale for this apparently ontologically oriented premise was cited as the capacity of the analyst in physics to delimit the 'number of significantly connected variables of different kinds' so that it is 'as if they formed a closed system for which we can observe and control all the determining factors' (pp. 3f). The result is the 'widely accepted interpretation of theoretical science as a "hypothetico-deductive" system ... [in] which the essence of *all* scientific procedure consists in the discovery of *new* statements ("natural laws" or "hypotheses") from which testable predictions can be derived' (p. 4, original emphasis).

Recognition of this claimed capacity of physical scientists still meant for Hayek that 'it would certainly be paradoxical to try to force methods made possible by these special conditions on disciplines regarded as distinct because in their field these conditions do not prevail' (ibid., p. 4). Moreover, such a methodological presumption 'may become a serious bar to the penetration of our understanding into fields where certainly at present, and perhaps forever, a different procedure may be our only effective means of obtaining guidance in the complex world in which we live' (p. 4. As we have seen above, on the terms of his own explicit understanding expressed elsewhere, subjectivist human science was, of course, the most obvious of these distinct fields and one to which the 'forever' extension just alluded to applies. However, he had now become reluctant to make too much of the human subjectivist dimension. His focus was instead on the notions of *relative* ontological complexity and consequent *degrees* of methodological difference between the fields of science. As we are to see, the differences involved were primarily of a quantitative kind, and his original emphasis on the qualitatively distinct ontology of human phenomena was to lapse.

One popular proposition concerning this shift of methodological perspective by Hayek is that his contact with Karl Popper had much to do with his emerging inclination to cast the human sciences as members of a common body of sciences. For Popper, any science is composed of a body of conjectural knowledge that satisfies the *universal* sequential demarcation criteria of falsifiability and refutability. These criteria were to be applied independently of any concern with the origins, human or otherwise, of the object under investigation. Having accepted this vision of what constitutes science in general, it is reasonable to suggest that this inclined Hayek to adapt his metatheoretical ideas to allow that the human sciences are distinctive only because they deal with the most complex of all phenomena. This having been said, the argument of such sciences must then be required to meet the same test of acceptability as applies in any other science. My inquiries will show that, in Hayek's intellectual evolution, there did emerge a gap between the analysis of the nature and role of subjectivism in generating the phenomena of the human sciences and the full recognition of the resulting ontological character of those phenomena in the methodology he advocated for the human sciences. But the extent to which this shift of metatheoretical orientation away from the demands of subjectivism can be attributed to the influence of Popper must remain unexplored in the present context.[3]

It is Hayek's definition of the degree of pattern complexity that becomes highly indicative here. For his purposes, he claimed, the degree can be expressed as 'the minimum number of elements of which an instance of the pattern must consist in order to exhibit all the characteristic attributes of the class of patterns in question' (ibid., p. 25). He went on to extend this to encompass some ontological considerations, but only as these affect the *quantitative* criterion. His belief was that, from the perspective of 'the minimum number of distinct variables a formula or model must possess in order to reproduce the characteristic patterns of structures of different fields (or to exhibit the general laws which these structures obey), the increasing complexity as we proceed from the inanimate to the ... animate and social phenomena becomes fairly obvious' (p. 26). The problematic confronted by 'theoretical explanations of the phenomena of the mind and society' was now one where 'individual events regularly depend on so many concrete circumstances that we shall never in fact be in a position to ascertain them all', with the consequent scientific limitation being that 'not only the ideal of prediction and control must largely remain beyond our reach, but also the hope remain illusory that we can discover by observation regular connections between the individual events' (p. 34).

The key notion of the 'degree of complexity' could, then, be attributed to any class of phenomena by virtue of the number of variables of which it is comprised and the number of variables that are thought to be pertinent in determining its identifiable form (ibid., pp. 8f). It is to be realized, Hayek explained, that, as the degree of phenomenal complexity increases in this sense, the capacity of analysts to deal with unique events in detail decreases. Under these circumstances, explanations and predictions could not 'refer to an individual event but always to phenomena of a certain kind or class; they will always state only some and never all the properties of any particular phenomenon to which they refer'. And, he continued, 'each property stated will be expressed not as a unique value or magnitude but as a range, however narrow, within which the property will fall' (p. 9; cf. p. 15). What is more, the increasing complexity of phenomena, in the human sciences especially, means giving up the notion that universally valid causal laws are the only legitimate foundation for scientific argument. Indeed, as he argued the point, 'the prejudice that in order to be scientific one must produce laws may yet prove to be one of the most harmful of methodological conceptions'. For, although the simplicity of argument demanded by formulating universally applicable laws may have its place, his view remained that 'there will always be fields where it can be shown that all such simple statements must be false and where in consequence also the prejudice in favour of "laws" must be harmful' (p. 42).

Hayek's position on this was that 'the description of scientific theories as "nomological" ... is appropriate only to those two-variable or perhaps three-variable problems to which the theory of simple phenomena can be reduced, but not to the theory of phenomena which appear only above a certain level of complexity' (ibid., p. 41). More expressly argued, 'we may well have achieved a very elaborate and quite useful theory about some kind of complex phenomenon and yet have to admit that we do not know of a single law ... which this kind of phenomenon obeys'. His opinion was explicitly that, 'though we possess theories of social structures, I rather doubt whether we know of any "laws" which social phenomena obey'. This means that 'the search for the discovery of laws is not an appropriate hall-mark of scientific procedure but merely a characteristic of the theories of simple phenomena' and that, where complex phenomena are concerned, 'the term "law" as well as the concepts of cause and effect are not applicable without such modification as to deprive them of their ordinary meaning' (p. 42).

The 'model building' method to which Hayek referred (ibid., pp. 14f) as consistent with these limitations involves first of all the specification of particular problems, for 'until we have definite questions to ask we cannot employ our intellect; and questions presuppose that we have formed some provisional hypothesis or theory about the events' (p. 22). In this respect, 'questions will arise at first only after our senses have discerned some recurring pattern or order in the events' (p. 23). Then it is appropriate to inquire 'to what extent our existing knowledge of the forces at work, or of the properties of some of the elements of the complex, may account for what we observe. We endeavour to find out whether this may be derived by deduction from what we know about the behaviour under simpler conditions of some of the factors involved' (p. 10). Here analysts are not required to '*invent* new hypotheses or constructs but merely to *select* them from what we know already about some of the elements of the phenomena' so that 'the observed facts thus come to "make sense" and to "fall into their places"' (p. 11, original emphasis). As far as predictions are concerned, although 'such theory does not tell us precisely what to expect, it will still make the world around us a more familiar world in which we can move with greater confidence that we shall not be disappointed because we can at least exclude certain eventualities' (p. 18). More than this, according to Hayek, we will be able to focus on 'the recurrence of abstract patterns', where 'the prediction that a pattern of a certain kind will appear in defined circumstances is a falsifiable (and therefore empirical) statement. Knowledge of the conditions in which a pattern of a certain kind will appear, and of what depends on its preservation, may be of great practical importance' (p. 28; cf. p. 40). This analytical result flows from the idea that, as active agents, 'even if we cannot control the external circumstances at all, we may adapt our actions to them. And sometimes, though we may not be able to bring about the particular results we would like, knowledge of the principle of the thing will enable us to make circumstances more favourable to the kinds of events we desire' (p. 19; cf. p. 36).[4]

Epistemologically assessed, such 'soft' theoretical endeavours as espoused in the above passages, as well as being conjectural, must rely upon convention for their continuing legitimation. Hayek saw it as a disadvantage for any science that insecure explanations in principle, dictated by the complexity of its object phenomena, were the limit of its capacity to provide understanding. This means especially that 'because such theories are difficult to disprove, the elimination of inferior rival theories will be a slow affair, bound up closely with the argumentative skill and persuasiveness of those who employ them. There can be no crucial experiments which decide between them' (ibid., p. 19). Moreover, as he reminded himself, albeit somewhat incongruously in the present context, there are sound *ontological* reasons to expect that some sciences will be bound permanently by these limitations. Thus it is 'especially where we have to deal with the extreme complexity of human affairs, the hope of ever achieving specific predictions of particulars seems vain', for it is '*the nature of the subject* [that] puts forever beyond our reach the sort of explanation of detail which would enable us to make specific predictions' (p. 20, emphasis added). Hayek rejected the notion that, as far as concerns human affairs, the analyst's mind can ever 'be equipped to deal with the full details of phenomena of any conceivable degree of complexity', a notion that 'certainly ceases to be true when we have to deal with some of the activities of man himself' (p. 21): that is, when we are doing human science in general, and economics in particular.

In the end, as a reflection of his lingering methodological ambivalence, Hayek concluded that the 'advance of science will ... have to proceed in two different directions' in order to make due allowance for the varying ontological exigencies of the object phenomena that will be met. So, 'while it is certainly desirable to make our theories as falsifiable as possible, we must also push forward into fields where, as we advance, the degree of falsifiability necessarily decreases'. Most especially, then, in the case of the human sciences such as economics, 'this is the price we have to pay for an advance into the field of complex phenomena' (ibid., p. 29). His emphasis elsewhere on the subjectivist origins of human phenomena confirms and makes the justification for this conclusion even more abundantly clear.[5]

NOTES

1. This reading should be compared with that of both Lawson (1994d) and Fleetwood (1995), who are intent upon identifying a period when Hayek can be understood as believing in an extreme 'hermeneutical foundationalism' in which interpretations and conceptual forms are all that exist for agents in representing their external world to themselves. All that agents 'know' about their world, and all that it comprises for them as a consequence, is effectively concept-*determined*. However, it is apparent from my findings that evidence exists to suggest that very early in his researches Hayek had formed a vision of agents contending with an existentially independent and intransitive world of reality. What should be appreciated when reading the ostensibly contrary evidence of Lawson and Fleetwood is that this vision in no way precludes the conduct of agents as having resulted from the interpretation *and influence* of the external structures and relationships they accept as relevant. For Hayek, agents must be depicted as necessarily having a concept-*dependent* vision of their external world. In forming this vision, they may well fail to represent the given reality completely or correctly because they rely on the mediation of an ultimately subjectivist mind. The result is that agents potentially exhibit a contingent remainder in their individual conduct that cannot be reliably or fully tied back to their situational conditions. This is not because they have a purely relativist vision, but because their interpretations and reasoning are fallible.
2. This reinforces what I have argued in note 1 above about Hayek's early recognition of an intransitive external real world that agents must confront and can only grasp by means of concepts. There is no question here of his believing that the world of agents is exclusively concept-determined.
3. There can be no doubt that Hayek knew of Popper's philosophy of science very early in his career (see Hayek, 1949, p. 33, n1; 1982, p. 323; 1994, pp. 49ff), even though his more specific, albeit always cryptic, references to its influence on him did not come until many years later (see Hayek, 1967, pp. viii, 4, n2, 4ff). Because of the ambiguity in these citations of Popper, the question of *when* Popper's influence on Hayek was first felt remains an open one. But it must be added by way of pointing to some direction of closure that some interpreters have found that there is much in Hayek's writings on the metatheory of the human sciences during the 1930s to 1950s that implicitly denies any Popperian connection (for example, Caldwell, 1992a, *passim*). I think that this has been made all too apparent in this and my previous chapters, where I have provided much exegetical evidence of the highly subjectivist ontology of human phenomena that Hayek tried to maintain in his early metatheoretical research. And, given the cryptic nature of the extant references to his connections with Popper, it is not surprising that a confusing situation concerning Hayek's Popperian status has been the result. The subject of their relationship has thus been given very different readings by scholars, with the main contenders in the resulting stoush being Hutchison (1981, pp. 214ff, 1992, 1994, pp. 216ff) and Caldwell (1992a, 1992b). Moreover, an additional complicating factor is that, even today, there is by no means any agreement on what actually constituted Popper's implied metatheory for economics or for the human sciences generally (see, for example, Hands, 1985, 1992; Blaug, 1985; de Marchi, 1988; Caldwell, 1991a). It is, therefore, doubtful if Hayek could have properly grasped the real significance of Popper's message as it applies to economics, whatever the extent of their contact.
4. Karl-Heinz Paqué (1990) critically examines the theoretical and empirical relevance of the methodology of 'patterns' and 'pattern predictions' that was suggested by Hayek as a

means of dealing with representations and prognoses in economics. His most general conclusion is that this methodology has nothing to offer economics as an alternative to its entrenched pseudo-physical scientism because it cannot be applied without ambiguity. In Paqué's own words, 'we must conclude that there is no such thing as pattern prediction, at least as long as we do not void the term "prediction" of any empirical meaning'. The reason is that, if 'we define a pattern as parametric, the pattern prediction boils down to an ordinary prediction', whereas if 'we define a pattern as nonparametric, the pattern prediction is not falsifiable, simply because it is not a genuine prediction at all but rather a particular way of describing and interpreting reality' (ibid., p. 292). This is a telling criticism and serves to emphasize the ambiguity of the links that Hayek provided between his subjectivist vision of agents' actions and the methodological demands of representing and accounting for their results with ontological integrity.

5. The extent to which Hayek should be designated a subjectivist with respect to his methodological conclusions has recently been debated in terms of the contrast between modernism and post-modernism. Burczak (1994a) establishes that one of the key characteristics of Hayek's subjectivism is the consequent implicit rejection of modernist claims to an objective, empiricist and rationalist economics, with its aims of accurate quantitative predictions. According to Burczak's reading, Hayek's emphasis on market processes and spontaneous order, based upon widespread subjectively held and differentiated agents' knowledge, renders his thought post-modern. In particular, Hayek's subjectivism is said to lead to a 'non-reductionist, non-essentialist methodological individualism' (ibid., p. 37) in which the theory of human agency is necessarily hermeneutic. Caldwell's (1994a) response seeks to de-emphasize the hermeneutic inclinations of Hayek's thought by pointing, first of all, to his later arguments that economics is a science of complex phenomena that does not ultimately differ from physical science in its methodology. Secondly, Caldwell reminds us of the objectivist, physiologically grounded individual psychology in the *Sensory Order* (Hayek, 1952) that Hayek might well have believed provided scientific foundations for his subjectivist vision of human agency. For Caldwell, there is a sense in which 'Hayek was thoroughly committed to the scientific world view' (Caldwell, 1994a, p. 309). In his reply to Caldwell's account, Burczak (1994b) agrees that 'Hayek was committed to a "scientific" subjectivism rather than to a "hermeneutic" subjectivism' (p. 315). However, in Burczak's view, there remains a tension in Hayek's ideas between this commitment and the need to understand the actual actions of human agents as the origin of the complex phenomena of the human sciences. In the latter endeavour, Burczak finds Hayek sustaining a post-modernist rejection of objective theory on the basis of the need to understand actions as responses to subjective beliefs, meanings and interpretations. For this reason, Burczak has him recognizing in true hermeneutical fashion that 'our knowledge of society is theory- and rhetoric-laden "all the way down"' (1994b, p. 316). In the exegetical evidence that I elicit on these matters, Hayek's metatheory for economics has all of the characteristics cited by these two scholars. The sense of this inconclusive debate may perhaps be best summed up by 'it all depends on where one looks' in the mass of Hayek's writings.

9. The 'radical' subjectivism of Lachmann

9.1 INTRODUCTION

In his obituary tribute to Ludwig Lachmann, Stephan Böhm reminds us that, although born and educated a German, 'with the possible exception of Ludwig von Mises, there is arguably no other economist who during the 1940s and 1950s thought of himself so self-consciously as an Austrian' (1991, p. 366). But he also draws our attention to another important characteristic of Lachmann's work: once the neoAustrian revival was under way, it became increasingly apparent that 'Lachmann's iconoclasm did not fit well with more moderate versions of Austrianism' (ibid., p. 367). And as Böhm's following pages go on to explain, the root of this iconoclasm was Lachmann's unswerving dedication to a 'radical' version of subjectivism and to exposing fully its ramifications for understanding economic phenomena. His subjectivist heterodoxy extended to a relentless critique of formalist methodology in economics and to its replacement by the modelling of market processes as kaleidic and continuous in form and indeterminate in outcome. For many neoAustrians, the prospect of a Lachmann-induced nihilism, ill-founded though belief in such a prospect may have been, was too much to contemplate (cf. Prychitko, 1994a, pp. 304f).[1]

The result has been that, in the 1970s revival and beyond, the most profound of Lachmann's metatheoretical insights have had a rather narrow and restrained influence. It has been the contributions of Mises and Hayek, instead, that have had most impact, in spite of what Lachmann saw as their failure, 'when around 1930 ... expectations made their appearance in the economic thought of the Anglo-Saxon world', to 'grasp with both hands this golden opportunity to enlarge the basis of their [subjectivist] approach' (Lachmann, 1976a, p. 58). This division within the world of Austrian subjectivism has been most notable in the contrasting analyses Lachmann and Israel Kirzner offer to account for market processes and outcomes (Vaughn, 1992, 1994, ch. 7). While Lachmann was trying to get beyond the limitations of the equilibrium paradigm, Kirzner has been intent upon identifying what remains of it in practice and attempting to provide an account of that remainder in terms of human action (see Böhm, 1992). The balance of their respective successes and failures cannot be explored here. But it might be said that

Lachmann left much to be done in meeting Kirzner's very real challenge through the aphorism that 'Paris does get fed', for 'when we look around at modern society, we can only be amazed at the extraordinarily intricate degree of division of labour and co-ordination characterizing it'. That is, for subjectivist economists, 'the question always has to be, how do we account for the extraordinary degree of co-ordination which has historically been observed in market society?' (ibid., pp. 103, 107). At the same time, though, it is apparent that Kirzner's own proffered answers have side-stepped the most crucial and intractable facets of subjectivism that Lachmann chose to emphasize: the role of uncertainty and the incorrigible need to act on the basis of expectations alone (Vaughn, 1994, pp. 145ff).

Lachmann came to the London School of Economics in the early 1930s, and there he was directly exposed to the cycle theories of Hayek. It was evidently the Austrian Paul Rosenstein-Roden who drew Lachmann's attention to the gap in Hayek's formalistic dynamic theories where subjective expectations should be.[2] And this was reinforced by his reading in Keynes's *General Theory* in 1936 that what matters most in understanding investment is the influence of expectations (Mittermaier, 1992, p. 10). So, from the mid-1930s onwards, it became Lachmann's lifetime crusade to rid economics of the false formalism that had been legitimated by a failure fully to recognize the implications of subjectivist economic agency.[3]

My intention in this chapter and the next is critically to examine the nature and extent of the subjectivism that underpinned Lachmann's vision of economics. The exposition is not intended to comprise an exposition of Lachmann's many and varied substantive contributions to economics as such, for this would require a much more extended study than is possible here. Also, as I am not concerned with the development of his thought, my critical analysis will treat his contributions more or less as one piece. To an extent, this is justified by my reading that, over the years, his subjectivist ideas in particular underwent little change. If anything, they simply became more definite. It will be my conclusion that the ostracism of the metatheoretical aspects of his thought by some neoAustrians has been a serious error of judgement, one that amounts to a denial of the subjectivist empirical realities of the capitalist economic system that theory should be accounting for. However, it will also become evident to just how limited an extent even Lachmann was prepared to confront and grasp the complete significance of subjectivist ontology in economics and to allow it free rein in influencing the redesign of its metatheoretical principles. His legacy for the neoAustrians is a version of subjectivism with increased scope that goes beyond the foundations provided by the earlier generations of Austrians. But it is still a legacy that left gaps to be filled and its often claimed 'radical' status needs to be treated with some caution.

Lachmann was an Austrian subjectivist in the sense that he picked up and ran with this vision of economics from very early in his research career. His economic inquiries generally, and those concerning its metatheoretical foundations in particular, always began from the extant literature of the Austrians from Menger onwards. But he was no hagiographer, and the Austrian luminaries all felt the point of his critical pen to one degree or another. He admired the general thrust of their contributions, but only to the extent that they sustained the subjectivist vision and its entailed demand that economics should eschew formalism. Any hint of a retreat to deterministic argument, metatheoretical or substantive, was set upon and shown to be inconsistent with the tenets of subjectivism. Mises and Hayek had both been critics of neoclassical formalism, most especially where it claimed to represent an understanding of exchange and markets. Lachmann joined them in this critique, but probed further than they had done into the subjectivist rationale for it. He made some endeavour, too, to provide an alternative subjectivist analysis of markets comprising open-ended processes that are the manifestations of collective human actions. In this effort, his contributions must be judged as of limited success beyond showing convincingly that there exists a case for pursuing such a non-equilibrium alternative on subjectivist grounds.

9.2 CONSIDERING THE AUSTRIAN ROOTS OF SUBJECTIVIST HETERODOXY

Over the years, Lachmann wrote a number of papers in which he investigated the distinctive nature of Austrian economics when compared to the orthodoxy that had grown out of the limited subjectivism of the 'marginalist revolution' of the 1870s. For the present purpose, three distinguishing aspects of the Austrians' perspective that he found of particular significance are pertinent. First, their emphasis was on the origin of all economic phenomena in individual human action as the essence of subjectivism. The antecedent classical economists had pursued an intellectual tradition of naturalism, objectivism, quantitative dominance and scientistic emulation of physical science methodology (Lachmann, 1977, pp. 49ff). Such metatheoretical predilections led them to model human agents as the homogeneous *homo oeconomicus*. This was a narrow and confining perspective, allowing only that 'as in nature, people *react* to the current external conditions of their economic existence: they *do not act*' (ibid., p. 51, original emphasis). By contrast, in Austrian economics, 'man *as an actor* stands at the center of economic events' (p. 51, original emphasis). This means that, although 'manifold quantitative economic relationships are also for the Austrian school in the first place the cognitive object of economic inquiry', these are not in themselves 'the ultimate objective'. What follows is the need for a deeper inquiry, 'for these relationships flow from acts of mind that have to be "understood", that is, their origin, their significance and their effects must be explained within the framework of our "common experience" of human action' (p. 51). The implication of subjective individualism here was reinforced by going on to make the point that, for Austrians, 'men are viewed as *highly unequal*', with each one having 'different needs and abilities', so that 'each economic agent through his action imprints his individuality on economic events' (pp. 51f, original emphasis).

One fundamental contrast with the Classicals was the shift of vision that interprets value as a substance embodied in commodities as a consequence of production to the notion of its being subjective and related to agents' perceptions of the valued commodity. That is, in the theory of value, 'the central concept of Viennese theory is *evaluation*, an act of mind. The value of a good now consists in a relationship to an appraising mind' (ibid., p. 52, original emphasis). But the demands of subjectivism went well beyond shifting the perception of value, and it was one of Lachmann's most often reiterated concerns that the Austrians had not taken the required extensions of the vision far enough. Mises, for example, he thought had not pursued with sufficient conviction the potential of subjectivism to reach into a more complete understanding of human agency, especially with respect to the problem of action under uncertainty. Mises had recognized the essentials of uncertainty and a kaleidic world: indeed, Lachmann at one stage read him as sharing with George Shackle certain common subjectivist principles. These were an 'emphasis on the spontaneous, and thus unpredictable nature of human action' and a 'rejection of mechanistic notions of time and probability', along with their agreement that 'a science of human action requires a methodology *sui generis*' (Lachmann, 1976a, p. 58). But as the advocate of praxeology and as a rationalist at the level of the essentials of human action, Mises had only allowed the intrusion of such subjectivism of time, uncertainty and expectations at the empirical level of analysis (Lachmann, 1982a, p. 37). For Lachmann, the import of what he called 'radical' subjectivism went far deeper, for it is 'a subjectivism of active minds. The mental activity of ordering and formulating ends, allocating means to them, making and revising plans, determining when action has been successful, all these are its forms of expression' (ibid., p. 37). By contrast, Mises was concerned only with the fact that agents choose different ends, and having done so are able to pursue them by rational action responses. This defied the true subjectivist problematic of understanding agents as choosing ends and applying means to their circumstances.

Beyond these principles, though, Lachmann's subjectivism retained a much greater emphasis on the nature of agents and the contingency of their involvement in generating the processes and outcomes of a market economy than could be found in much of the extant and emerging Austrian literature. First of all, it was the extension of subjectivism to encompass agents' expectations to which Lachmann drew attention. The Austrians had failed to take up this dimension of human agency with any seriousness of purpose; instead they 'treated the subject rather gingerly' even though it surfaced from time to time in their work (Lachmann, 1976a, p. 58). Secondly, the notion that agents must act in the absence of knowledge rather than just with incomplete knowledge was a radical step forward in subjectivist understanding. For agents, expectations are a substitute for knowledge. As such, they cannot be fitted into the Austrian idea of the market as comprising a knowledge distribution process (ibid., p. 59). It was a simple fact of human existence that 'all economic action is ... concerned with the future, the more or less distant future', and that 'the future is to all of us unknowable, though not unimaginable' (p. 55). That the origin of expectations must lie in the individual interpretation and imagination means that, by their very nature, they must diverge between agents in a way that makes it difficult to propose any forces that can bring about their convergence (p. 59; cf. Rizzo, 1992a, p. 125).

The second fundamental distinguishing characteristic of the Austrians was their emphasis on the essential status of time in subjectively rooted economic processes. This distanced them from the burgeoning models of static equilibrium in which time and process had no explicit role and the focus was only on contrived outcomes. The Austrians' treatment of the market as a process constituted from the collective actions of human agents followed from this rejection of such timeless models. But here Lachmann was concerned, too, to reject any implication that such a process could comprise any *necessary* tendency towards equilibrium. By contrast with their contemporaries who developed the 'Lausanne school' of general equilibrium, the Austrians treated their common grounding in subjective value theory quite differently from a methodological perspective. Lachmann's challenge was to reveal 'those characteristics of the Austrian style of thought to which formalistic analysis cannot do justice' (Lachmann, 1977, p. 53). One crucial consequence of the formalistic predilections of the Lausanne group was the need to avoid the explication of human action set in real time. It was argued by Lachmann that 'it is certainly not overstating the case if we say that the real disagreement concerns, in the first place, the significance attributed to the element of time'. While the Lausanne vision was confined to a 'framework of timeless statics', the Austrian vision '*requires time for its full meaning*'. And 'this is not just a matter of the level of abstraction; it is much more than that', for 'the Lausanne theory of equilibrium not only does not require time; it requires time's exclusion' (ibid., p. 54, emphasis added).

The Austrians' focus on time was essential because 'all human action is only possible in time' and it is human action that is the origin of the processes that they view as the main objects of economic inquiry. Thus it is market transactions, 'undertaken in the course of time, that are their real objects of interest, since conscious human action is bound to plans, and all plans require a time dimension' (ibid., p. 54). In their vision of the economic world, when 'one takes one's orientation from reality', 'economic plans depend on the economic calculations of each agent. The interplay of economic plans accounts for the market phenomena'. A world of explicit time is one of continuing changes, so there is a 'continual need ... to adapt economic plans to these changes' and, in such a world, 'a general condition of equilibrium cannot be achieved' (p. 55). By contrast, the formalistic functions that represent agents' behaviour in building up a general equilibrium outcome are simply matters of logic. In the timeless static world, 'man as economic agent does not stand at the center of economic life' because, every day, 'human acts shape the real world anew'. In the case of plans, it must be assumed that 'all conceivable plans are already "given" from the start!' and to use them thus 'as "data" one must first divest them of their nature as mental acts' (p. 56).

A third characteristic that distinguished the Austrians was their recognition that, because of the human subjectivist origins of its phenomena, economics demands a methodology *sui generis* and distinct from that which had come to dominate science generally. It is this human origin of phenomena to which economists can turn when pursuing methodology, for it enables them to elicit 'inside' understandings of the decisions and actions involved. Because they are agents themselves, they can gain interpretive insight into the origin and logic of plans devised by agents when making choices and taking decisions about actions. In Lachmann's view, 'the approach is justified by the fact that all human action, at least insofar as it is of scientific interest, is oriented to plans. Plans are logical constructs immanent to the course of action. A plan serves the economic agent as a guideline; he orients himself to it. The social sciences can thus use plans as a means of interpretation' (ibid., p. 58). Further, 'the economic plan of an individual ... [is] the prototype of the scheme of thought lying at the base of action' (p. 62).[4]

What appealed to Lachmann especially in the Austrian approach was the metatheoretical primacy given to 'the methodological independence of the theoretical social sciences of the natural sciences by stressing the cardinal importance of *means* and *ends* as fundamental categories of human action' (ibid., p. 95, original emphasis). In this vision of independence, the Austrians' 'ideas and aims' were argued to be 'always directed not only toward the discovery of quantitative relationships among economic phenomena but also toward an *understanding* of the meaning of economic actions' (p. 46, original emphasis). It was his conviction, then, that such methodology 'which aims at discovering the *meaning* of things, apparently conflicts with most methods used in and suitable to the natural sciences' (p. 49, original emphasis). And it became the 'characteristic of the trend of thinking of the Austrian school' that '*Verstehen* (understanding) ... [was] introduced as a method into the theoretical social sciences' (p. 47). Lachmann's emphasis here was thus on the gradual development within Austrian writings from Menger onwards of '*understanding* as a *theoretical method*, that is, as a method for the interpretation of *typical courses of action with the aid of thought designs*, for example, economic plans'. For Austrians, 'the thought design, the economic calculation or economic plan of the individual, always stands in the foreground of theoretical interest' (p. 47, original emphasis).

In each of these three respects, the Austrians had set themselves apart metatheoretically from the mainstream in ways with which Lachmann had much empathy. As the argument to follow will show, however, their divergence from the established orthodoxy was not always to the extent that he judged to be appropriate. Nevertheless, these characteristics reappeared in his writings as the main frame of reference for his own extended and more 'radical' subjectivism.

9.3 THE HUMAN AGENT IN ECONOMIC ACTION

It was in his 1943 paper, 'The role of expectations in economics as a social science' (1977, pp. 65ff), that Lachmann presented in bold relief the main tenets of what would become the foundations of his subjectivist approach to economics. In it, he set the stage for his subsequent contributions to subjectivism generally and, from then on, the developments were largely elaborations of these seminal ideas. He was concerned to demonstrate with as much cogency as possible that the ontology of economic phenomena is constituted by their origin in the subjective actions of human agents. This meant rejecting the mechanistic depiction of agents as determinate automatons upon which the neoclassical 'pure logic of choice' depends. A subjective theory of economic action would be required to replace the image of agents as reacting deterministically with one in which the subjectivism of volitionally active minds and creative decisions and actions are emphasized by giving due attention to the role of uncertainty and expectations (ibid., pp. 69f). Such a subjectivism would then have to be made an integral element in accounts of economic phenomena (cf. Kirzner, 1992b, pp. 49f).

In Lachmann's vision of agents, deliberation and planning are the preliminaries to action. And, as 'a prerequisite to making a plan, we [as active agents] have to draw a mental picture of the situation in which we are going to act, and ... the formation of expectations is incidental to the drawing of this picture'. Inevitably, in such a subjective analysis, it will need to be realized that the 'picture of the situation will be drawn differently by different individuals confronted with the same observable events' (Lachmann, 1977, p. 72). This is because agents are both innately different and have had different biographical profiles of cumulative experience influencing their cognitive processing. Their interpretations of the past and present will be different. What is more, then, these interpretations must be made prior to forming the expectations that will be manifested in the drawing of the picture of the imagined future environment through which planned action is to be carried out, along with the potential scenarios of results that could follow from that action. Incorporating such expectations in economic analysis means, as Lachmann recognized, that 'economic action concerned with the future ... is often decided upon in a penumbra of doubt and uncertainty, vague hopes and inarticulate fears, in which ultimate decisions may well depend on mental alertness, ability to read the signs of a changing world, and readiness to face the unknown' (p. 65).

At the same time, such recognition demands that the expectations formed by agents in order to cope with these uncertainties and vagaries of their position be explained. Expectations cannot legitimately be treated as mere data, for their existence and composition are a reflection of the interpretations by means of which agents must operate in an economy undergoing perpetual change. So 'nothing will be achieved in the way of an inductive study of expectations until people's expectational responses to the facts of the situation are made *intelligible* to us, until we are able to understand *why* the acting and expecting individuals interpreted a set of facts in the way they actually did' (ibid., p. 68, original emphasis).

Two characteristics of human agency shape the plans made prior to action: first, 'all human action is directed towards purposes'; and secondly, 'all human activity is problem-solving' (ibid., p. 68). These mean that active agents are required to plan what they intend to do in accordance with the given internal and external means at their disposal to solve the problem consistently with their chosen ends. Thus the plan is 'a product of the mind, [and] *is* both the common denominator of all human action and its mental pattern', so that 'it is by reducing "action" to "plan" that we [as analysts] "understand" the actions of individuals' (p. 69, original emphasis). This reference being to analysts interpreting the interpretations of agents, Lachmann made due allowance for the necessity and practical viability of introspection and extrapolation: 'Plan is the *tertium comparationis* between our mind and the mind of the person who acts.' But in understanding human action in this way, analysts must realize that even a properly constituted and consistent individual plan can fail because it was built upon false expectations about aspects of the future upon which its success would have depended (p. 69). On this basis, Lachmann believed that expectations would remain for analysts a very real contributing factor to the indeterminate nature of capitalist economic processes. His metatheoretical reasoning here was, though, that 'we need not deplore unduly the indeterminateness of expectations, for it is *intelligibility* and not *determinateness* that social science should strive to achieve' (p. 68, original emphasis). In the case of human activity, 'to make an action intelligible means to show not only its purpose, but also the general design of the plan behind it'. But, in the real 'world of imperfect foresight in which no plan can meet all contingencies all human activity is bound to be indeterminate; in this respect expectations are simply on a par with everything else' (pp. 71f).[5]

As a matter of specific concern, the most important of all subjectivist theses for Lachmann was that of expectations and their implications for understanding human agency in economics. In his 1956 book, *Capital and its Structure* (1978c), he devoted Chapter II to working up his ideas on this aspect of agency (ibid., pp. 20ff). He began with the assertions that 'expectations reflect economic experience and are affected by changes in it' and that they 'always embody *problematical* experience, i.e. ... experience which requires *interpretation*' (p. 20, original emphasis). Thus 'it is the task of the theory of expectations to elucidate the problems our experience ... sets us in judging the uncertain future, as well as to clarify the *modus operandi*' (pp. 20f). In such a theory, that is, it is fundamental to recognize that, while 'experience is the raw material out of which expectations are formed', for agents 'not all material is equally useful, not all experience is equally relevant to a given situation'. There exists, therefore, a '*subjectivism of interpretation*' that enters 'the acts of mind by which we select those portions of our experience we allow to affect our judgement of the future' (p. 21, original emphasis).

But the next step in Lachmann's argument warrants critical scrutiny. He made the point that the subjectivism of interpretation in forming expectations 'yields provisional judgements to be confirmed by later experience, imperfect knowledge capable of being perfected' (ibid., p. 21). And, he went on, expectations 'reflect an attempt at cognition and orientation in an imperfectly known world, ... [they] embody imperfect knowledge to be tested and improved by later experience. ... [Thus] our present expectation, to be revised later on as experience accrues, is not only the basis of the action plan but also a source of more perfect future knowledge' (p. 23). Two puzzles are posed in these passages. First, in forming expectations there is a dimension of the agents' situation about which nothing can be known: 'knowledge' of the future is not just 'imperfect', it is non-existent and any claim to have it is but a figment of the agent's imagination. Secondly, as agents, we cannot learn from experience with the potential of definitude suggested here. Revision of plans will be induced by disappointed and changing expectations, but those new expectations are just as much founded on uncertainty as any previous ones. There can be no incremental approach to any perfect knowledge even of the past, for there is nothing static ultimately to know in this sense once time is allowed to make its continuous changes. And, because the future is always new in some respects, expectations errors will continue for ever new reasons.

Of all his antecedents and contemporaries, Lachmann made it apparent that it was George Shackle that he admired the most (cf. note 3) and that the main reason for this admiration was Shackle's preparedness to confront the chronically subjectivist problem of agent expectations. Throughout Lachmann's writings, the influence of his sometime English colleague can be detected. But the precise nature of this influence, especially as it involved the expectations problematic, can be read most directly from the one piece that Lachmann wrote in which Shackle was the focus of attention. In 1959, he devoted a review article to Shackle's De Vries Lectures, published as *Time in Economics* in 1958. In the article, entitled 'Professor Shackle on the economic significance of time' (1977, pp. 81ff), what appealed to Lachmann was Shackle's rendering of time as a complex exigency of economic theory and the emphasis that he gave to the kaleidic nature of the real world in which agents make decisions and act. Rather than being shown as responding mechanically and deterministically to given and static conditions, agents were shown by Shackle as having to act on the subjective basis of expectations in the face of uncertainty. He denied the possibility of treating time as just a homogenous situating continuum analogous to space. Agents located in time are not homogeneous and they all change with every inevitable and irrevocable shift *forward* in time. For each unique individual, time is experienced as a sequence of 'moments-in-being' (ibid., pp. 81ff). And, as Lachmann understood, although 'the human mind can … transcend the present moment in imagination and memory, … the moment-in-being remains nevertheless always *self-contained* and *solitary*' (p. 83, original emphasis). Each existential moment is also subjective and unique, so that it makes no sense to try to understand agency by comparing an agent's situation at different points in time: 'it is impossible to compare human actions undertaken at different moments in time. For no two moments can be "in being" together' because the existence of one precludes the existence of the other. Thus, 'in describing the phenomena of human action, time cannot be used as a co-ordinate because we lack an identifiable object which "passes through time". Man with his "feelings", preferences and the content of his consciousness changes in an unpredictable fashion' (p. 83).

Nevertheless, Lachmann was critical of this discontinuous vision of the agent's consciousness when it is set in time (ibid., pp. 84ff). There are some elements of discontinuity affecting the mental make-up of agents to be dealt with in understanding human agency, especially those associated with the dynamics of the imagination, with 'the creative power of the mind and our inability to predict its acts', and those that arise because agents cannot avoid 'interpreting experiences, acquiring knowledge, planning and revising plans' (p. 85). But his fear was that, 'if we were to take Professor Shackle's thesis literally, there could be no testing the success of plans, no plan revision, no comparison between *ex ante* and *ex post*. In fact planned action would make no sense whatever' (p. 84). It was concluded that 'Professor Shackle's strong emphasis on the subjective nature of economic action ... deserves every support' (p. 85), but that this support must be qualified by the need to recognize elements of *continuity* in the subjectivity of agents' minds which allow some meaning to be given to the intertemporal observations of patterns of human action. The consequent search was for some threads of continuity in the time flow of agents' experience so that plans can be made and revised by comparing outcomes with intentions. This was found first of all in the existence of means available to pursue ends as transportable through time. The view was that Shackle's thesis could apply 'to human ends, of which we are unable to postulate any continuous existence in time', but such discontinuity need not apply 'to our knowledge of the adequacy of means to ends' (p. 84). It was also found in the 'acts of mind' of agents, for the 'human mind is continuous' to a degree sufficient to make intertemporal comparisons of the bases of actions viable (pp. 84f). And, although it seems to have been denied by Shackle, there could also be a continuity of agents' preferences (p. 85).

A further theme to be given some attention by Lachmann when reflecting on Shackle's contributions was that of 'the relationship between knowledge and expectations' and the entailed matter of devising a theory of how expectations are formed (ibid., p. 90). The problematic to be confronted is that subjectivism in economics brings with it the need to realize that 'what men will do in a given situation depends largely on their interpretation of it and on the direction of their imagination' (p. 92). Lachmann's suggestion was to focus on the premise that 'all prognosis which is more than mere guesswork must be linked to the diagnosis of the existing situation' (p. 90). Practically relevant though this suggestion may be, it should be recognized as bringing to light more issues than it resolves about the real nature of the expectations formation predicament. A reading of Shackle should have discouraged any use at all of such notions as those again used by Lachmann in relating expectations to 'an imperfectly known world' and 'imperfect knowledge to be tested and improved by later experience' (p. 90). The simple facts of life are that expectations about the future are epistemologically of an irrevocably and incorrigibly different status from any knowledge of what currently exists or what did so in the past. In comparison, expectations have no 'knowledge' content at all that can be in any sense 'incomplete' or 'imperfect' or 'corrected'. These were Shackle's most fundamental messages, but they were defied by such mixed up conclusions as the following: 'Our present expectation, to be revised later on as experience accrues, is not only the basis of any plan of action we may contemplate but also *a source of more perfect future knowledge*' (p. 91, emphasis added). Expectations are so used and revised, but they can have nothing to do with perfecting 'knowledge' of the future or even knowledge in the future.

Some hint of recognition of these ambiguities was present in the qualification that the 'testing' of expectations has to be 'made in a world which not merely changes, but whose change is not governed by any known law' (ibid., p. 90). This means that expectations can never have any durability once time is permitted to elapse because, to the extent that expectations are based on accumulated knowledge, expectations must change with the inevitable change of knowledge over time (pp. 92f). In relation to business expectations, too, 'a good deal will depend on interpretation of experience, i.e. on creative acts of the mind, and that the knowledge yielded will be imperfect' (pp. 90f). Well may this be so, but the *imperfect* knowledge is still confined to that which has already been experienced. And it is true that knowledge dynamics are continuous in the sense that 'any experience made conveys knowledge to us only insofar as it fits, or fails to fit, into a pre-existent frame of knowledge' (p. 91). But at the same time it remains true, too, that 'the frame of knowledge in terms of which we interpret a new experience is always "private and subjective". Knowledge always belongs to an individual mind', so that from all perspectives, static and dynamic, 'expectations and the knowledge they reflect are always subjective' (p. 91).

Understanding human phenomena subjectively is complicated by the fact that 'all human action takes place within a context of "intersubjectivity"; our common everyday world ... in which the meanings we ascribe to our own acts and to those of others are typically not in doubt and taken for granted' (Lachmann, 1990a, p. 138). The challenge for analysts is to interpret and elucidate the meanings actually ascribed to actions and phenomena by the situated agents who generate them, where such 'interpretation of economic phenomena ... has to take place within a horizon of established meanings, with one such horizon for each society. Our phenomena observed have to be placed within an order constrained by this framework' (ibid., p. 139). In what was, in retrospect at least, a remarkable piece of insight, Lachmann had recognized these crucial facets of economic agency in his 1937 article, 'Uncertainty and liquidity preference'. His focus was directly on the origin of collectively generated phenomena as the products of *situated and conditioned* individual action. Such phenomena are 'made intelligible by reference to the similarity of the conditions under which different individuals have to act'. These conditions may be 'either of a subjective (psychological) or an objective (institutional) nature'. So it is, he reasoned at the time, that 'men may act identically, either because they are all subject to the same mass-psychological influences or because they all have to operate within the same institutional framework' (Lachmann, 1937, p. 296).

It is indeed unfortunate that Lachmann chose not to maintain his pursuit of these pregnant observations as the core of his later subjectivist metatheory. It was not to be the last thing he wrote about the situational containment of agents, but not much detailed development was to follow (cf. Mongiovi, 1994, pp. 264ff). At the same time, in the 1937 paper, Lachmann was exposed to an idea that he did carry forward. He was expressly concerned with the nature and implications of uncertainty for agents and their economic conduct, where uncertainty had the sense of an *absence* of future knowledge. It was the existence of such uncertainty that indicated to him that economics should be mindful of the contrast between 'our world of frictions and unforeseen changes' and 'a frictionless world of perfect foresight' (Lachmann, 1937, p. 297). This was a contrast about which he was to have much more to say in the future.

Lachmann returned to these themes when he gave some attention to institutions in his book, *The Legacy of Max Weber* (1970), several decades later. In this work, institutions were depicted as a means of delimiting the individual qualities and collective results of human action with which analysts must contend. He envisaged drawing out of Weber's scattered remarks about institutions some theory of how they evolve to meet the needs of assisting human agents to deal with the more intractable facets of their situations, such as uncertainty (ibid., pp. 9, 12ff). His stated ambition was 'to investigate the nature, functions and structural relationships between institutions' (p. 50), but this ambit intention was never realized to any degree that could be considered sufficient fully to establish their role in understanding situated human agency.

Most relevant for the present purpose is Lachmann's intended attempt to extract an account of the way institutions serve to *facilitate and condition* human action. That is, because 'human action in society is interaction', which means that 'each plan must take account of, among many other facts, favourable and unfavourable, the plans of other actors ... [that] cannot all be known to the planner', it follows that 'institutions serve as orientation maps concerning future actions of the anonymous mass of other actors. They help the planner by making the social world a little less uncertain than it would be otherwise' (ibid., pp. 12f). In this endeavour, Lachmann's intentions were consistent with just the understanding of institutions that is compatible with and complementary to individualism and subjectivism, for, quite clearly, his concern with institutions arose because he recognized that agents must act in concert with and cognizant of others. In this dimension of their situations, agents confront the elements of unpredictability in what others will do. Because of this uncertainty, some form of established containment is needed to render tractable their mandatory dealings with others (p. 49). As he argued the point, 'an institution provides a means of orientation to a large number of actors. It enables them to co-ordinate their actions by means of orientation to a common signpost' (pp. 49f). Individual actions are oriented to and a result of plans. Institutions act as means of orienting these plans in an endeavour to give them the maximum chance of being devised consistently with those of others (p. 50). In addition, it is the coherence and permanence of institutions which provides orientations that assist agents in 'reducing the uncertainty of the future which enshrouds all human action', as well as helping them to 'overcome the limitations of ... [their] ignorance of the present' (p. 70). The argument was, then, that institutions effectively provide 'rules of the game' by means of which agents may orient their plans of action. But these rules cannot determine actions. Rather, 'the rules of the game constitute a set of orientation points, limiting the range of action of each player but also permitting him, because his rivals' actions are equally subject to limitation, to guess with greater confidence what they will do' (p. 61). Nonetheless, it remains the case that 'within these limits human action here as elsewhere remains free. ... Norms as such cannot determine a concrete outcome' (p. 61).[6]

In his discussion of institutions, Lachmann dealt with understanding subjective human agents by situating them in a conditioning and constraining environment. In the end, this approach fell well short of what would be required fully to grasp the role of institutions in giving some shape to otherwise wholly volitional and capricious human agency. He was well aware that agents do not pursue their purposes in isolation and on their own whims and wills, and that, as a consequence, human action is not entirely indeterminate. In this same vein, he must have been aware that the divergence of expectations that was so important in his argument against equilibrium would not be unbounded under these conditioning circumstances. However, in this direction of his inquiries he missed an opportunity to expand his subjectivism to include a more complete representation of the structured interaction of agents with their environment.[7] His analysis of human agency in situ was thus left with some degree of ambiguity because of his failure to be more specific about the nature and degree of the influence agents could imbibe from their multidimensional surroundings (cf. Rizzo, 1992a, pp. 127f).

NOTES

1. Lachmann's extended and 'radical' subjectivism left a number of the neoAustrian followers of Mises and Hayek to struggle to keep what they saw as this impending nihilism at bay. Leland Yeager, for example, warns against exaggerated representations and uncritical acceptance of subjectivist insights (1987, pp. 21f). His comments that it is common for advocates to 'lapse into overstating the subjectivist position so badly as to risk discrediting

it' and that 'more important than subjectivism for its own sake is getting one's analysis straight' beg all the questions in this matter. Cryptic though they are, the suggestion in these passages seems to be that, once subjectivism reaches a point where conformity to its demands gets in the way of 'sound' analysis, it can and should be dispensed with. One of my theses, reinforced by reading Lachmann, is that subjectivist implications should not be treated as sort of 'optional' in this way. The demands of the ontological principles posited by a properly defined subjectivism are logically prior to and thus binding on choices that can be made about adhering to analytical niceties. Moreover, the type of derisive remarks made by Yeager in response to Lachmann's revelations concerning the kaleidic nature of economic phenomena rather smacks of 'shooting the messenger' (Yeager, 1987, p. 27). In Don Lavoie's well-founded view, such expressions of 'alarm' about the nihilistic import of the doctrine 'only shows how many Austrians had not yet worked out the implications of their own principle of subjectivism' (1991, p. 484, n14). This is an assertion that is consistent with much of what I have to say in this chapter and the one that follows.

2. As was shown in the chapters above, Hayek was not unaware of the problem of subjective expectations, and even of the need to consider them in the formal context. It must be concluded, though, that ultimately he did not pursue the matter to the extent required to expose their complete significance for economic analysis.
3. Alongside him in London was George Shackle and, by the early 1940s, they were both dedicated subjectivists confronting the puzzles of uncertainty and expectations in the behaviour of economic agents. Although Shackle went his own way in forging a 'radical' subjectivism (1972, 1979), there remained a lifelong parallelism between the direction and substance of their work. Indeed, their writings have come to comprise almost alone the history of 'radical' subjectivist economics since the 1940s. Although this story cannot be told here, its relevance emerges in the fact that, when their 'lonely' intellectual paths crossed over the years, Lachmann drew much by way of confirmation and reinforcement of his own subjectivism from what the Englishman was doing. The strongest evidence of this came after the late 1950s when, as one biographer notes, 'once he had embraced Shackle's brave critical enterprise against neoclassical orthodoxy, he backed him without reserve and saw him as an ally in the struggle to revive the Austrian School'. It was Shackle's deep understanding of the subjectivism of expectations that induced Lachmann to want 'to build a bridge between Shackle and the Austrians' (Mittermaier, 1992, pp. 9, 11; cf. Lachmann, 1976a, 1977, pp. 81ff, 1990b). And, it should be added, the great respect that Lachmann had for Shackle was reciprocated. A 1970 letter from Shackle included a reference to his 'profound admiration' for Lachmann and the observation that 'our ways have lain apart, but we have converged in thought to a degree which gives me immense consolation and encouragement in the face of the inimical climate of our time to our subjectivist views' (quoted by Mittermaier, 1992, p. 17).
4. In an interesting aside, prompted by the fact that Lachmann understated the intersubjective and conditioned situation of the human agent he read about in the work of Alfred Schutz, Warren Samuels makes the point that there is much more to action than the plan from which it stems (Samuels, 1994, p. 323). This is an important suggestion, for, as will become increasingly apparent below, Lachmann placed very heavy reliance on the plan as *the* key to understanding human agency, to the neglect of just those other factors that Schutz had emphasized.
5. When we look at Lachmann's vision of subjectivism as it appeared some decades later, we find him confirming his belief in these seminal principles. In his 1990 paper, 'G.L.S. Shackle's place in the history of subjectivist thought' (1990b), he identified subjectivism as 'a research programme of the social sciences which aims at elucidating social phenomena in terms of their *inherent meaning*, i.e. in terms of their meaning to actors' (p. 3, original emphasis). He saw in this claim a number of further qualities that need to be made explicit. First, the subjectivist ontology of human phenomena means that 'elucidation of meaning is a typical research procedure of the social sciences', and this demands an alternative methodology from that in the physical sciences. Secondly, 'social phenomena are the result of the interaction of actors conscious of the purposes they pursue. To actors, therefore, their action has ascertainable meaning, though not the same for all participants'. Thirdly, 'choice

is the prototype of social action' and this is a subjectivist understanding that respects 'the autonomy of the human mind'. Fourthly, 'the research programme of subjectivism is thus incompatible with determinism in all its forms, in particular that of the General Equilibrium model' (p. 3).

6. In these arguments, the game analogy used by Weber was not subjected to critique and Lachmann did not recognize that institutional rules need not be like those of formal games: the former can be much more flexible and leave a greater degree of contingency in human agency than the analogy might suggest. For the most part, games and institutions rely on the volitional conformity of participants with the rules, but in the case of many games much less room for interpretation of the rules per se is allowed than is possible in most institutions. That is, the predictability of human actions in formal games, although by no means perfect, is greater than that which might emerge from agents operating within institutions.
7. Unfortunately, whatever its merits more generally, as it turned out, in this part of Lachmann's book on Weber, he confined his attention to only three matters somewhat remote from the more immediate issue of understanding how agents engage and use institutions (Lachmann, 1970, pp. 51f): first, the nature and implications of institutional change, where he was concerned about its potential for social disruption (pp. 88ff); secondly, the integrated structure of the institutional order; and thirdly, the need for maintenance of an institutional order. He also provided a discussion of the origins of institutions (pp. 61ff), including the distinction that can be drawn between institutions as undesigned products of individual actions and as the products of conscious construction (p. 69). Here he has been criticized by Gary Mongiovi for failing to give due attention to those institutions that are the products of agents' desire deliberately to provide for increased coordination of their actions, and for neglecting how the power structures that are embodied in institutions may affect agents' actions (Mongiovi, 1994, pp. 265f). Steven Horwitz's response (1994a, pp. 279ff) mitigates in favour of Lachmann, perhaps with rather too much enthusiasm (pp. 280, 285, 287), but the shortfalls cited by Mongiovi remain. I am of the same opinion as Karen Vaughn here when she concludes that Lachmann said 'many tantalizing things about institutions without developing a theory of the relationship between action and institutions that generates confidence in the relative beneficence and coherence of the market order'. This means, she continues, that he 'still has not solved his problem of order. He has just moved it to another level of social interaction' (Vaughn, 1994, p. 157). And even in his magnum opus on markets, *The Market as an Economic Process*, (Lachmann, 1986a) she reads him as allowing 'the role of institutions [to] recede into the background. It forms an indispensable presence, but is not a conscious focus' (Vaughn, 1994, pp. 157f).

10. Lachmann's kaleidics

10.1 A KALEIDIC VISION OF ECONOMICS

For Lachmann, the substantive content of economics that he saw as most immediately affected by the demands of subjectivism was capital theory and the theory of market processes. Two of his major works were respectively devoted to these themes: his 1956 book, *Capital and its Structure* (1978c), and his 1986 book, *The Market as an Economic Process* (1986a). In its own way, each of these works also set out the more general subjectivist caveat that we should be wary about the equilibrium predilections of orthodox economics. Once economics shifts its focus from the individual agent to any collective consequences of their actions, the notion of an equilibrium becomes impossible to apply in any sense that maintains contact with the real processes of the economy. The theses of these contributions were reinforced in several shorter pieces published in the intervening years (several of which are reprinted in Lachmann, 1977). In the analyses to follow, attention to this literature must be confined to its import for critically assessing how, and the extent to which, Lachmann's 'radical' subjectivism penetrated into his substantive contributions.[1]

10.1.1 Equilibrium puzzles

Lachmann apparently saw himself as an advocate for and defender of free market capitalism, but he was concerned that orthodoxy had misrepresented the nature of free markets and what they could achieve. It was his belief that their merits and limitations warranted a more properly explicated understanding and defence in order to forestall the calls for interventionist strategies by governments (Lachmann, 1977, pp. 113, 114, 118, 150f). His general thesis was that markets cannot legitimately be depicted in equilibrium terms because of the subjective origins of the processes that constitute them. Orthodoxy had exaggerated the role of equilibrium and the implied homogeneity and consistency of actions by human agents who comprise the market's participants. Intrusions of scientism into market analysis have meant there is 'little room for a discussion of market processes or of the actions causing them. Even less attention is given to those mental acts from which these economic actions spring'. In these respects, then, 'neoclassical formalism ... does not find it a congenial task to explain economic phenomena in terms of underlying plans and actions'. Rather, 'it abstracts from ... these and, following the example of the natural sciences, substitutes the functional determination of magnitudes, within a closed system characterized by simultaneous equations, for causal explanation' (ibid., pp. 112f, cf. pp. 120, 121).

As far as Lachmann was concerned, the appropriate target of the critique of equilibrium was its misuse in applying it to any economic entity beyond the individual agent. His view was that equilibrium is a notion 'which makes very good sense when confined to individual agents', including households and enterprises as collectives of like-minded individuals with a common purpose. It is the existence of more extended 'human interaction' that contributes to the breakdown of the notion (ibid., p. 149). Thus '"equilibrium of the industry" is a difficult concept to handle. Equilibrium of the "economic system" is a notion remote from reality. ... Equilibrium of an economic system in motion, "equilibrium growth", borders on absurdity' (p. 150). The message was that what might be possible as a state of internal consistency within an individual agent's set of plans cannot be transferred to the inter-agent world without specific justification: to do so represents 'the vice of formalism' (p. 189).[2]

In reality, agents act on the basis of plans, and while individual agents can be in equilibrium with respect to their own intentions and prospects, at the collective level 'room must be left for the unavoidable inconsistency of plans. We must be able to speak not only of unsuccessful plans and malinvestments, but also of the revision of such plans' (ibid., p. 122). This inconsistency was attributed to the subjective and variegated nature of plan formation by different agents. They follow different interpretations of existing situations and knowledge, and thus form different expectations about the future: 'The market as a whole is fed by a broad stream of knowledge, which, although it flows constantly, provides each person with different information. ... In an uncertain world, in which economic agents are dependent on their expectations, a general coherence of plans is almost impossible' (p. 123). Lachmann also adhered to the belief that any tendency towards equilibrium in markets may well be disrupted by the joint and mutually interdependent effects of unexpected changes and inconsistent agents' plans (pp. 189f). Thus 'what ... will in reality frustrate the equilibrating forces is the divergence of expectations inevitable in an uncertain world, and its corollary, the inconsistency of plans. Such inconsistency is a permanent characteristic of a world in which unexpected change is expected to recur' (p. 190). He granted that, alongside these disruptive market forces, there can exist some price and quantity adjustments that are equilibrium-directed. But what is equilibrating in one market may upset the process in another market. Any claim of a general tendency towards equilibrium must establish that these forces are *inherent* in the market processes, that they can be maintained simultaneously and consistently across all markets, and that on balance the equilibrating forces outweigh the disruptive forces (pp. 190f).

Another requirement is that this equilibrium tendency can be shown to be consistent with the information dissemination function of market processes: 'Equilibrium theory, in order to affirm the existence of a strong tendency towards it, has to assume that correct information about equilibrium prices and quantities is readily distilled from market happenings and available to all participants' (ibid., p. 192). Only then can the adjustments induced by agents' decisions be rapid and correctly directed. The subjectivist response from Lachmann here was: 'In reality ... information will spread slowly because not all participants have the same ability to assess the informative significance of the events they observe' (p. 192). This is complicated by the fact that observed events must be assessed as temporary and random or as permanent and systemic; and by the need to assess information as of temporary or durable relevance. Waiting for confirmation makes it all too late (p. 192). So, while there maybe equilibrating tendencies in the form of information flows, 'it is in reality bound to be a rather slow process, likely to be hampered by the divergence of expectations and overtaken by unexpected events' (p. 192).

In understanding markets, then, the moot point is the extent to which the agents involved are or are not able to act in ways that bring about a convergence of their individual plans towards consistency. As Lachmann argued the point, the difficulty is subjectivist in that 'what men adjust their plans to are not observable events as such, but their own interpretations of them and their changing expectations about them' (Lachmann, 1986a, p. 4). Time changes knowledge through information flows and these change expectations and plans for action. Agents will see 'the need for continuous re-orientation evidently requiring a stream of information all of which becomes obsolete after a time interval which may vary from an after-dinner hour to a generation. What needs emphasis is that information has to be interpreted by active minds, "signals" decoded without the help of a permanent code book' (p. 19). The forces of competition which are experienced by agents result in a mix of coordination and discoordination of plans. Particular market relations are interdependent with others, so that change in one that aims to coordinate may well affect the others in ways that discoordinate (p. 5: 'In the first place, revision of plans in the direction of convergence requires a common diagnosis of the present disequilibrium situation. *Divergence of interpretation* will prevent it. Secondly, convergence requires that agents expect each other to revise their plans in this direction. *Divergence of expectations* may prevent this' (p. 56, original emphasis). To these insights was added the third, that 'it is of course always possible that unexpected change will compel or induce some agents (for example by offering them new opportunities) to abandon their plans and start altogether new ones' (pp. 56f). So it is that, while the market process 'is kept in motion by unexpected change and divergent expectations', it is this 'divergence of interpretation ... [that] lends the market process shape and direction' (p. 57).

For similar reasons to those canvassed above, Lachmann was intent upon extending the critique of equilibrium to the dynamic context and denying the relevance of any growth equilibrium set in an artificially structured time sequence. He rejected growth equilibrium analysis in any of its guises on the grounds of a lack of realism: first, the assumed instantaneous real sector supply adjustments required if equilibrium is to be maintained over time in response to changes in demand patterns (Lachmann, 1977, pp. 184ff); secondly, the related implicit assumption that producing agents have perfect foresight, an assumption 'that deprives the model of growth equilibrium of any resemblance to the market process of the real world' (ibid., p. 186). The reality is that, when set in a context of an expanding economy, agents will always have some degree of divergent expectations and the plans they form on these bases are thus bound to be inconsistent and partially bound to fail for that reason. But 'continuous equilibrium requires continuous success of plans. We have to conclude therefore that in an uncertain world in which expectations diverge and the plans based upon them cannot be consistent with one another the particular type of dynamic equilibrium known as "growth equilibrium" is impossible' (pp. 187f). In any proper comprehension of macrodynamics, the role of human agents was to be retained, and subjectivism requires that this role be constructed around the key exigencies of individual plans, expectations and actions (cf. Lachmann, 1973, pp. 39ff). The import of this subjectivist perception of macrodynamic problems was to render dubious the notion of growth equilibrium in any form.

10.1.2 Subjectivism and the theory of capital

Lachmann saw his book, *Capital and its Structure*, as a reaction to what he referred to as a 'low ebb' of Austrian economics in 1956. Writing in the Preface to the second edition of the work in 1977, he recalled that 'the 1950s were a bad time for subjectivists. The role of expectations in economic theory, except for Shackle's pioneering efforts, was hardly appreciated'. Thus his book was a 'gesture of defiance to the spirit of the age'. The vision to be pursued was that, in economics, 'Austrians in general accepted that we must start with the individual and proceed by exploring the, often unintended, consequences of its maximizing endeavours' (Lachmann, 1978c, p. viii). To this end, his intention was to 'infuse a dose of subjectivism' into the theory of capital and to bring methodological individualism to bear on it so as to 'relate capital phenomena to individual choices' (ibid., pp. viiif).

Fundamentally, the premise of the book was the claim that 'the two greatest achievements of our science within the last hundred years, subjective value and the introduction of expectations, became possible only when it was realized that the causes of certain phenomena do not lie in the "facts of the situation" but in the appraisal of such a situation by active minds' (ibid., p. xv). In this respect, capital must be envisaged as a heterogeneous stock, and the task of theory becomes 'explaining its composition in terms of individual choice' and to provide for and understand that 'within the limits set by technology, each such combination reflects the production plan of its owners and managers'. The plans associated with the combinations will vary because 'the divergence of expectations makes for some variety' (p. ix). It followed that Lachmann's approach here was 'not towards the "objective" and quantifiable, but towards the subjective interpretation of phenomena' (p. xv). The challenge was to devise 'an approach to capital problems which is both realistic and directly based on the definition of economic action: realistic in that we deal with the world of unexpected change; directly based on the definition of economic action in that we start from the fact that capital resources are scarce resources *with alternative uses*' (pp. 7f, original emphasis). His intention was that, rather than focus on the static state outcome of equilibrium theory, he would concern himself 'with the "path" which men have to follow in building up capital combinations and using them' (p. 8n). That is, capital theory must 'explain why capital resources are used in the way they are; why in a given situation some alternatives are rejected, others selected; what governs the choice or rejection of alternative uses when unexpected change compels a revision of plan' (p. 8).

In this endeavour, Lachmann intended to 'employ the method of process analysis based on plans and those entrepreneurial decisions which accompany their success and failure'. In doing so, he advocated the rejection of mathematical expression of the argument. The fear here was of implying the relevance of determinism, for such methods allow dynamic analysis 'to degenerate into a series of economically irrelevant mathematical exercises' (ibid., p. 15). Specifically, 'to assume that entrepreneurial conduct in revising plans at the end of successive periods is, in any objective sense, *determined* by past experience and thus *predictable*, would mean falling into a rigid determinism which is quite contrary to everyday experience'. So, in modelling the human agents, he rejected the notion of 'behavioural functions' and 'reaction equations' as too deterministic. The reality is that 'all human conduct is ... moulded by experience, but there is a *subjective* element in the *interpretation* of experience to ignore which would be a retrograde step' (p. 14, original emphasis). Indeed, to apply any such rigid representations of agents 'is simply to deny that entrepreneurs are capable of interpreting historical experience, i.e. experience that does not repeat itself. In other words, to make these assumptions is to say that entrepreneurs are automata and have no minds' (pp. 14f).

Any analysis set in time, as capital theory must be, and any analysis involving processes, including entrepreneurial activity, will demand the use of expectations. Their formation represents an 'entrepreneurial interpretation of past experience' and 'a moment in the acquisition of knowledge'. It comprises 'those acts of the entrepreneurial mind which constitute his "world", diagnose "the situation" in which action has to be taken, and logically precede the making of plans ...' (ibid., p. 15). The consequently required vision of capital theory was one comprising process analysis that emphasizes the exigencies of human agency. It must represent the continuous making of plans by agents on the basis of expectations and the consequent remaking of plans because of unanticipated changes in their environment induced by the very actions that were taken, along with the emergent reactions of other agents (p. 18). Thus expectations formation within the context of inter-agent relations that comprise the market processes as they relate to capital must be accounted for in two steps: one has as its focus the individual agent: 'to describe the structure of the mental acts which constitute the formation of expectations'; the other brings in the collective interdependence of agents: 'to describe the process of interaction of a number of individuals whose conduct is orientated towards each other' (p. 23). The latter step brings out 'problems of *consistency*, both interpersonal and intertemporal' in the sense that, in deliberating, choosing and acting, 'different people may hold different expectations at the same time; the same person may hold different expectations at different times. These are quite insoluble problems as long as we regard expectations as independent of each other' (p. 24f, original emphasis).

The idea of process analysis itself is heavily dependent upon such a subjectivist perspective in which, individually, agents must be presumed to act consistently in accordance with their plans. But unlike equilibrium analyses, there is no assumption that these plans and actions will be collectively consistent. 'On the contrary, we take interpersonal inconsistency for granted and study its effects' (ibid., p. 40). So, even allowing that *individuals* will be in equilibrium in this sense, the problem remained that their collective actions are not directed towards consistency by any centralized constructive force analogous to the mind in the market-place. But having said that, due recognition was then given by Lachmann to the fact that 'the market serves to produce interpersonal consistency, but [that] it does so *indirectly* by modifying the conditions of action of the individuals'. In this respect, 'the market is no substitute for the decision-making unit' (p. 40, original emphasis). The mixed messages about the status of equilibrium in markets, where process analysis is defined such that it 'combines the equilibrium of the decision-making unit, firm or household, with the disequilibrium of the market' (p. 40), is taken up in the next subsection.

10.1.3 Markets as processes of human agency

In writing his 1986 book, *The Market as an Economic Process*, Lachmann explicitly believed that 'the Austrian revival of recent years brought forth a commitment to radical subjectivism' (1986a, p. x). The immediate import of this belief was that his primary attention was to be given to understanding 'the market regarded as an economic process, that is, an ongoing process, impelled by the diversity of aims and resources and the divergences of expectations, ever changing in a world of unexpected change' (ibid., p. x). Consequently, his vision of the market was one in which 'no market process has a determinate outcome' because it is a continuing process that builds on its own past agent dynamics comprising the interaction of the plans and actions of its participants. This subjectivist approach meant that 'at any moment the actor's mind takes its orientation from (but does not permit its acts to be dictated by) surrounding facts as seen from its own perspective, and in the light of this assessment decides on action, making and carrying out plans marked by the distinction between means and ends. This perspective applies to the future as imagined, as well as to the past as known' (p. 4).

Thus, if our aim is to understand human agents in their market actions, we must focus on the fact that they all 'seek to achieve ends by the use of means, but ends are usually problematic, even while they are "given", while the suitability of the means we command, relative to other means we do not, but might perhaps acquire, is always problematic'. The consequent 'choice between alternative courses of action is a central problem of human action and requires for our comprehension of it a theory of choice' in which determinateness cannot be a feature. In making choices and planning for action, agents must be assumed to act rationally in the 'original commonsense meaning' of bringing individual potentials for reason and 'experience interpreted by reason to bear on one's circumstances' (ibid., pp. 114f).

The backdrop for Lachmann's subjectivist critique of market orthodoxy was the widespread acceptance of Walrasian General Equilibrium. In this vision of markets, the crucial role of the imaginary auctioneer is to provide all the information about circumstances needed by omnipotent agents in order that their actions are fully equilibrating (ibid., pp. 43ff, pp. 111ff). Lachmann viewed the orthodox economists as obsessed with determinate outcomes to an extent that forced their analysis into a twofold distortion when representing the human agency. First, 'there is no longer any scope for the variety of human action. Instead of men who pursue a variety of ends by means more or less rational we only find "agents" to whom rationality of action means nothing more than the maximization of some given function'. On this basis, 'we are told nothing at all about how agents became acquainted with these functions, or how changing knowledge would affect them, or what they would do if they came to doubt their permanent character' (p. 113). More generally, what needed emphasis here was that no attention is paid to the problematic of 'circumstances' itself: what constitutes them and how are agents to grasp their contents? In the face of scarce and costly information, and in the presence of an unknowable but vital future, these are not innocent questions.

Secondly, 'the modern "theory of choice" ... which has to eschew indeterminateness at any cost, has made the word denote a situation in which, with given preferences and market prices, there literally *is nothing to choose*'. In reality, 'choice is the prototype of indeterminate action', for it exists only where the agent 'faces a number of courses of action between which he has to *choose*, so that the outcome of his action cannot be known until he has made his choice' (ibid., p. 113, original emphasis). The subjectivist strategy to be pursued was referred to as a 'retreat from determinateness' because 'the task of economic theory ... is to make the world of human action intelligible to us' and such a world offers 'little scope for determinateness' (p. 114).

So it is that the rejection of the auctioneer device calls forth the need explicitly to question 'how men in a market economy acquire, use, store and replace the knowledge daily required for successful action in market place, workshop and household. All these are typical activities of the human mind and have to be treated as such if we are to understand what is going on' (ibid., p. 44). But this appreciation of the need to understand knowledge dynamics per se is complicated by the subjectivism of the *use of knowledge*. In particular, 'changing situations have to be *interpreted* before they are acted upon, and ... it as a rule takes time and effort to collect the material required for such interpretation' (p. 44, original emphasis). It is in the nature of deliberative human action that it is 'problem solving' and any understanding of knowledge use in economics must establish the 'status of knowledge within the means–ends scheme' that is to be attributed to agents as the basis of their planning and action. The challenge for economics in which information plays an explicit part is to recognize that 'problem-solving activity involves interpretation of whatever is "given" to us with regard to the problem at hand'. The challenge for economics then involves 'applying knowledge to interpretation on two levels: while the economist has to interpret observed action in terms of the agents' knowledge as reflected in their plans (their means–ends schemes), these agents themselves have to interpret their own daily experience in the same terms' (p. 49).

This is a summary of the 'double hermeneutic' problematic of economics as a human science in the sense that 'the economist has *to reflect on the agents' reflections* on what and what will not fit into their means–ends schemes', which in terms of the handling of information means that 'he has to interpret changes in knowledge germane to action observed by tracing them back to those acts of the agents' minds by which they lifted out of their stream of experience those particles which might be of use in their practical pursuits' (ibid., p. 49, emphasis added).

One further matter that drew Lachmann's attention was the need in discussions such as the above for a more subtle treatment of any relevant distinction between information and knowledge. In defining these terms, he endeavoured to get beyond the most commonly accepted flow–stock analogy. *Information* was defined as 'the tradable material embodiment of a flow of messages'. *Knowledge* was defined as 'a compound of thoughts an individual is able to call upon in preparing and planning action at a given point of time'. The extension envisaged was that information takes on the quality of a 'socially objective entity' and knowledge remains a 'private and subjective compound of thoughts' (ibid., p. 49; cf. Lewin, 1994, p. 250 n4). This lends itself to the idea that information is traded while knowledge is not, but it does not remove the subjectivist dimension from information in that its use requires interpretation: 'for each ... unit of information has to be *digested* before it can be used in practice' (Lachmann, 1986a, p. 50, original emphasis). And it also irrevocably links the use of information to existing knowledge: 'Such interpretation of information is of course an activity. It requires acts of our minds, and each human mind performs it in a different way. One reason for this is obviously that different individuals have at each point of time different stocks of knowledge. Information that fits into one man's stock may not fit into another's' (ibid., p. 50). In addition, there will exist differences in abilities to make use of information for reasons other than those linked directly to knowledge differences. Most significantly, it is information acquisition and interpretation that brings obsolescence and change in knowledge as it is applied in plans for action (pp. 50, 52f). But the problem of plan revision is one which goes beyond mere reaction to the inflow of relevant information. Plans have an inertia in the sense that their revision is a matter of conscious subjective decision and action (p. 54).

In the end, 'what needs emphasis is the *subjective* character of all activity concerned with information and knowledge, as contrasted with the necessarily objective nature of the information market' (ibid., p. 50, original emphasis). A pertinent observation about this passage is that due recognition might well have been given by Lachmann to more of the meaning and import of his own insight. To begin with, he might have emphasized the fact that information and some parts of knowledge as market commodities cost resources to generate, disseminate and acquire. They are traded in one form or another between agents and institutions, often through explicitly commercial undertakings. Thus the availability to, and the use by, agents of information and knowledge are themselves a matter of economic decision making in three senses. First, their availability is a matter of government or private agents providing the structures and operational facilities required to service other agents' needs. Whether this is, and remains, sufficiently economically and/or socially beneficial will be measured by the sociopolitical judgement of government agents or by the profits (or other measures of return) yielded to private agents.

Secondly, the decision by individual user agents to take up this available information and knowledge, or to gather it themselves as part of their own operations instead, is also a matter of economic judgement. It is about the balancing of pecuniary and other costs against the benefits perceived. So it is, then, that agents may knowingly choose to operate with *technically* suboptimal information and knowledge inputs for the economic reasons that follow from these criteria. The effects of this possibility are compounded by the fact that some such desirable input elements may not be available at all, independently of economic considerations. This comes about mostly because much information and knowledge is highly personalized and subjective in its form and, therefore, cannot be gathered or processed in any consistent and reliable manner. For example, in making strategic decisions it would be desirable for agents to know about the expectations and intentions of other agents with whom they must deal. Such information just cannot be gathered reliably at any cost. Moreover, certain information and knowledge is consciously kept secret by individual agents in order to preserve the benefits that they realize therefrom. Whatever the desires of other agents, this information, too, will be difficult, if not impossible, to obtain without resort to clandestine, and thus costly and risky, means.

Thirdly, all the above considerations are rendered even more insecure by the fact that decisions about obtaining and using information and knowledge must be made ex ante to the substantive decisions they affect. Combined with this is the fact that once a particular choice is made, it is single valued, making all potential alternative choices and actions redundant. Together these facts of life for agents mean that it is simply impossible for them to know ex ante, when it really matters, what the optimum decision about obtaining information and knowledge is. This will not even be clear after the choice is made and the results of the action are in, because the 'otherwise situation' of some different decision in the matter ex ante cannot be tested ex post. It is all too late.

10.2 METHODOLOGY IN A KALEIDIC WORLD

Throughout all the arguments about human agency and about the subjective origins of economic phenomena that have been canvassed above, Lachmann maintained his concern to establish and defend two specific methodological characteristics of economics. First, he was adamant that any methodology must deliver accounts of phenomena that identify the essential character of their ontological origins in the actions of human agents. In the case of the market process, for example, if the ontological perspective is to be subjectivist, then the intention must be to 'attempt to provide the market process with a firm foundation in methodology' while making due allowance for the essential condition that 'needless to say, this [methodology] has to conform to the postulate of methodological individualism, or *subjectivism*, which sees in spontaneous human action the mainspring of economic events' (Lachmann, 1986a, p. 19, original emphasis). It was fundamental to Lachmann's scattered remarks about a specific methodology for economics that 'the object of Economic Science is Human Action'.

At the same time, he was aware that any such science must confront the problem that humans can exercise free-will, meaning that their action responses will always be volitional and in part, at least, indeterminate. Economics is a science that cannot be 'deterministic' in its arguments for this reason, and this presents some peculiar problems for designing its theory (Lachmann, 1977, pp. 166f). For economists, Lachmann went on, all 'phenomena have, in the first place, to be interpreted as the manifestations of the human mind, of decisions to seek certain ends with given means. ... In fact the business of the economist consists of very little else but asking what human choices have caused a given phenomenon' (ibid., p. 168). And, it is a simple fact of ontology that no phenomena outside the human realm have this origin, an origin which sets the metatheoretical challenge of the human sciences apart from those of the natural sciences for this reason alone. As he explained the point, while natural science defines its object world in terms of its continuity and uniformity, this cannot be so for the human sciences. For the latter, the very essence of existence of its phenomena lies in human action that has as its purpose, and is directed at, continuously inducing change. Any continuity to be included must have its origin and nature explained, or it must be artificially imposed (p. 169).

Secondly, he was just as adamant that, nonetheless, economics is and must remain a human *science*, and he took some steps to define what this implied. In 1950, he suggested a 'triple thesis' concerning what it meant for the discipline to be a science: 'Economics is a Science'; Economics is 'a Social Science'; Economics is 'an Analytical Social Science' (ibid., p. 166). The challenge was to say what these theses could mean in more detail once accurately representing the subjectivist ontology of economic phenomena becomes the essential criterion for the design of methodology. His claim was that 'by saying that Economics is a Science I mean economists endeavour to establish *systematic generalisations about observable phenomena*' (p. 166, original emphasis). The 'analytical' quality of the human sciences was summed up by Lachmann in these terms: 'The *modus operandi* of all sciences consists in analysing complex phenomena into their elements', but in the case of the human science 'where causation is our quest, the elements of our analysis must be the causes of the phenomena observed. Only where we can account for all the necessary and sufficient conditions can we claim to have grasped all the elements of the problem' (p. 172).

Integral to this challenge was a proper understanding of *causality* in the human context (ibid., pp. 169f). Causality has a role in the philosophy of natural science, but the particular point made here was that the use of the notion in accounting for human action and its observed consequences cannot be identified through any analogy that associates it with the regularities of the natural world. Although not couched by Lachmann in just these terms, his message was that, whereas the apt questions to be asked about a natural event are empirical and concerned with *how* it happened, the appropriate inquiry for the human realm is *why* an event occurred in the purposive sense of a response to the question '*for what humanly attributable reason*?' Except in theology, such ontologically oriented '*why?*' questions that ask for reasons of any sort have no place in the natural realm. The human sciences are subjectivist because 'our object of study is the pattern of the relationships between decisions and the practical carrying out of these decisions, the co-ordination of means and ends' (p. 169). Their emphasis must be upon the *human causality* of phenomena: decisions and choices by agents comprise mental processes that are to be treated as causes of phenomena that result from the planned coordination of logically prior means and ends. In Lachmann's words, 'the social scientist ... not merely *describes* but *explains* social phenomena by reducing them to acts of the mind. We may therefore say that the "causes" of these phenomena are our choices, co-ordinated in the form of plans' (p. 170, original emphasis). Indeed, in his explanation, this focus on a specific mode of causality represented a superiority of the human over the natural sciences, with its origins in the subjectivity of human agency: 'In the social sciences the quest for final causes is a meaningful enterprise, and in it lies their superiority' (p. 171). Such status flows from the claim that these sciences 'can go beyond mere description and correlation, and render the social world *intelligible* by reducing the phenomena of human action to the irreducible cause: human choice' (p. 171, original emphasis).

A key problem of ontology affecting the nature of economic methodology arising from these analytical claims remained the lack of any 'laws' to depend upon in representing and predicting human conduct (Lachmann, 1986a, p. 29). The mere inclusion of a means and ends logic as the form of purposeful human action cannot overcome the subjectivist influences that are the roots of economic phenomena. In the logic of such argument, the 'truth is purely abstract and formal truth. The means and ends it connects are abstract entities'. By contrast, 'in the real world the concrete means used and ends sought are ever changing as knowledge changes and what seemed worthwhile yesterday no longer seems so today' (ibid., p. 31). It remained the case, though, Lachmann believed, that the means–ends orientation of planning was still to be seen as 'our indispensable frame of reference for the explanation of action' because 'plans are comprehensive means–ends schemes' (pp. 49, 53). Ultimately and incorrigibly, nevertheless, 'the main obstacle to our generalizing effort lies in the unknowable quality of the future' (p. 31). While it may be acceptable to make some limited generalizations about past events, this is not much help concerning predictions about a future that is based on unknowable expectations. Thus the economist must confront the reality that 'the social world, unlike the solar system, is impelled by forces as mutable as thoughts and that no Newtonian model fits it' (p. 32).

Two issues raised here relating to Lachmann's methodological analyses require comment: one is the problematic of predictions in economics and the other is the inclusion of agents' plans in understanding and thus representing human action. Concerning the nature and legitimacy of predictions, he posed and sought an answer to the legitimate, albeit loaded, question 'of what use ... is economics if economists are unable to predict?' (Lachmann, 1977, p. 89). In doing so, he adopted a scepticism that flowed from the extent of 'future knowledge' demanded in making predictions, a demand that just cannot be met for the reason that the very concept is without meaning. That is, 'if subjectivism teaches that prediction of future events is impossible because the future is unknowable and will in fact itself only be created by active minds, what are economists to do?' (Lachmann, 1990a, p. 6). But to the question, 'Does our inability to predict the unknowable future entail our inability to make any contribution whatsoever to the resolving of economic problems of our own day and society?', Lachmann's response was: 'Not so.' The grounds for this response were that, even in a kaleidic economy, 'the past does indeed have a bearing on all action concerning the future, but it is a subtle bearing, reflecting all the nuances of subjective interpretation' (ibid., p. 7).

Moreover, two further aspects of economics were elicited in defence of at least a limited capacity to deal with predictions. First, it was reiterated that the real objective of economics was to provide 'inside' accounts of phenomena that facilitate understanding, that provide 'schemes of interpretation' that 'enable us to understand better certain predicaments of the past and present' (Lachmann, 1977, p. 89). In this sense, he believed, economics should savour its superiority over natural sciences in being able to 'give an intelligible account of the world with which they are dealing. Secondly, a merit claimed for economics is its capacity to provide accurate 'negative predictions' in which certain future outcomes are ruled out as inherently impossible independently of any 'knowledge' of the present or future circumstances.

Nevertheless, the conclusion could only have been one that confirmed a qualified scepticism to the effect that 'economists should, in our view, openly admit that they are unable to make positive predictions about the world' (ibid., p. 89). This was an unnecessarily pessimistic claim even for a 'radical' subjectivist, for, as Lachmann well realized, much more could be done to understand and represent the delimited predictions that economics must be capable of making if it is to have anything but an ex post descriptive content.[3]

In addressing the methodological requirements for theory to be capable of delivering such limited predictions, Lachmann's emphasis was on the plan as the ontological key that is common to all human action and phenomena. In order to appreciate the reason for this particular emphasis, we should begin by recognizing the two potential methodological strategies to which he gave prominence because they are consistent with the fundamental requirement that object ontology should be prior to, and the guiding criterion for, methodological design. These were, first, the procedures required in order to achieve *understanding*, *Verstehen*, in the sense of making observed economic phenomena intelligible as the rational products of human agency in some carefully defined and delimited sense. And secondly, as complementary to the objective of *Verstehen*, he espoused the procedures of *typification*: forming type categories that capture discursively the essential observed elements of agency and its results in order to overcome the analytical intractabilities of dealing with the specific details of individual examples of phenomena. These issues were given their most comprehensive analysis in Lachmann's book on Weber (1970).[4] But, amongst his later contributions that touched further on these themes, one that also warrants attention here is that in which he briefly tackled the idea of hermeneutics as a methodological extension of, and a further complement to, the more general pursuit of *Verstehen* (1990a).

In the context of his critique of Weber, one of Lachmann's priorities was to launch a defence of *Verstehen* as the methodological objective of the human sciences, for it was it was apparent to him that the influence of Weber as an advocate of the 'method of *understanding*' had been shut out of economics by the dominance of neoclassical formalism (1970, p. 2, original emphasis). For Lachmann, an essential metatheoretical premise for analysts in the human sciences should be that the methodology they choose allows the ontological nature of the object human phenomena to be grasped and represented accurately in discursive accounts of their origins (pp. 10f). The consequent difficulty that confronts the attempt to transfer physical science methodology to human inquiry is that 'human action cannot be regarded as mere reaction to stimulus' and cannot, therefore, be ascribed the regularity required by the procedures involved (p. 11). Only one element is common to all self-conscious human action, namely the plan, and Lachmann reasoned that any chance of developing a universal methodology for the human sciences must be worked up from this element. It is a simple fact, he believed, that 'the correspondence between plan and action which ... provides an almost "natural" conceptual basis for the study of human action has no counterpart in nature. A claim for the methodological autonomy of the social sciences, such as Weber endeavoured to establish, is thus most strongly substantiated when we base it on the existence of this correspondence' (p. 12). Most essentially, then, starting from the plan could serve our need to adopt 'as our fundamental concept a notion germane to human action, a notion, that is, in which the meaning of action is preconceived even before the very moment at which the course of action begins to unfold' (p. 29). It was this preconceived status of the intention to act which gives the plan its fundamental status: 'the distinguishing characteristic of the causal explanation of human action lies in the fact that the "effect" of action in its imagined form, i.e. as "purpose", precedes the actual course of action, and thus has to be regarded as a cause. In human action, as in nature, cause precedes effect. ... The essence of the matter is that the end sought, in its mental form, must precede the end achieved as an observable event' (p. 33).

In recognition of this crucial status of the plan, Lachmann introduced his version of the 'praxeological method' in which the key ontological premises to be met were, first, that 'human action exists in mental form, as plan, before it takes place in space and time ... [so that] we may regard action as the unfolding of a mental scheme' (ibid., p. 40); and, secondly, that 'human action is free within an area bounded by constraints' (p. 37). The result must be that, relative to the deterministic arguments of the natural sciences, 'praxeology requires a more flexible form of thought, an "open" analytical framework which will nevertheless permit us to ascertain the boundaries of action. Orientation is the pivotal concept within this framework' (pp. 37f). It was on this basis that Lachmann saw the task of human science as 'to explain observable social phenomena by reducing them to the individual plans (their elements, their shape and design) that *typically give rise to them*' (p. 31, emphasis added). Individual actions in terms of the purposes and plans involved are thus subsumed within 'the elements common to all these plans, such as norms, institutions and sometimes institutionalized behaviour'. The argument here was one in which he was concerned to indicate the situational containment of human action in its typical forms. It is the explanation of 'recurrent patterns of action ... [that is] the essential subject-matter of all social sciences' (p. 22). Thus 'the plain fact is that every recurrent pattern of events, anything we should feel at all entitled to call a "structure", requires explanation in terms of permanent forces as well as in terms of concrete historical circumstances. Interpretation is needed in the former as well as the latter type of explanation' (p. 23).

So, when the focus is shifted explicitly to the pursuit of *Verstehen* in human sciences, it is the need for *typification* which requires immediate attention: 'There seems to be no reason why a method which is useful in the explanation of individual action should be less so in the explanation of *classes of such action*' (ibid., p. 22, emphasis added). The principle of such an approach was that 'in praxeological theory we are concerned with the typical *points of orientation* of typical courses of action', where the elements of such orientations will be imbedded in a plan. Along with these elements, 'the plan must *inter alia* contain directives for action in space and time' (p. 38, original emphasis), presumably typified ones for analytical purposes.

More specifically in relation to understanding market processes, Lachmann advocated typification as necessary because 'the multitude and variety of market processes seems to us to call for a central concept of a special kind, an *ideal type* to which various actual market processes can be compared in such a fashion that the various characters they exhibit permit us to study them in terms of proximity and distance from it'. In this approach, 'we abstract from a mass of unnecessary detail' while at the same time 'we actually *accentuate* the features we wish to study' (Lachmann, 1986a, p. 19, original emphasis). Forming types is thus a mix of abstraction and accentuation: 'A type, ... constructed for whatever purpose, must bear some relation to an aspect of reality. The relation of course need not, and as a rule will not be that of a mirror image, certainly not in the case of an ideal type, the origin of which may be found in our imagination. Nevertheless, a comparison with reality must be possible' (ibid., p. 35). The reference here to the role of the analyst's imagination signalled the distinction between the *real type* and the *ideal type* (p. 36). The real type is a distillation of qualities from observed experience alone, especially in history. The ideal type may have the input of the analyst's imagination. Most importantly, although there can be no rules for their construction, ideal types are expected to 'serve the purpose of helping us to understand the past, to make relations between events, in particular sequences of events, *intelligible* to us by providing, as it were, fixed points around which real events can be located in terms of proximity and distance' (p. 36, original emphasis). To this end, they must be relevant to the inquiry at hand.

But whatever the merits of the typification strategy elicited by Lachmann, a number of inherent difficulties required attention as part of any advocacy of it for economics. One potential source of misuse to which he did draw attention related to the fact that schemes of analysis applying ideal types are 'by their nature contrivances of our minds designed to serve as points of comparison for events that have really happened'. The danger comes in 'ascribing to them a "higher" reality which often finds an expression in such words as "normal" or in the belief that in our scheme we have somehow succeeded in distilling the "essence" of history while real events constitute "deviations" from it'. All this, he added, 'of course is [a] misuse of ideal types' and that 'ideal types and the reality they are to illuminate must not be confused' (ibid., p. 37). These claims open up a number of metatheoretical conundrums that require careful attention. Was he actually ruling out realism as a premise of inquiry in human science as a result of the implications of the appellation 'ideal'? His use of Walrasian General Equilibrium as an example of the way the ideal type can be made out to be effectively real may allow us to resolve this issue (p. 37; cf. pp. 40ff, 43ff). It is possible that what he was ruling out was only the extrapolation of real-world qualities to what were consciously devised as abstract and imagined constructions, as the ideal of the general equilibrium model had been. An indication of this interpretation came a page or so later: 'Economists who believe that they can test models built from ideal types, products of their minds, by predicting events in the real world must evidently hope to have contrived them in such a fashion that they reflect the "essence" of reality, if not the whole of it' (pp. 39f). The potential was there, then, for ideal types to be constructions which directly reflect essential real-world qualities, and this suggests that Lachmann had at least some inclinations towards realism.

What remained confused and begging for clarification in Lachmann's exposition was the *potential of types*, whatever we call them, actually to contribute to a realist analysis of human phenomena. As has been argued elsewhere (Oakley, 1997b, ch. 6, 1997c), this Weberian strategy has problems of its own that were left untreated here. The most crucial limitation of Weber's approach to a discursive understanding and explanation of empirical phenomena by means of ideal types concerns the viability of the comparisons with reality required in order to expose and 'add back' the relevant individual dimensions to the ideal constructs. The logical fallacy of this procedure is a consequence of Weber's own adopted position that no intellectual grasp of reality is possible without the mediation of concepts. Any reality against which the comparison must be made is necessarily itself already a conceptual construction, so the comparison is between one conceptual construction and another. Such an analyst-dependent exercise cannot, therefore, provide any empirical contact or confirmation for the ideal type in the manner suggested by Weber and taken up by Lachmann. The conclusion that what results is necessarily tainted with relativism and must fail any test of 'objectivity' seems difficult to avoid. A further limitation present in both Weber's and Lachmann's treatment of the typification process is that neither of them recognized that active subjective agents themselves must make use of types in order to cope with their complex life-world. Lachmann's contacts with the work of Alfred Schutz should have enabled him to see the vital import of this aspect for any application of the typification strategy.[5] In sum, Lachmann left much to do with respect to the formulation and application of the typification methodology, and he also failed to reflect upon the unresolved difficulties that these procedures present.

He briefly extended the scope of his methodological inquiries in his 1990 paper, 'Austrian economics: a hermeneutic approach' (Lachmann, 1990a). In this paper, the issue was 'if modern Austrians were to succeed in replacing the neoclassical paradigm – an embodiment of desiccated formalism – by a body of thought more congenial to the spirit of hermeneutics, what exactly might they hope to accomplish?' (ibid., p. 135). Hermeneutics was thus envisaged as a response to the failures of neoclassicals to confront the subjectivist nature of economic action, for 'in its essence Austrian economics may be said to provide a voluntaristic theory of action, not a mechanistic one' (p. 136). By contrast, 'the fundamental flaw of neoclassical methodology lies in the confusion of action with reaction. Man in action is seen as a bundle of dispositions and not the bearer of thought' (p. 144). In these arguments is found the opening for hermeneutics as an alternative vision of methodology that can handle the subjectivist origins of human phenomena that have no counterpart in nature.

Through a reiteration of some of the key characteristics of human agency, Lachmann was able to address the question: 'Why hermeneutics?' His answer was that our need is 'for conceptual schemes more congenial to the freedom of our wills and the requirements of a voluntaristic theory of action than anything we have at present'. The ensuing question was thus: 'Is hermeneutics likely to assist us in this endeavour?' and this called initially for some answer to the question: 'What is hermeneutics?' (ibid., pp. 137ff). He explained that its origins are to be found in the interpretation of texts as human products by means of applying the tenets of critical rationalism, for 'what texts and phenomena of action have in common is that they both are utterances of human minds, that they have to exist as thoughts before they become manifest as observable phenomena'. Economic phenomena are observable in this sense, but 'our observations need an interpretation of their context if they are to make sense and to add to our knowledge. Only meaningful utterances of a mind lend themselves to interpretation' (p. 138). Once again, though, Lachmann's exposition gave only the barest indications of the desired direction of methodological developments that include hermeneutics. Here, too, much remained to be done.[6]

NOTES

1. Another related substantive concern that flowed from his subjectivist inquiries was Lachmann's sustained critique of the idea that somehow macroeconomic phenomena could be explained on their own terms. This was the theme of a pamphlet he wrote for the Institute of Economic Affairs, *Macroeconomic Thinking and the Market Economy*, which carried the indicative subtitle, *An essay on the neglect of the micro-foundations and its consequences* (1973). In this piece his basic critical objective was to reject the representa-

tion of macroeconomic phenomena without explicated foundations in microeconomic behaviour. These foundations require an individualist and subjectivist understanding of the collective and interdependent human agency that generates the phenomena. Without such foundations we are left with a macroeconomic formalism with insufficient depth to facilitate understanding (ibid., pp. 15f). More specifically, though, there was much on his mind in this piece concerning doctrines of the period, especially the rise of Cambridge neoRicardianism as he understood it. Indeed, the argument was perhaps too much a victim of its context and the dominance of polemic left little scope for any serious contribution to the development of more solid subjectivist foundations for the phenomena of the macroeconomy. For this reason it will not be considered further here.

2. Formalism was accused by Lachmann elsewhere of 'evading the whole problem of *how plans are made*, a problem which is of crucial significance to subjectivism'. And, in the same vein, the question of '*how* ... lists of alternative plans *ever came into existence* is ... ruled out of order as falling outside the sphere of economic questions!' (1977, p. 157, emphasis added). From here, the analysis was of the struggle in economics between 'methodologies' of formalism and subjectivism (ibid., pp. 155ff). The focus was on the handling of the two crucial dimensions of subjectivism: agents' plans as the bases for action and expectations as the bases of plan formation. But there is a sense in which this comparison is incongruous, because subjectivism does not have the immediate methodological connotations that are associated with formalism. Formalism in economics is a method of expression that makes demands on the form in which its objects are represented and treated that are not consistent with their ontological realities. Subjectivism is a metatheory in which maintaining the ontological origins of economic phenomena in human action is given priority over methodological design. Nonetheless, the two aspects of vision applied to economics are certainly opposed and incompatible and should be contrasted on that basis.
3. In his review of Lachmann's *The Market as an Economic Process*, Terence Hutchison expresses the critical concern that such 'radical scepticism' could further the notion of the 'Austrian dogma of total unpredictability' in relation to the actions of human agents and the phenomena they create. Such an extreme vision, he fears, must lead to 'a thorough-going nihilism regarding the guidance of economic policy by economic theory' (Hutchison, 1987, p. 232). His alternative view is that some caution is warranted when employing subjectivist premises as the basis for economic theory so as to ensure that its usefulness is enhanced rather than destroyed altogether. It must be said here that these caveats are significant and warranted. The point at issue, as he advises, 'cannot be, and never has been, a question of total and precise prediction and predictability, but one of more or less accurate or inaccurate, qualified or unqualified, prediction and predictability'. And the reason for this is itself ontological: 'If men were totally unpredictable to one another, they would certainly be less than human. Fortunately for the human race, we find ourselves neither mutually, totally predictable nor totally unpredictable'. What remains as the challenge after making due allowance for all the subjectivist characteristics that underpin economic phenomena is the question, 'can economists slightly reduce the inaccuracy of predictions in certain relevant areas, so that slightly less unsuccessful policies can be achieved?' (ibid., p. 232). But all this still poses further crucial matters concerning human agency in economic theory and the use of theory for predictions that, although demanding urgent recognition and resolution, cannot be pursued in the present context.
4. In actual fact, Lachmann set out to rework Weber's ideas around the notion of the plan, as 'something more closely akin to human action and society' (Lachmann, 1970, p. 3), *in place of the notion of the ideal type*: that is, to identify and develop 'a new starting point, based on the method of interpretation, for a theory of action, namely *the plan*' and 'inspired by the Weberian notion that action derives its meaning from the mind of the actor' (ibid., p. 9, original emphasis). He correctly read the ideal type as Weber's 'fundamental concept of a theory of human action which seeks to interpret meaningful action' (p. 11), but then went on to confuse the issue with some quite incongruous interpretations. These incongruities involved both the interpretation of the ideal type itself and the use of it attributed to Weber. As Lachmann put it, albeit cryptically, the 'ideal type was really meant by Weber as

a measuring-rod, a device to bring order into a mass of facts. As such it has nothing to do with the intelligibility of human action' (pp. 11f). The effect of this reading was to situate the ideal type as an element of *methodological* importance that can retain its *complementary* relevance in a subjectivist metatheory that is founded on the essential ontological principle that agents act on the basis of plans. From this perspective, the import of the very next sentence is difficult to sustain: 'We propose to replace it [the ideal type] by the notion of the *plan*' (p. 12, original emphasis). So, although he had touched on the crucial point that the ideal type is part of a methodological strategy required to deal with the wide variations in the individual actions that contribute to the generation of human phenomena, he went on anyway to espouse the need to *replace* the ideal type with the plan. This was one of the most problematical outcomes of Lachmann's efforts here.

5. Lachmann's treatment of Schutz has been considered by Roger Koppl. (1994a). Koppl's concern is to establish that, while Lachmann had paid considerable attention to the subjectivism of Shackle (cf. note 3 in Chapter 9, above), he had not pursued fully the distinctive vision of phenomenological subjectivism offered by Schutz: he 'curtsied to Schutz, but he walked with Shackle' (ibid., p. 289). Indeed, it is Koppl's reading that Lachmann had begun by being sceptical about Shackle's perception of agents' conduct as rather isolated and discontinuous, a scepticism that may be ascribed to the adoption of Schutz's strongly intersubjective situation of agents. But, subsequently, according to Koppl, Lachmann let this scepticism drop and he missed out on much in Schutz that could have increased the penetration of his subjectivism (pp. 294ff). My assessment of Lachmann agrees with Koppl's in this important respect. However, I would want to extend the critique and argue that Lachmann elicited from *neither Schutz nor Shackle* the full value of their respective metatheories and that his subjectivist legacy was all the poorer as a consequence. Moreover, I am inclined to agree with Warren Samuels when he suggests that the complementarity between Schutz and Shackle may have been underestimated by Koppl (Samuels, 1994, pp. 322f).
6. An extensive literature addressing the nature of Lachmann's shortfall in hermeneutics and its implications has emerged since the 1970s resurgence of Austrian economics (Ebeling, 1986; Lavoie, 1986, 1990a, 1990b, 1990c, 1994; Madison, 1988, 1990). David Prychitko (1994a) provides us with a summing up of the relevance of these developments for interpreting the legacy of Lachmann in particular. His key point is that Lachmann's hermeneutics turned out to be too narrow and not 'radical' enough in the light of the subsequent work done on the contributions of Hans-Georg Gadamer and Paul Ricoeur in the literature just cited (ibid., pp. 308ff). Most significantly, their development of a phenomenological hermeneutics meant extending the source of meaning ascribed to an action beyond the beliefs and intentions of the agent concerned. For analysts, understanding action, giving it intelligibility, has to transcend the historicism of the plan from which it stemmed and allow for a 'mutual relationship' between themselves as interpreting subjects and the record of action as their object (p. 309). Understanding in this sense generates meaning, rather than merely identifying it in the agent's psyche and reproducing it discursively. One practical indicator of this need for transcendence is the existence of unintended consequences of actions, for these were not part of the agent's plan and yet they are integral to the full meaning of the action. Lachmann was well aware of this, but the implications of the external and intersubjective sources of such consequences for understanding action were not followed through (pp. 313f).

11. Subjectivism: the legacy

PREAMBLE

The potential for establishing a neoAustrian economics grounded on the principles of subjectivism was carried into the period after World War II by the work of Mises virtually alone. By then he was in the United States, and it was his *Human Action*, along with his seminar series at New York University, that constituted the focus for those economists who took an interest in such heterodoxy. He had few followers during the 1950s and 1960s and his influence on economic thought and practice was minimal. In the same period, Hayek had also appeared on the American scene, but as a political theorist more than specifically as an economist. By then, as we have seen, his writings coming out of the University of Chicago had a broader focus that combined economics with libertarian political philosophy, albeit one in which the key influences of subjectivism were still in evidence.

It was not until the 1970s that any attempt was made to salvage and return to a serious discussion of subjectivist economic ideas (cf. Lachmann, 1982b; Vaughn, 1990, 1994, chs 5 and 6). The meaning of subjectivism that had been left incompletely formulated by Menger was again the centre of attention amongst a small group of economists. From the outset, the intellectual leaders of the revival were Mises and Hayek, through both their personal presence at several key conferences and the renewal of interest in their complementary rather than identical written contributions (Kirzner, 1994c, pp. xiff). Lachmann played the role of 'devil's advocate' in promoting subjectivism as the founding metatheoretical element to be developed, but it soon became apparent that his open-minded and 'radical' subjectivism carried a different message for the understanding of economic processes from that espoused in the contributions of the main Austrian duo.

The legacies of subjectivist metatheory for economics that I have identified in the writings of the several Austrian contributors above vary widely in scope and content, in spite of their common origins in the thought of Menger. Nonetheless, each in his own way provided something for the founding of the neoAustrian revival. Mises must be judged to be the main initiator and founder of this modern revival, and he also provided many of the subjectivist ideas that Hayek and Lachmann were to take up and run with alongside him.

But both of these latter authors broke from the confines of Mises's thought and produced independently revised visions of subjectivism in economics. These were sometimes complementary and sometimes conflicting, both with respect to the work of their antecedent and as between themselves. Ultimately, all three authors had different degrees and kinds of influence in shaping the revival. My objective has been to ascertain the strengths and weaknesses of, and the key differences between, the subjectivist legacies that these major figures of the Austrian heterodoxy left for their neoAustrian followers to grapple with.

11.1 MISES

The reading of Mises elicited in Chapter 3 above leaves neoAustrians with mixed results to apply as his most fundamental contributions to the potential for a subjectivist economics. There were a number of key alternative philosophical orientations that may be identified in his writings on subjectivist principles, and these resulted in the philosophical ambivalence that he displayed in formulating his praxeology. More specifically, I have shown that there were indications of Kantian and neoKantian epistemological roots and orientations to be found in his writings, and these were juxtaposed to passages in which Mises emphasized the ontology of Aristotelian realism and dealt with its epistemological implications. At the same time, a distinction can be drawn between two levels of analysis that appear in his writings. One is the pure thesis of praxeology as an ontology of rational human action, and the other is the study and explanation of observed economic phenomena. I argued in this respect that the distinction enabled Mises ultimately to establish the meaning of the tenets of praxeology as necessarily manifested within the reality of observed economic phenomena. This gives us some potential insight into his own way of steering a coherent course between the alternative and incompatible philosophical positions concerning ontology and epistemology to which he adhered from time to time. However, as I have also made apparent, the requirement that agent rationality be given an *ontological* a priori status is not readily defended once the contingent realities of human agency are examined. It is quite evident that Mises was aware of these realities, but he chose not to link them to the rationality thesis upon which his subjectivist economics essentially depended.

That it was Mises's intention to confine praxeology to the role of the existential foundation for understanding observed economic actions and phenomena has been made clear in my analysis. However, the ontological and epistemological status to be ascribed to its logical arguments appear to be much less definite when the totality of his thought is assessed. There is no denying that he remained ambivalent about the uneasy mix of epistemological consequences of working with the unreal conceptual forms that stem from neoKantianism alongside the realist categories required to meet the demands of Aristotelian essentialism. Whether he was conscious of it or not, the heritage that he left for his followers comprises an ambiguous and incompatible mix of arguments in which the concepts of praxeology were sometimes ontologically sterile and sometimes replications of living forms claimed to be actually discoverable in empirical phenomena. I have concluded that it is reasonable to respond to these imprecisions in Mises's thought by giving priority to the realist inclinations that appear in his understanding of economic ontology and epistemology. For this to be accepted by neoAustrians would require an agreement that the maximum sense of his praxeology is made if it is perceived as expressing a rational ideal upon which to ground an understanding of the conduct of active, subjective agents. As Mises was aware, any such grounding always requires the immediate qualification that the actual conduct of agents will be observed in some imperfect but nonetheless explicable empirically manifested form. His vision of human agents, that is, can be understood to include facets that deny any realism to an ontology of purely rational action, even when accounting for the essentials of economic phenomena.

As the evidence that I have set out indicates, it was the immediately ontological interpretation of the axioms of human action, and the contingencies of such action thus exposed, that rendered indefensible the rationalist foundations for subjectivism that Mises was inclined to pursue. Contrary to what he expressly sought to do at a number of points in his writings, he was unable to provide rational action with a sustainable defence as an ontologically relevant axiom. As a consequence, he failed to give his praxeology a cogent realist grounding and left its appropriate epistemological status unresolved. This metatheoretical ambivalence of Mises left the way open for the factionalization of the neoAustrian revival that was to follow. In the end, the insights that we recognize as comprising Mises's metatheoretical legacy for neoAustrian economics are confined to a compendium of pertinent observations concerning the subjectivist problematic at issue. Beyond that, he left much to be done to provide a complete and cogent alternative to the established foundations of orthodox economics.

11.2 HAYEK

My extensive inquiries above have indicated a number of Hayek's contributions to the development of a subjectivist economics that stand out, along with several important matters that remained inconclusive. It is quite evident that he had a real commitment to subjectivism throughout the shifting orientations of his life's work and that he believed this metatheoretical principle could provide the proper foundation for valid accounts of phenomena that comprise the economic problem. Even his earliest writings as a formalist orthodox economist with a difference were punctuated by frequently occurring references to the subjectivist nature of the economic problem. In these works he left behind him some highly suggestive argument about the primary exigencies of human agency as these affect economics. I refer here especially to his initial consciousness of the real-time dimension of economic action and the consequent need for agents to deliberate, decide and plan on the basis of expectations that may turn out, to varying degrees, to be right or wrong. After a brief period of assuming agent omniscience in matters of decision making, Hayek came to realize that such expectation failures could be a fundamental endogenous source of disruption to the equilibration process. His acquired sensitivity to the dimensions of the problem that emerge directly from the deliberated actions of individual human agents made his pursuit of the lodestone of equilibrium increasingly difficult to justify. He eventually turned away from this formalist orientation of his first academic work precisely because of a growing awareness that subjectivist premises could not find their proper place within the methodological constraints imposed by orthodox, scientistic analyses. Evidence from Hayek's own writings indicates that it was this increasing realization that a subjectivist ontology demands explicit and integrated recognition in defending a methodology for economics that led him into an exploration of metatheoretical issues.

As I have read them, certain aspects of Hayek's continuing research served to highlight the subjectivist substance that he felt was missing from his early analyses. His message that individual agents deliberate and make plans on the basis of their personal and specialized knowledge is of fundamental significance for understanding individual human agency. Vital prior questions about the planning process that warrant answers include the following: what can and do agents know about their circumstances; what capacities for deliberation and calculation do agents bring to their circumstances; and how do agents actually cope with their future circumstances about which they can know nothing ex ante? On the subject of agents' knowledge, Hayek's contributions were significant but incomplete. His involvement in the socialist calculation controversy had emphasized to him the false leads that could be given concerning market analysis by the presumptions of perfect competition. What became apparent to him was that the effect of applying the essentials of subjectivism as he understood them was to separate the resulting metatheoretical perspective from the pseudo-subjectivism of orthodox microeconomic analyses. A consequence of this was to enable him to form a different vision of the market that ostensibly stressed its processes as comprising collectives of individual agent actions.

Hayek's critique of the imposed world of perfect competition, with its focus on the 'pure logic of choice' and logically entailed collective equilibrium states, was well directed and telling. In these analyses, the human agent is modelled as *homo oeconomicus*, the puppet-like, but omnipotent, being who mechanically responds to preferences and circumstances with a logical rationality and precision of choice that is actually entailed by the premises and conditions established by assumptions. In particular, Hayek emphasized appropriately that orthodoxy had thus avoided the problematics of two fundamental issues of free markets: first, agents' acquisition and use of knowledge; and secondly, the process by which competitive interactions of individual agents bring about equilibrium tendencies or outcomes. Merely positing different patterns of preferences, and positing maximum utility as the singular human objective, are not sufficient conditions to render the depiction of decision and choice processes truly subjective. On the contrary, in the determinism of the imposed 'logic of choice', all the knowledge agents require is presumed given to them and the ends and means manifested in their conduct are preordained so that agency, and indeed choice itself in the strict sense, are not present. Indeed, agents are actually portrayed as omniscient beings who have no need to pursue knowledge and for whom deliberations and time are of no explicit concern, for the required optimizing actions and the future are logically entailed and carry no uncertainty.

Once we leave the world of imposed equilibrium logic, there is in this sort of analysis no indication of just what the processes of human agency are that can bring spontaneous order of some degree to otherwise uncoordinated and potentially disparate actions of the market's independent constituent agents. Hayek made more explicit the role of the 'division' of individual agents' knowledge in market activities, but this did not add all that is required for us to know how, as a matter of actual processes, the order that characterizes market outcomes is generated. His awareness of the subjectivist problematic was, though, sufficient to lead him to refer only to a *tendency* for free market competition to generate coordinated outcomes. As he saw things, this step substituted an empirical claim for the logical one that was employed by orthodox analysts. Well may this be so, but understanding the empirical phenomenon of a collective tendency that results from independent human actions still demands a cogent account of how those actions are determined and how they actually link up. He was moved to admit at one point at least that he could not provide such an account. The best argument he could devise was that agents acting in markets constitute a 'self-organizing system' in which feedback adjustments to individual plans and actions brought about by price signals and a process of learning will move the system increasingly towards a fully coordinated outcome. Here again the argument lacks cogency. No detailed or precise argument was ever presented in defence of the implied informational richness of the prices upon which agents are expected to rely so heavily when making decisions. Moreover, the presumption of the simplistic analogy from the mechanical world, as Hayek applied it, is that the entities involved in the mutual adjustment, and what they have iteratively to learn about so to adjust, are all unchanging during the coordination period. For if agents themselves, and/or what it is they have to learn to gain adequate knowledge, have their own dynamics of change, then the 'self-organizing' capacities of the system can no longer be invoked without some more penetrating analytical defence.

Alongside all of this argument, Hayek had developed and was carrying forward his vision of what constitutes human agents and their agency. Most essentially, the image of the agent he presented was formed within his detailed theory of human psychology. In this theory, the mental structures and processes in which human actions originate have an irreducible physicalist dimension that accounts for them through their links to the genetic and physiological structures and processes of agents' brains. But, as he made very apparent, in order to understand action, it is not possible to rely exclusively upon pursuing the intricacies of these neurological connections in isolation. One of the reasons for this was the straightforward fact that any hypotheses about brain functions that were posited at that time could only result from mere speculation, for they remained untestable by any anatomical or physiological investigations. But the importance of Hayek's psychological endeavours for economics does not depend upon the veracity or otherwise of his physicalist analyses. Rather, it is the accompanying subjectivist insight into the experiential and conditioned origins of agents' mental make-up that warrants further attention.

Even at this most fundamental level of their representation, agents could not be understood in isolation from their cumulative biography of experiences and their current environmental conditions. These environmental conditions consist of all facets of the existentially independent world in which agents live. They include all kinds of inherited and pre-existing entities, ranging from physical objects to the virtual world of social institutions and relationships. Hayek explained this conclusion quite early in his career by the idea that the very constitution of their cognitive processes is a direct product of these past and present external conditions. Acting agents were thus depicted as existentially integrated into and intimately part of the independent and prior structures of their surrounding conditions. This positioning of agents within an inherited external environment that their actions had helped to construct meant that the mediation of their minds in interpreting 'facts' about reality arriving as sensory inputs was an active rather than a passive process. Mental structures and functions were always the joint products of current experience and the cumulative residue of past experience. More specifically, real objects from the external world, be they physical or virtual in their presence, are experienced by agents, not as immediate existential qualities in themselves, but as phenomenal composites of already established mental categories that select and classify the sensory flows into the brain. Their immediate sensory experience is thus shaped by an existing mental order, the composition of which is itself the product of cumulative past experiences. In this sense, for active subjective agents *all perception is interpretation* and all knowledge is in the form of some abstract 'theory' about and/or model of the physical or other realities of their past and present experience. In this way, they represent to themselves in phenomenal form what they understand about the aspects of their environment upon which they choose to focus their attention.

In Hayek's theory of the agent, then, the cognitive structures of the mind were not depicted as a set of innate and given mental categories in the Kantian manner. Agents' responses to their circumstances at any point in time are in part human species specific and in part genetico-physiologically and biographically specific to the individual. Over time, some degrees of change in agents' cognitive make-up and in their situational response patterns are always in progress as a consequence of their continuing engagement with and experience of a changing external environment. The actual dynamics involved here were explained by Hayek as comprising incongruities between the pre-existing mental apparatus and the sensory experiences with which it is confronted. The cognitive system possessed by agents will progressively undergo a reclassification process affecting the linkages that handle sensory inputs, a process that is stimulated whenever they meet with conflicting experiences that introduce inconsistent elements into their model of the external world. In addition to these experiential effects, agents may also choose self-consciously to expand the reach of their knowledge by learning in one form or another.

One of the crucial consequences of this theory of the agent for Hayek's subjectivism is that it rendered the physical realm of external reality and the mental realm of phenomenal reflection as separated but always related. The links between them enabled him to envisage agents' deliberations and actions as everywhere the joint products of their cognitive make-up and capacities, their knowledge and their current situational environment. From the mid-1940s onwards, Hayek's subjectivism included a concept of individualism that embraced the fact that agents are always situated within and function through some set of contemporary situational conditions. These conditions exist externally and prior to any attention from those agents. He devoted considerable space in his writings over the remainder of his life to developing this thesis and its implications for a subjectivist understanding of economic actions by individuals and the resulting spontaneous collective outcomes. What was apparent to him was that any spontaneity of coordination between independent individuals was somehow the product of like agents shaping their volitional actions in accordance with the common rules and directions inherent in their institutional and social situations. The collective outcome is thus not planned in any sense by any one individual, but each contributes to it by acting in conformity with a given pattern of structural and relational conditions. Their experience and deliberative reason tells them that so to proceed in their choices and actions will deliver the best result for them individually that they can expect under the circumstances.

Hayek's rationale for this claim was a product of his rejection of absolute constructive rationalism in the human realm. He found rationalism to have two dimensions of limitations, one of which relates to individual agents and the other to the origins of the environmental structures within which they live. Both limitations were integral to his subjectivist understanding of situated human agency. First, it was a simple fact of human being that individual agents cannot be thought of as able optimally to deal with their circumstances by depending upon their own cognitive and rational capacities. The world they are required to contend with is simply too complex for them to acquire full knowledge of their circumstances and then to apply the range of cognitive processes required to make fully rational sense of them. As intellectually limited and fallible beings, they must somehow find means by which that intractable complexity can be mitigated in order to make sensible and satisfying decisions. It is for this purpose that they turn to the pre-existing structures and relationships around them for guidance. The resulting potential for coercion is minimized by the fact that, although agents thus choose to forgo the pure volition of their actions, they remain free to pursue their own motivations, preferences and purposes. The crucial talent that agents have in this respect was specified by Hayek as their capacity to form categorical abstractions that give a manageable order to their circumstances and coherent direction to their plans and actions. These mental formations are reflections of the rules manifested by the various institutional and social structures that surround them, and agents may or may not be consciously aware of their details.

Second, and complementary to the first point, the institutions and social structures confronted by agents have evolved by a process of functional selection rather than by any conscious design and construction that depended upon the rationality of particular agents. Active agents inherit a situational pattern that works for them in the above sense because its very existence means that this must be so. But, within their limited capacities, agents have little option but to make the best use of the pattern they reasonably can, even if any of them find it individually less than ideal as the means to their particular ends. Institutional and social change is predominantly evolutionary and slow. But Hayek was prepared to grant that it can also be induced in a more programmatic way by the interventions of political authorities. In neither case, though, are *individual* agents able to do much about changing the immediate situational conditions within which they must act. There exists very little scope for them unilaterally to apply their reason to the redesign of their environment, however much they may wish for this to be done and however clear they may be about what is to be done.

Sometimes implicit in Hayek's argument, albeit in passing, were hints at a third limitation of the rationalist conception of human agency. Human agents engaging in cognitive and physical actions do so on the basis of accumulated stocks of knowledge about, newly acquired information flows concerning, and biographically conditioned interpretations of, their individual circumstances. It was one of Hayek's most emphasized points that understanding human action demands an understanding of all facets of the sources, nature, limitations and use of knowledge and information, and of the subsequent processes of their interpretation. But he was also well aware of the need to give due attention to the fact that human action takes place in a *real-time* setting where the future looms large. Such action circumstances demand that agents form *expectations* as a vital part of their prior cognitive process. Deliberations and actions take place in present time, but their consequences will emerge in future time, so that agents confront and must find some way of dealing with incorrigible *uncertainty*.

What Hayek failed to pursue with anywhere near enough depth of subjectivist insight are the specific implications that these facts of life for agents have on the ontology of their deliberation and decision processes, and thus on the resulting actions and outcomes that are generated. It may well be that individual agents apply their accumulated knowledge and their limited reasoning capacities to what they know of their individual circumstances. But this argument leaves unanswered important questions about the nature of the knowledge of circumstances and about the nature of the reason applied by agents.

As the uncertain future is crucially involved in all deliberated economic decisions of pecuniary significance, such deliberations confront agents with an *absence of knowledge* about the relevant circumstances, for these have yet to eventuate. Their only means of handling these situations is to reason through imagination about what the future circumstances could be like and how they might provide the conduit through which present actions will be transmitted and reach their outcome. Some future scenarios in this sense will, on the basis of past experience, seem be more feasible than others. All agents can do is to apply existing knowledge and their capacities to reason to *constructing* the potential circumstances and consequences. From amongst the possible and feasible scenarios, agents must then choose only one and live with its outcomes, for better or for worse. Moreover, the world they confront, and its potential future directions and conditions, are characterized by patterns that cannot be replicated by any closed probability distribution. Agents' imaginations and choices ensure that their future is non-ergodic because the range of potential outcomes is virtually limitless. They may reason that applying some stochastic method to selecting a future is the best way to go, but the probability patterns used must be devised and imposed by the agents themselves. For all his pursuit of the knowledge issue as it affects human agency, these were matters that Hayek chose to leave without the attention they warrant. Nonetheless, no complete subjectivist analysis of economic phenomena can legitimately avoid facing up to the very real methodological and epistemological difficulties raised by these aspects of the reality with which it must deal.

As a result of recognizing such difficulties, it has become an integral part of some subjectivist approaches to human scientific inquiry to espouse hermeneutics as comprising one defensible principle upon which to base methodology. Hermeneutic procedures in human science are concerned to provide an interpretive understanding of the meaning structures devised by agents and upon which they base their actions. Subjective agents are presumed by analysts to act on the basis of interpretations of their problems and situational environment by means of their multidimensional cognitive characteristics and abilities. The crucial point is that hermeneutics explicitly directs the analyst of human phenomena to give priority to ontological integrity, for it *begins* from the notion of agents as voluntaristic but limited, purposeful and situated beings. Agents must deliberate and make choices on the basis of their own, individual interpretations and understandings of the problems and environments that they confront. Hayek made much of this access to 'specialist' knowledge of acting individuals when analysing the role of knowledge in collective agency. Whatever may be the limitations of agents' understanding that come from lack of information and/or shortcomings of their cognitive capacities, their actions as individuals are to be understood as the result of the meaning *they* attribute to the environment and to the *telos* of the pursuit of *their* objectives. Such an approach makes the demand that analysts try to grasp the objects of their inquiries in a manner that incorporates an explicit representation of the understanding that agents themselves have of their own deliberations and action.

That is, as Hayek implicitly recognized, economists must contend with a 'double' hermeneutic in the sense that their science is not only, in itself, essentially a process of forming understanding, but also has as its object the understanding that active economic agents themselves have of their own agency in all its dimensions. The import of this for economics is that, in order to claim an understanding of observed phenomena, economic analysts are not entitled to assign to them whatever meaning suits their own cognitive capacities and/or purposes, be they substantive or methodological. So, although analysts who aim to understand what observed agents do can only operate by means of their own cumulative and subjectively conditioned cognitive capacities, the meaning assigned by them to the various actions observed must be consistent with, even if not limited to, what those observed take to be the meaning involved. And it is also incumbent upon analysts to face up to the facts of agents deliberating and acting under uncertainty. This puts them in the difficult position of representing realistically the various facets of the process of determining choices as it must take place in the absence of any sufficient knowledge of circumstances.

A subjectivist methodology will necessarily involve procedures that depend upon analysts identifying and representing the mental exigencies of other agents, especially where the latter must act under uncertainty, and there is the ever-present danger of succumbing to relativism and, possibly, to scientific nihilism. In this connection, a number of seriously difficult and unresolved metatheoretical puzzles are raised. Extreme idealist forms of subjectivism, in which any structure human agents perceive in the object world around them is taken to be exclusively the result of their cognitive inclinations and capacities, cannot constitute an adequate response. Nor can extremes of objectivism that would want to eliminate subjectivist dimensions and render agents as automatons acting in a world that is entirely independent of their conceptual formations. What is of concern here is rather a dualistic puzzle. On the one hand, analysts must decide the extent to which they believe the forms of the object circumstances confronted by active subjectivist agents, including such virtual structures as institutions and social relationships, are intransitive and existentially independent of the agents' concepts of them. On the other hand, they must be concerned about the extent to which these agents' conceptual interpretations of life-world phenomena can be shown to be shaped and directed by these pre-existing ontological structures and relationships. What is more, the avoidance of an individualist relativism requires that effects of situations in this sense have some typical characteristics that are common to all agents in some particular category. The result is that some tricky matters relating to the meaning and significance of realism as a metatheoretical ideal appear alongside subjectivism and hermeneutics in economics. Realism, in its simplest guise, requires that agents, both as acting subjects and as observing analysts, assume an independent existential status for all entities they confront. Subjectivism in the form being pursued in the present context presumes that agents comprising a particular category of interest to economists will adapt their conduct in some common manner to make the best use of the relevant situational entities with which they are presented, given the interpretations of them that they are able to make.

Although Hayek showed some degree of sensitivity to each of these concerns, my conclusion is, nevertheless, that in two crucial and closely related respects his subjectivist legacy fell short of its own potential to direct economics away from its scientistic orthodoxy. The first of these relates to his establishing that the particular ontological character of the economic problem is essentially the consequence of the relevant phenomena having their origins in the exigencies of human agency. In doing so, however, he failed fully to include in his subjectivist portrayal of agents and their agency several of the most essential *defining* characteristics, and these incompletely treated characteristics were just those that have since been shown to comprise the most contingent and thus analytically intractable ontological dimensions of human agency.

In particular, he did not give due recognition to the creative mental processes of active agents that constitute such an integral and important part of the 'deep' ontology underpinning object actions or events. The need for creativity and imagination on the part of deliberating agents stems directly from the unavoidable exigencies of real time that beset the action process. But, as I have already noted above, the actual deliberation and choice procedures set in time, with all the attendant difficulties for both active agents and observer analysts to contend with, were simply not part of Hayek's treatment of the agency issue. Having posited his minimalist subjectivist image of the economic agent, he moved straight on to situate such agents in structured environments that direct and shape their action responses to particular circumstances. He envisaged actions as entirely voluntarist, with the qualification that the immediate situations in and through which they must act, comprising the rules and directions thrown up by institutions, structures and social relations, all have an existential form that is prestructured and given for them individually. From this realist perspective, he was aware, too, that all these dimensions of the surrounding world contain and constrain, as well as providing facilities for, agents' chosen actions. Imagined future outcomes of alternative actions are rendered feasible or not by the exigencies of these situations as far as they are able to know and understand them.

Be all this influence of situational containment and constraint, direction and facilitation on agency as it may, there is no avoiding the contingent remainder that will characterize all deliberations and actions carried out by individual agents. As Hayek's understanding of the demands of subjectivism enabled him to realize, this contingent dimension can only be mitigated for analytical purposes if some typification and classification of agents, actions and events are employed as a mode of generalizing and regularizing the processes and outcomes of human agency. He drew attention to this technique of analysis in his own way by means of the concept of 'patterns' of events, but he gave only limited emphasis to the details of its implications for theory construction.

What is suggested by this theoretical strategy is that explanations and the predictions derived from them, as they follow from subjectively grounded hermeneutical understandings of human deliberations and actions, require strict methodological and epistemological circumscription. It should be stressed in this respect that typified explanations are always prior to, and never reducible to, predictions as such. In particular, they should be limited to a degree of specificity sufficient to identify an event as qualitatively typical of its class. The requirement then is only that they remain consistent with the limited degree of quantitative and temporal regularity exhibited by that class of event. That is, the accuracy and reliability characteristics of predictions cannot be expected to transcend those of the explanatory arguments from which they are devised.

Hayek was sensitive to methodological qualifications such as these, even though the reach of his analyses in this direction must be judged to have been too limited. More specifically, what Hayek believed should be accepted is that the sort of predictions to be made are not able to be as quantitatively or temporally specific about *individual* events as those possible in astronomical observations or in physics experiments. They can never be so because of the unique contingency that plagues human action by virtue of the *volitional, imagined and creative* foundations upon which it is ultimately based. Such contingency, and the openness of consequent phenomena, remain at the individual agent level irrespective of the containment and constraints that may flow from the situations within and through which action is undertaken. These are implications of any fully subjectivist interpretation of human agency, as Hayek showed himself to be aware, but his awareness was desultory for the most part and he did not pursue them with the warranted vigour.

The particular limitations to which I have just been pointing were directly linked to the second shortfall that I wish to identify. Having understated the intricacies and contingencies of representing active human agents in his analyses, Hayek was able to give some legitimacy to retaining a methodological stance in economics that did not break completely with the established norms of the physical sciences. He could do so because he came to envisage individual and collective phenomena of human agency as merely very complex analogues of physical phenomena. In making this move away from the demands of subjectivism as he had recognized them, the basis for the 'in principle' and 'pattern' conditioning of methodology in economics was changed to one of mere quantitative intractability. Epistemological limitations applying to explanations and predictions concerning such complex physical events as the weather and tidal patterns were just like those applying to human phenomena under this interpretation. Were he to have carried through into his portrayal all of the exigencies of human agency to which he had drawn attention, albeit often in passing and without due elaboration, the degrees of complexity notion might have appeared less of a satisfying conclusion. No such concern only with *degrees* of epistemological distinction based on quantitative profiles can encompass the unique qualitative contingency of human action as I have specified it above. Had Hayek been more prepared to recognize and cater for this incorrigible element in the generation of human phenomena, he might have been moved to take the joint implications of hermeneutics and realism more seriously, and to accept the consequent methodological deviations and epistemological limitations that were entailed.

My reading of Hayek suggests that, in spite of its rich potential, the treatment of subjectivism he developed was, in the end, not sufficiently 'radical' to bring that potential to fruition. This assessment applies both to his reflections on the ontology of economic phenomena and to his derivation of the methodological principles required to ensure consistent ontological integrity in consequent analyses. It would be left to others to bring subjectivist economics increasingly towards recognizing the full metatheoretical implications of the direction in which he had moved it.

11.3 LACHMANN

There can be no doubting Lachmann's bona fides as an 'Austrian' subjectivist, but just what his legacy for neoAustrians comprised, and just what its most durable and relevant elements are, remains a matter of opinion.[1] Here I draw together some of the most significant contributions to a subjectivist legacy that I have identified in his writings. The metatheoretical foundations for economics that I found him to have espoused were characterized by just the two key ontological elements that subjectivism demands: first, all economic phenomena have their origins in individual human action; and second, all human action takes place in real time. And, in explicit recognition of these subjectivist ontological principles, he rejected the methodology that mainstream economics had adopted. Economics as a human science could not make legitimate use of the procedures of inquiry that were suitable for the realm of nature. Orthodoxy had managed to do so only by distorting the ontological features of economic phenomena so as to allow formalist modes of expression to have any meaning. Because economics is concerned with real-world human action, the objective of methodology must be primarily to *understand* the generation of its phenomena in the sense of finding human reasons for their appearance at a particular time and place. Such an objective, and the process of interpretation that it requires, immediately takes us beyond anything that can or needs to be achieved by natural science, where knowledge is confined to the way in which events occur within a universally consistent, regular and stable environment.

Agents who carry out economic actions do so with self-conscious deliberation that employs specific cognitive processes; they do not merely react to given and known circumstances, but rather act creatively in the face of limited knowledge and uncertainty with the intention of meeting certain goals. They can 'know' their circumstances only through interpretation based on experience and cognitive capacities. Action is a process that both occupies time and requires agents to recognize the exigencies of time in the form of a perfidious future. There can be no knowledge of the future, so that this missing link in agents' knowledge of their 'circumstances' must be filled in by expectations. Actions must be preceded by plans created in the minds of agents on the basis of their expectations and their purposes. This must be so, because actions are deliberated and relate to a future yet to unfold in reality. Expectations must be formed, in part at least, on the basis of agents' knowledge of the present and past. They possess some accumulated knowledge and can draw on more in the form of flows of new information made available to them, usually at a cost.

Agents vary in their talents when it comes to the processes of deliberation in which knowledge and experience are applied in devising expectations that are to be the bases of a singular choice and action in response to each circumstance. Agents are fallible in their actions. They plan in partial ignorance and with delimited skills, and they form expectations about future conditions as best they can. Ex ante, they may feel satisfied that they have planned optimally for each action and that their planned actions are consistent with each other in terms of the scarce resources needed. That is, they may enjoy a state of present individual equilibrium, but this state is one that will most probably be more or less disappointed because their actions will have some unexpected consequences and will fail fully to realize their goals. The demand will be for some degree of change on the part of agents in their next 'round' of deliberations, choices, plans and actions.

But, as Lachmann was well aware, another crucial dimension of subjectivism stems from the fact that agents rarely act in isolation from other agents and they never do so in a situational vacuum. In several dimensions, economic action is social action. Agents act in concert, interact, with relevant others around them to constitute collective actions. Such situated actions are carried on through what may be labelled generically as institutions to which agents 'belong' in some sense, or in which they just 'participate'. In each aspect of these external involvements with others, agents seek to mitigate their limited capacities as economic agents and to reduce the uncertainty they confront in making choices and decisions. Institutions, broadly considered, shape individual human actions by delimiting their scope, by conditioning their form and by facilitating their performance. Individually, agents draw on the facilities made available to them by institutions, and voluntarily accept the conditions and constraints the rules place upon their actions. Agents also act with some consciousness of the responses of a wider range of yet other relevant agents within their situations. This brings them into an often unconscious extended set of social relationships with unknown people upon whom they depend for their economic well-being.

Within this range of interdependencies and dependencies, individual actions take on a much greater potential for unanticipated personal consequences. And, collectively, agents' actions will generate outcomes for all agents that no individual could have anticipated. For these reasons, Lachmann followed Shackle in referring to the world of economic events as kaleidic: the appearances of observed phenomena have a protean form that flows from ever-changing causes in the subjectivism of human actions. In the human realm, the efflux of time changes everything to a degree and in ways that matter profoundly to agents who every day must pursue their material needs anew.

In spite of its kaleidic nature, Lachmann was well aware that the market capitalist system in reality delivers collective outcomes that are closer to order than to chaos. Individual actions can bring unanticipated results, and collective actions bring results that cannot be predicted exactly and contain outcomes that no individual could have foreseen. But the inclination towards order means that some containment and constraint of human actions must be in place such as to ensure an inclination towards systemic cohesion. The most probable sources of this regularizing influence on economic agency are the situational structures and conditions within and through which agents operate. Lachmann realized this very early in his research, and his inclusion of institutions in the later analysis of agency had the potential to develop these insights further. Unfortunately, this potential was not pursued and he never clarified how subjectivist economists should deal analytically with the nature and origin of regularities in an otherwise kaleidic system.

For Lachmann, one crucial consequence of this kaleidic vision of the economy was that it ruled out the legitimate use of any form of equilibrium arrangement as a core state when representing and accounting for observed phenomena (cf. Mongiovi, 1994, p. 261).[2] And, moving from inquiries that relate to static or stationary conditions to those that relate to dynamic conditions means that equilibrium can have even less legitimacy. Individual agents have the potential to satisfy themselves that they have reached a state of equilibrium, albeit only temporarily. They can believe, rightly or wrongly, that their plans are consistent and can all be successfully carried out with the resources available to them. The concurrent presumptions must be that other relevant agents will behave as expected and that emergent future conditions will turn out as expected. But, at the collective level, the success of individual plans will depend upon their overall consistency with each other, of the potential for which no individual can have any knowledge at all. The unanticipated outcome of plans will be an unpredictable mix of success for some and disappointment for others from this wide range of sources. So it must be, Lachmann believed, that equilibrium is not possible because of the fact that agents plan and act on individual interpretations of and expectations about their circumstances. These will inevitably diverge and the resulting plans will most probably be collectively inconsistent from the outset. What will happen ex post will be another 'round' of the same thing, but now with changed present circumstances and changed prospects for the future. The notion of a tendency towards equilibrium is, therefore, also ruled out by virtue of agents having to learn about their mistakes in an ever-changing environment. Their planning and action responses could just as well be more divergent as less so 'next time' round. To repeat one of Lachmann's key aphorisms concerning equilibrium convergence: 'In the first place, revision of plans in the direction of convergence requires a common diagnosis of the present disequilibrium situation. *Divergence of interpretation* will prevent it. Secondly, convergence requires that agents expect each other to revise their plans in this direction. *Divergence of expectations* may prevent this' (1986a, p. 56, original emphasis).

Lachmann chose as examples of his kaleidic economic vision the problematics of capital and of market processes. In each case, a subjectivist treatment demanded that all of the above exigencies of human agency and potentials for disruption to equilibrium provide the incorrigible foundations for the inquiry. With respect to devising a theory of real capital formation and use, the focus had to shift to agents' subjective choices concerning means of production on the basis of individual expectations. It is then the fallibility of such choices in the face of a host of uncertainties that renders the sphere of capital so unstable and unpredictable in its several dimensions. As far as markets are concerned, the crucial consequence of subjectivism is the demand that analytical attention shift from outcomes to processes that generate those outcomes and, with this, that the artificial devices of *homo oeconomicus* and the 'auctioneer' be replaced by depictions of agents who must act in partial ignorance of the past and present and complete uncertainty and ignorance about the future. Lachmann was sceptical about the capacity of markets to provide the knowledge and information agents would require in order to plan and act consistently. Not only are these things scarce resources, but their acquisition and use by agents involve highly subjective and insecure procedures. Nonetheless, agents in markets must make choices that are real, but it is apparent that the choices they make and the consequences for themselves and others will be indeterminate. Indeterminacy in markets takes the form of continuous disequilibrium and the improbability of any tendency towards an equilibrium for all the subjectivist reasons canvassed above.

Finally, what are we to make of the quite desultory treatment by Lachmann of the methodological revisions required to make economics into a subjectivist science of human action? As we have seen, his implied methodological platform comprised the procedures needed to achieve understanding, *Verstehen*, in the sense that economic phenomena are rendered intelligible to analysts. But all phenomena have their origins in the actions of *individual agents* conditioned by their environment at a particular time and place. Each observation will be unique in its human causation and form as a consequence. Understanding of any human event will require the analyst to interpret the conduct of the agents involved on the basis of the observed evidence available to them. Lachmann accepted and defended this analytical situation as one that could involve the method of hermeneutic inquiry. That is, economic inquiry could take a form analogous to the reading of a text in the sense that both processes are concerned with objects that are the products of purpose-driven human minds. But, if at the same time economics is to retain the scientific status that he believed it should have, analysts have to do better than mount inquiries that deliver ex post descriptions of particular events.

In order to meet the implied demand for generalizations, he followed Weber in recommending the method of typification. This is a procedure that Lachmann viewed as mixing abstraction from particular detail and accentuation of essential characteristics. By forming categories of agents and the types of outcomes that their plans and actions generate, some general accounts of economic phenomena that transcend the unique are possible. Such an approach also allows predictions to be made about future events within very delimited boundaries. But these methodological suggestions, and they were little more than that in Lachmann's all-too-brief expositions, entailed some necessary assessment of the epistemological status to be attributed to the resulting representations. One of the options here is that of realism, and he at least hinted at a belief that, rather than being mere abstractions, types could express the essential existential qualities of real-world actions and events. However, as with other facets of the methodology fit for subjectivist inquiry and understanding, this issue was left without further attention.

Lachmann's subjectivism had a scope that was certainly more extensive than that of his Austrian antecedents and contemporaries. Whether it was more 'radical' depends upon the extensions and emphases that are thought most needed. Lachmann's subjectivism gave more thorough attention to the variegated nature of human agents, but failed to penetrate into the deeper recesses of decision making in the face of uncertainty. He also chose not to follow up the potential that situations in all their many dimensions have to contain, constrain and facilitate human action. And while his adamant belief was that subjectivism as an ontological principle demands the redesigning of economic methodology, in the end, his suggestions were indicative but not substantive. On all fronts, Lachmann's 'radicalization' of subjectivist economics left much for his neoAustrian followers to do (cf. Vaughn, 1994, pp. 160f). In this respect, he joined Mises and Hayek, about whose legacies I have been led to similar conclusions.

NOTES

1. This is clear from the range of views expressed by contributors to the 'Symposium: Ludwig Lachmann and his contributions to economic science' published in Boettke *et al.* (1994, pp. 229ff). Some of these views are referred to below.
2. Mongiovi provides an interesting potential extension of Lachmann's scant treatment of institutional constraints that shape human agency. His suggestion is that we need to recognize a core of necessary relationships within the capitalist production and market structure that would, if they could be realized, provide for a balanced reproductive outcome. This alternative 'Classical–Marxian' vision of equilibrium conditions (see Walsh and Gram, 1980) is one to which Lachmann, amongst others, failed to give warranted credence (see Oakley, 1990, for a critique of Schumpeter from this perspective). Although this is not the place to elaborate, I am in *qualified* agreement with the thrust of Mongiovi's conclusion that, if the capitalist economy is modelled in accordance with the 'Classical–Marxian' vision, 'there is ample scope for the introduction of institutional and subjective considerations, including expectations, outside the core, while the core itself exposes the coordinating forces which prevent the kaleidic process of human history from deteriorating into chaos and disorder' (Mongiovi, 1994, p. 268). My main reticence here, which is confirmed in the work of Adolph Lowe (1976, 1977), concerns the status to be given to the 'coordinating forces' that Mongiovi envisages as inherent in the 'long-period' outcome of fully free market operations (Mongiovi, 1994, p. 267). Lachmann's views on the matter, sending some belated caveats to Mongiovi, were expressed in correspondence that I had with him in 1985 (Lachmann, 1985) concerning my paper on Schumpeter and the 'Classical–Marxian' alternative to the Walrasian model of equilibrium (Oakley, 1985; see also 1990, ch. 4). He explicitly rejected *any* equilibrium state of market capitalism that is claimed to be the product of coordinated and consistent actions on the part of agents. One of his pertinent comments to me was that 'I always understood that to C–M ['Classical–Marxian'] adherents classical equil. is a "centre of gravitation". *You evidently think otherwise*, but [you] should warn your innocent readers' (emphasis added). Other penetrating comments in the same vein that are relevant here were that the failure to ensure the explicit and integrated inclusion of expectations shows us 'how artificial is the C–M world in which these problems vanish from sight!'; and 'a scheme such as C–M which ignores ... [the subjective theory of capital], in fact any "objective" capital theory, can tell us nothing about the real world'. In particular, he stressed that relying on human agency to ensure the required reproductive replacement and expansion of the real capital stock through market operations is not something that can be taken for granted. It is 'a highly problematic endeavour, an activity of the mind, at which some men are better than others. (You have to admit the inequality of men)'. And, contrary to Mongiovi's suggestion (1994, p. 271), Lachmann would have none of the idea of traverses between growth paths, for he argued that, 'once we are off the steady state path, there is no telling what the subsequent outcome will be', and we should not be concerned about states that just cannot be reached by any known combination of agents' actions anyway (cf. Lowe, 1976, 1977). Apropos all these key points, Lachmann went on to conclude that 'what we need is a theory of Market Processes', to which he added the cryptic rider, 'which as yet we have not got'. Perhaps this remark reflected his lack of complete satisfaction with his efforts in *The Market as an Economic Process*, which he had sent to me in page proof form and was about to be published.

Bibliography

Addleson, M. (1984), 'Robbins's *Essay* in retrospect: on subjectivism and an economics of choice', *Rivista Internazionale di Scienze Economiche e Commerciali*, 31.

Addleson, M. (1986), '"Radical subjectivism" and the language of Austrian economics', in Kirzner (ed.).

Barry, N.P. (1979), *Hayek's Social and Economic Philosophy*, London: Macmillan.

Barry, N.P. (1990), 'The road to freedom: Hayek's social and economic philosophy', PPE- Lectures, Lecture 2, Department of Economics, University of Vienna, May.

Bianchi, M. (1994), 'Hayek's spontaneous order: the "correct" versus the "corrigible" society', in Birner and van Zijp (eds).

Birner, J. (1994), 'Introduction: Hayek's grand research programme', in Birner and van Zip (eds).

Birner, J. and R. van Zijp (eds) (1994), *Hayek, Co-ordination and Evolution: His Legacy in Philosophy, Politics, Economics and the History of Ideas*, London: Routledge.

Blaug, M. (1985), 'Comment on D. Wade Hands, "Karl Popper and economic methodology: a new look"', *Economics and Philosophy*, 1.

Boettke, P.J. (1994a), 'Introduction: Ludwig Lachmann and his contributions to economic science', in Boettke *et al.* (eds).

Boettke, P.J. (ed.) (1994b), *The Elgar Companion to Austrian Economics*, Aldershot: Edward Elgar.

Boettke, P.J., I.M. Kirzner and M.J. Rizzo (eds) (1994), *Advances in Austrian Economics*, vol. 1, London: JAI Press.

Böhm, S. (1982), 'The ambiguous notion of subjectivism: comment on Lachmann', in Kirzner (ed.).

Böhm, S. (1985), 'The political economy of the Austrian School', in P. Roggi (ed.), *Gli economisti e la politica economica*, Naples: Edizioni Scientifiche Italiane.

Böhm, S. (1986), 'Time and equilibrium: Hayek's notion of intertemporal equilibrium reconsidered', in Kirzner (ed.).

Böhm, S. (1989), 'Subjectivism and PostKeynesianism: towards a better

understanding', in J. Pheby (ed.), *New Directions in PostKeynesian Economics*, Aldershot: Edward Elgar.
Böhm, S. (1990), 'The Austrian tradition: Schumpeter and Mises', in Hennings and Samuels (eds).
Böhm, S. (1991) 'L.M. Lachmann (1906–90): a personal tribute', *Review of Political Economy*, 3 (3).
Böhm, S. (1992), 'Austrian economics and the theory of entrepreneurship: Israel M. Kirzner interviewed by Stephan Boehm on 2 May 1989', *Review of Political Economy*, 4 (1).
Böhm, S. (1994), 'Hayek and knowledge: some question marks', in Colonna *et al.* (eds).
Böhm-Bawerk, E. von (1994), 'The historical vs the deductive method in political economy' [1891], in Kirzner (ed.) (1994).
Burczak, T.A. (1994a), 'The postmodern moments of F.A. Hayek's economics', *Economics and Philosophy*, 10 (2).
Burczak, T.A. (1994b), 'Reply to Bruce Caldwell: can subjectivism be non-hermeneutic?', *Economics and Philosophy*, 10 (2).
Caldwell, B.J. (1988), 'Hayek's transformation', *History of Political Economy*, 20 (4).
Caldwell, B.J. (ed.) (1990), *Carl Menger and his Legacy in Economics*, Durham: Duke University Press.
Caldwell, B.J. (1991a), 'Clarifying Popper', *Journal of Economic Literature*, XXIX.
Caldwell, B.J. (1991b), 'Comment on Lavoie', in de Marchi and Blaug (eds).
Caldwell, B.J. (1992a), 'Hayek the falsificationist? A refutation', *Research in the History of Economic Thought and Methodology*, 10.
Caldwell, B.J. (1992b), 'Reply to Hutchison', *Research in the History of Economic Thought and Methodology*, 10.
Caldwell, B.J. (1994a), 'Hayek's scientific subjectivism', *Economics and Philosophy*, 10 (2).
Caldwell, B.J. (1994b), 'Four theses on Hayek, in Colonna *et al.* (eds).
Caldwell, B.J. and S. Böhm (eds) (1992), *Austrian Economics: Tensions and New Directions*, Boston: Kluwer Academic Publishers.
Coats, A.W. (1983), 'The revival of subjectivism in economics', in J. Wiseman (ed.), *Beyond Positive Economics?*, London: Macmillan.
Colonna, M., H. Hagemann and O.F. Hamouda (eds) (1994), *Capitalism, Socialism and Knowledge: The Economics of F.A. Hayek*, vol. II, Aldershot: Edward Elgar.
Craver, E. (1986), 'The emigration of the Austrian economists', *History of Political Economy*, 18 (1).
Cubeddu, R. (1993), *The Philosophy of the Austrian School*, London: Routledge.

de Marchi, N. (ed.) (1988), *The Popperian Legacy in Economics*, Cambridge: Cambridge University Press.

de Marchi, N. and M. Blaug (eds) (1991), *Appraising Economic Theories: Studies in the Methodology of Research Programs*, Aldershot: Edward Elgar.

de Vries, R.P. (1994), 'The place of Hayek's theory of mind and perception in the history of philosophy and psychology', in Birner and van Zijp (eds).

Dolan, E.G. (ed.) (1976), *The Foundations of Modern Austrian Economics*, Kansas City: Sheed & Ward.

Earl, P.E. (ed.) (1988), *Psychological Economics: Development, Tensions, Prospects*, Boston: Kluwer Academic Publishers.

Earl, P.E. (1992), 'Shearmur on subjectivism: discussion', in Caldwell and Böhm (eds).

Ebeling, R.M. (1981), 'Mises' influence on modern economic thought', *Wirtschaftspolitische Blätter*, 28 (4).

Ebeling, R.M. (1986), 'Toward a hermeneutical economics: expectations, prices and the role of interpretations in a theory of the market process', in Kirzner (ed.).

Ebeling, R.M. (1987), 'The roots of Austrian economics', *Market Process*, 5 (2).

Ebeling, R.M. (1988), 'Expectations and expectations formation in Mises's theory of the market process', *Market Process*, 6 (1).

Ebeling, R.M. (1990a), 'Introduction', in Mises.

Ebeling, R.M. (1990b), 'What is a price? Explanation and understanding (with apologies to Paul Ricoeur), in D. Lavoie (ed.), *Economics and Hermeneutics*, London: Routledge.

Endres, A.M. (1988), 'Subjectivism, psychology and the Modern Austrians: a comment', in Earl (ed.).

Fleetwood, S. (1995), *Hayek's Political Economy: The socio-economics of order*, London: Routledge.

Foss, N.J. (1995), 'More on "Hayek's Transformation"', *History of Political Economy*, 27 (2).

Frowen, S.F. (ed.) (1995), *Hayek the Economist and Social Philosopher: a Critical Retrospect*, London: Macmillan.

Giddens, A. (1979), *Central Problems in Social Theory: Action, Structure and Contradiction in Social Analysis*, London: Macmillan.

Grassl, W. and B. Smith (eds) (1986), *Austrian Economics: Historical and Philosophical Background*, London: Croom Helm.

Gray, J. (1984), *Hayek on Liberty*, Oxford: Basil Blackwell.

Haberler, G. (1981), 'Mises's private seminar', *Wirtschaftspolitische Blätter*, 28 (4).

Haberler, G. (1990), 'A Vienna seminarian remembers' [1981], in Littlechild (ed.), vol. I.

Hands, D.W. (1985), 'Karl Popper and economic methodology: a new look', *Economics and Philosophy*, 1.

Hands, D.W. (1992), 'Falsification, situational analysis and scientific research programs: the Popperian tradition in economic methodology', in N. de Marchi (ed.), *Post-Popperian Methodology of Economics*, Boston: Kluwer Academic Publishers.

Hayek, F.A. von (1926), 'Hayek on Wieser', in Spiegel (ed.) (1952).

Hayek, F.A. von (1928), 'Intertemporal price equilibrium and movements in the value of money', reprinted in Hayek (1984).

Hayek, F.A. von (1929), *Monetary Theory and the Trade Cycle*, trans. N. Kaldor and H. Croome, 1933, reprinted Clifton, New Jersey: Kelley, 1975.

Hayek, F.A. von (1931), *Prices and Production*, London: Routledge & Kegan Paul; 2nd revised and enlarged edn 1935.

Hayek, F.A. von (1933) 'The trend of economic thinking', *Economica*, 13.

Hayek, F.A. von (1934) 'Hayek on Menger', in Spiegel (ed.) (1952).

Hayek, F.A. von (1939a), *Profits, Interest and Investment and Other Essays on the Theory of Industrial Fluctuations*, London: Routledge & Kegan Paul.

Hayek, F.A. von (1939b), *Freedom and the Economic System*, Public Policy Pamphlet No. 29, Chicago: University of Chicago Press.

Hayek, F.A. von (1941), *The Pure Theory of Capital*, London: Routledge & Kegan Paul.

Hayek, F.A. von (1944), *The Road to Serfdom*, London: Routledge & Kegan Paul.

Hayek, F.A. von (1949), *Individualism and Economic Order*, London: Routledge & Kegan Paul.

Hayek, F.A. von (1952), *The Sensory Order: an Inquiry into the Foundations of Theoretical Psychology*, London: Routledge & Kegan Paul.

Hayek, F.A. von (1955), *The Counter-Revolution of Science: Studies in the Abuse of Reason*, New York: The Free Press of Glencoe.

Hayek, F.A. von (1960), *The Constitution of Liberty*, London: Routledge & Kegan Paul.

Hayek, F.A. von (1967), *Studies in Philosophy, Politics and Economics*, London: Routledge & Kegan Paul.

Hayek, F.A. von (1973a), 'The place of Menger's *Grundsätze* in the history of economic thought', in Hicks and Weber (eds).

Hayek, F.A. von (1973b), *Law, Legislation and Liberty: a New Statement of the Liberal Principles of Justice and Political Economy*, vol. 1, *Rules and Order*, London: Routledge & Kegan Paul.

Hayek, F.A. von (1976) *Law, Legislation and Liberty: a New Statement of the*

Liberal Principles of Justice and Political Economy, vol. 2, *The Miracle of Social Justice*, London: Routledge & Kegan Paul.

Hayek, F.A. von (1978), *New Studies in Philosophy, Politics, Economics and the History of Ideas*, London: Routledge & Kegan Paul.

Hayek, F.A. von (1979), *Law, Legislation and Liberty: a New Statement of the Liberal Principles of Justice and Political Economy*, vol. 3, *The Political Order of a Free People*, London, Routledge & Kegan Paul.

Hayek, F.A. von (1982), 'The Sensory Order after 25 years', in Weimer and Palermo (eds).

Hayek, F.A. von (1983), *Knowledge, Evolution and Society*, London: Adam Smith Institute.

Hayek, F.A. von (1984), *Money, Capital and Fluctuations: Early Essays of F.A. Hayek*, ed. R. McCloughry, Chicago: University of Chicago Press.

Hayek, F.A. von (1989), *The Fatal Conceit: the Errors of Socialism*, ed. W.W. Bartley, Chicago: University of Chicago Press.

Hayek, F.A. von (1992), *The Fortunes of Liberalism: Essays on Austrian Economics and the Ideal of Freedom*, ed. P.G. Klein, London: Routledge.

Hayek, F.A. von (1994), *Hayek on Hayek: An Autobiographical Dialogue*, ed. S. Kresge and L. Werner, London: Routledge.

Hennings, K. and W.J. Samuels (eds) (1990), *Neoclassical Economic Theory, 1870 to 1930*, Boston: Kluwer Academic Publishers.

Hicks, J.R. and W. Weber (eds) (1973), *Carl Menger and the Austrian School of Economics*, Oxford: Clarendon Press.

Hodgson, G., M. Tool and W. Samuels (eds) (1994), *The Elgar Companion to Evolutionary and Institutional Economics*, Aldershot: Edward Elgar.

Horwitz, S. (1994a), 'Subjectivism, institutions and capital: comment on Lewin and Mongiovi', in Boettke *et al.* (eds).

Horwitz, S. (1994b), 'Subjectivism', in Boettke (ed.) (1994b).

Hutchison, T.W. (1981), *The Politics and Philosophy of Economics: Marxians, Keynesians and Austrians*, Oxford: Basil Blackwell.

Hutchison, T.W. (1987), 'Review of Lachmann, *The Market as an Economic Process*' (1986), *Economic Journal*, 97.

Hutchison, T.W. (1992), 'Hayek and "Modern Austrian" methodology: comment on a non-refuting refutation', *Research in the History of Economic Thought and Methodology*, 10.

Hutchison, T.W. (1994), *The Uses and Abuses of Economics: Contentious Essays on History and Method*, London: Routledge.

Jacobi, N. (1990), 'Metaphilosophy and methodology in economics', *Methodus*, 2 (2).

Jaffé, W. (1976), 'Menger, Jevons and Walras de-homogenized', *Economic Inquiry*, XIV.

Johnston, W.M. (1972), *The Austrian Mind: an Intellectual and Social History 1848–1938*, Berkeley: University of California Press.

Kauder, E. (1957), 'Intellectual and political roots of the older Austrian School', *Zeitshcrift für Nationalökonomie*, XVII (4).

Kirzner, I.M. (ed.) (1982), *Method, Process and Austrian Economics: Essays in Honor of Ludwig von Mises*, Lexington, Massachusetts: Lexington Books.

Kirzner, I.M. (ed.) (1986), *Subjectivism, Intelligibility and Economic Understanding: Essays in Honour of Ludwig M. Lachmann on his Eightieth Birthday*, London: Macmillan.

Kirzner, I.M. (1992a), *The Meaning of Market Process: Essays in the Development of Austrian Economics*, London: Routledge.

Kirzner, I.M. (1992b), 'Subjectivism, freedom and economic law', *The South African Journal of Economics*, 60 (1).

Kirzner, I.M. (1994a), 'Introduction', in I.M. Kirzner (ed.) *Classics in Austrian Economics: a Sampling in the History of a Tradition*, vol. I, London: William Pickering

Kirzner, I.M. (1994b), 'Introduction', in I.M. Kirzner (ed.) *Classics in Austrian Economics: a Sampling in the History of a Tradition*, vol. II, London: William Pickering.

Kirzner, I.M. (1994c), 'Introduction', in I.M. Kirzner (ed.) *Classics in Austrian Economics: a Sampling in the History of a Tradition*, vol. III, London: William Pickering.

Koppl, R. (1994a), 'Lachmann on Schutz and Shackle', in Boettke *et al.* (eds).

Koppl, R. (1994b), 'Ideal type methodology in economics', in Boettke (ed.) (1994b).

Lachmann, L.M. (1937), 'Uncertainty and liquidity preference', *Economica*, 4.

Lachmann, L.M. (1970), *The Legacy of Max Weber*, London: Heinemann.

Lachmann, L.M. (1973), *Macroeconomic Thinking and the Market Economy*, London: Institute of Economic Affairs.

Lachmann, L.M. (1976a), 'From Mises to Shackle: an essay on Austrian economics and the kaleidic society', *Journal of Economic Literature*, XIV (1).

Lachmann, L.M. (1976b), 'On the central concept of Austrian economics: market process', in Dolan (ed.).

Lachmann, L.M. (1976c), 'On Austrian capital theory', in Dolan (ed.).

Lachmann, L.M. (1976d), 'Toward a critique of macroeconomics', in Dolan (ed.).

Lachmann, L.M. (1976e), 'Austrian economics in the age of the neo-Ricardian counterrevolution', in Dolan (ed.).

Lachmann, L.M. (1977), *Capital, Expectations and the Market Process: Es-*

says on the Theory of the Market Economy, Kansas City: Sheed Andrews & McMeel.

Lachmann, L.M. (1978a), 'Carl Menger and the incomplete revolution of subjectivism', *Atlantic Economic Journal*, VI (3).

Lachmann, L.M. (1978b), 'An Austrian stocktaking: unsettled questions and tentative answers', in Spadaro (ed.).

Lachmann, L.M. (1978c), *Capital and its Structure*, Kansas City: Sheed Andrews & McMeel.

Lachmann, L.M. (1982a), 'Ludwig von Mises and the extension of subjectivism', in Kirzner (ed.).

Lachmann, L.M. (1982b), 'The salvage of ideas: problems of the revival of Austrian economic thought', *Zeitshrift für die gesamte Staatswissenschaft*, 138.

Lachmann, L.M. (1983), 'John Maynard Keynes: a view from an Austrian window', *The South African Journal of Economics*, 51 (3).

Lachmann, L.M. (1985), 'Correspondence with Allen Oakley', mimeo.

Lachmann, L.M. (1986a), *The Market as an Economic Process*, Oxford: Basil Blackwell.

Lachmann, L.M. (1986b), 'Austrian economics under fire: the Hayek–Sraffa duel in retrospect', in Grassl and Smith (eds).

Lachmann, L.M. (1990a), 'Austrian economics: a hermeneutic approach', in D. Lavoie (ed.), *Economics and Hermeneutics*, London: Routledge.

Lachmann, L.M. (1990b), 'G.L.S. Shackle's place in the history of subjectivist thought', in S.F. Frowen (ed.), *Unknowledge and Choice in Economics*, London: Macmillan.

Latsis, S.J. (1972), 'Situational determinism in economics', *British Journal for the Philosophy of Science*, 23.

Latsis, S.J. (1983), 'The role and status of the rationality principle in the social sciences', in R. Cohen and M. Wartofsky (eds), *Epistemology, Methodology, and the Social Sciences*, Boston: D. Reidel.

Lavoie, D. (1986), 'Euclideanism versus hermeneutics: a reinterpretation of Misesian apriorism', in Kirzner (ed.).

Lavoie, D. (1990a), 'Introduction', in D. Lavoie (ed.), *Economics and Hermeneutics*, London: Routledge.

Lavoie, D. (1990b), 'Understanding differently: hermeneutics and the spontaneous order of communicative processes', in Caldwell (ed.).

Lavoie, D. (1990c), 'Hermeneutics, subjectivity and the Lester/Machlup debate: toward a more anthropological approach to empirical economics', in W.J. Samuels (ed.), *Economics as Discourse: An Analysis of the Language of Economists*, Boston: Kluwer Academic Publishers.

Lavoie, D. (1991), 'The progress of subjectivism', in de Marchi and Blaug (eds).

Lavoie, D. (1994), 'The interpretive turn', in Boettke (ed.) (1994b).
Lawson, T. (1988), 'Probability and uncertainty in economic analysis', *Journal of Post Keynesian Economics*, 11 (1).
Lawson, T. (1989), 'Realism and instrumentalism in the development of econometrics', *Oxford Economic Papers*, 41 (1).
Lawson, T. (1994a), 'Why are so many economists so opposed to methodology?', *Journal of Economic Methodology*, 1 (1).
Lawson, T. (1994b), 'Critical realism and the analysis of choice, explanation and change', in Boettke *et al.* (eds).
Lawson, T. (1994c), 'Realism, philosophical', in Hodgson *et al.* (eds).
Lawson, T. (1994d), 'Realism and Hayek: a case of continuing transformation', in Colonna *et al.* (eds).
Lawson, T. (1994e), 'Methodology', in Hodgson *et al.* (eds).
Lawson, T. (1996), 'Hayek and Keynes: a commonality', *History of Economics Review*, 25.
Lawson, T. (1997), *Economics and Reality*, London: Routledge.
Lewin, P. (1994), 'Knowledge, expectations and capital: the economics of Ludwig M. Lachmann', in Boettke *et al.* (eds).
Littlechild, S.C. (1979), 'Comment: subjectivism or radical subversion?', in Rizzo (ed.).
Littlechild, S.C. (ed.) (1990), *Austrian Economics*, 3 vols, Aldershot: Edward Elgar.
Lowe, A. (1976), *The Path of Economic Growth*, Cambridge: Cambridge University Press.
Lowe, A. (1977), *On Economic Knowledge*, enlarged edn, Armonk, New York: M.E. Sharpe.
Madison, G.B. (1988), 'Hermeneutical integrity: a guide for the perplexed', *Market Process*, 6 (1).
Madison, G.B. (1990), 'Getting beyond objectivism: the philosophical hermeneutics of Gadamer and Ricoeur', in D. Lavoie (ed.), *Economics and Hermeneutics*, London: Routledge.
Madison, G.B. (1994), 'Phenomenology and economics', in Boettke (ed.) (1994b).
Mäki, U. (1988a), 'On the problem of realism in economics', *Fundamenta Scientiae*, 9 (2/3).
Mäki, U. (1988b), 'How to combine rhetoric and realism in the methodology of economics', *Economics and Philosophy*, 4.
Mäki, U. (1990), 'Scientific realism and Austrian explanation', *Review of Political Economy*, 2 (3).
Milford, K. (1994), 'In pursuit of rationality: a note on Hayek's *The Counter-revolution of Science*', in Birner and van Zijp (eds).

Milford, K. (1995), 'A note on Hayek's analysis of scientism', in Frowen (ed.).

Mises, L. von (1958), *Theory and History* [1957], London: Jonathan Cape.

Mises, L. von (1960), *Epistemological Problems of Economics* [1933], translated by G. Reisman, Princeton: D. van Nostrand.

Mises, L. von (1962), *The Ultimate Foundation of Economic Science: an Essay on Method*, Princeton: D. van Nostrand.

Mises, L. von (1966), *Human Action: a Treatise on Economics* [1949], 3rd rev. edn, Chicago: Henry Regnery Company.

Mises, L. von (1969), *The Historical Setting of the Austrian School of Economics*, New Rochelle, New York: Arlington House.

Mises, L. von (1978), *Notes and Recollections*, trans. H.F. Sennholz, South Holland, Illinois: Libertarian Press.

Mises, L. von (1990), *Money, Method and the Market Process: Essays by Ludwig von Mises*, edited with an Introduction by Richard M. Ebeling, Norwell, Massachusetts: Kluwer Academic Publishers.

Mises, L. von (1994), 'Market' [1961], in Kirzner (ed.) (1994c).

Mittermaier, K.H.M. (1992), 'Ludwig Lachmann (1906–1990): a biographical sketch', *The South African Journal of Economics*, 60 (1).

Mongiovi, G. (1994), 'Capital, expectations and economic equilibrium: some notes on Lachmann and the so-called "Cambridge School"', in Boettke *et al.* (eds).

Oakley, A.C. (1985), 'Schumpeter and the Classical–Marxian tradition: two views of the generation of capitalist motion', *Research Report or Occasional Paper Series*, No. 114, Department of Economics, University of Newcastle.

Oakley, A.C. (1990), *Schumpeter's Theory of Capitalist Motion: A Critical Exposition and Reassessment*, Aldershot: Edward Elgar.

Oakley, A.C. (1994), *Classical Economic Man: Human Agency and Methodology in the Political Economy of Adam Smith and J.S. Mill*, Aldershot: Edward Elgar.

Oakley, A.C. (1997a), 'Epistemological problems of human agency in Mises's subjectivism', *History of Economics Review*, No. 26.

Oakley, A.C. (1997b), *The Foundations of Austrian Economics from Menger to Mises: a Critico-historical Retrospective of Subjectivism*, Aldershot: Edward Elgar.

Oakley, A.C. (1997c), 'Human agents and rationality in Max Weber's social economics', *International Journal of Social Economics*, 24 (7/8/9).

Paqué, K.-H. (1990), 'Pattern predictions in economics: Hayek's methodology of the social sciences revisited', *History of Political Economy*, 22 (2).

Parsons, S. (1990), 'The philosophical roots of modern Austrian economics: past problems and future prospects', *History of Political Economy*, 22 (2).

Prychitko, D.L. (1994a), 'Ludwig Lachmann and the interpretive turn in economics: a critical inquiry into the hermeneutics of the plan', in Boettke *et al.* (eds).

Prychitko, D.L. (1994b), 'Praxeology', in Boettke (ed.) (1994b).

Rizzo, M.J. (ed.) (1979), *Time, Uncertainty and Disequilibrium*, Lexington, Massachusetts: Lexington Books.

Rizzo, M.J. (1992a), 'Equilibrium visions', *The South African Journal of Economics*, 60 (1).

Rizzo, M.J. (1992b), 'Afterword: Austrian economics for the twenty-first century', in Caldwell and Böhm. (eds).

Rizzo, M.J. (1994), 'Time in economics', in Boettke (ed.) (1994b).

Runde, J.H. (1988), 'Subjectivism, psychology, and the modern Austrians', in Earl (ed.).

Samuels, W.J. (1994), 'Comments on papers by Roger Koppl and David Prychitko', in Boettke *et al.* (eds).

Shackle, G.L.S. (1972), *Epistemics and Economics: a Critique of Economic Doctrines*, Cambridge: Cambridge University Press.

Shackle, G.L.S. (1979), *Imagination and the Nature of Choice*, Edinburgh: Edinburgh University Press.

Shackle, G.L.S. (1981), 'F.A. Hayek 1899–', in D.P. O'Brien and J.R. Presley (eds), *Pioneers of Modern Economics in Britain*, London: Macmillan.

Shand, A.H. (1980), *Subjectivist Economics: the New Austrian School*, The Pica Press.

Shearmur, J. (1986), 'The Austrian connection: Hayek's liberalism and the thought of Carl Menger', in Grassl and Smith (eds).

Shearmur, J. (1990), 'From Hayek to Menger: biology, subjectivism and welfare', in Caldwell (ed.).

Shearmur, J. (1992) 'Subjectivism, explanation and the Austrian tradition', in Caldwell and Böhm (eds).

Shearmur, J. (1994) 'Hayek and the case for markets', in Birner and van Zijp (eds).

Shearmur, J. (1996), *Hayek and After: Hayekian liberalism as a research programme*, London: Routledge.

Smith, B. (1986a), 'Preface: Austrian economics from Menger to Hayek', in Grassl and Smith (eds).

Smith, B. (1986b), 'Austrian economics and Austrian philosophy', in Grassl and Smith (eds).

Smith, B. (1990a), 'Aristotle, Menger, Mises: an essay in the metaphysics of economics', in Caldwell (ed.).

Smith, B. (1990b), 'The question of apriorism', *Austrian Economics Newsletter*, 12 (1).

Smith, B. (1990c), 'On the Austrianness of Austrian economics', *Critical Review*, 4.

Smith, B. (1994), 'The philosophy of Austrian economics', *Review of Austrian Economics*, 7 (2).

Smith, B. (1995), 'The connectionist mind: a study of Hayekian psychology', in Frowen (ed.).

Spadaro, L.M. (ed.) (1978), *New Directions in Austrian Economics*, Kansas City: Sheed Andrews & McMeel.

Spiegel, H.W (ed.) (1952), *The Development of Economic Thought: Great Economists in Perspective*, New York: Wiley & Sons.

Streissler, E.W. (1969a), 'Structural economic thought: on the significance of the Austrian School today', *Zeitschrift für Nationalökonomie*, 29.

Streissler, E.W. (ed.) (1969b), *Roads to Freedom: Essays in Honour of Friedrich A. von Hayek*, London: Routledge & Kegan Paul.

Streissler, E.W. (1990), 'The intellectual and political impact of the Austrian school of economics' [1988], in Littlechild (ed.), vol. I.

Streissler, E.W. (1994), 'Hayek on information and socialism', in Colonna *et al.* (eds).

Sweezy, A.R. (1933–4), 'The interpretation of subjective value theory in the writings of the Austrian economists', *Review of Economic Studies*, 1.

Vaughn, K.I. (1990), 'The Mengerian roots of the Austrian revival', in Caldwell (ed.).

Vaughn, K.I. (1992), 'The problem of order in Austrian economics: Kirzner vs. Lachmann', *Review of Political Economy*, 4 (3).

Vaughn, K.I. (1994), *Austrian Economics in America: The Migration of a Tradition*, Cambridge: Cambridge University Press.

Walsh, V. and H. Gram (1980), *Classical and Neoclassical Theories of General Equilibrium: Historical Origins and Mathematical Structure*, New York: Oxford University Press.

Weimer, W.B. (1982), 'Hayek's approach to the problems of complex phenomena: an introduction to the theoretical psychology of *The Sensory Order*', in Weimer and Palermo (eds).

Weimer, W.B. and D.S. Palermo (eds) (1982), *Cognition and the Symbolic Process*, vol. 2, Hillsdale, New Jersey: Erlbaum Associates.

Wieser, F. von (1967), *Social Economics* [1914, 1924], trans. A.F. Hinrichs [1927], New York: Augustus M. Kelley.

Wieser, F. von (1983), *The Law of Power* [1926], trans. W.E. Kuhn, Lincoln, Nebraska: Bureau of Business Research, University of Nebraska-Lincoln.

Wieser, F. von (1994), 'The nature and substance of theoretical economics' [1911], in Kirzner (ed.) (1994a).

Yeager, L.B. (1987), 'Why subjectivism?', *Review of Austrian Economics*, 1.

Index